THE EASY GOSPEL FAKE BOOK

Melody, Lyrics and Simplified Chords

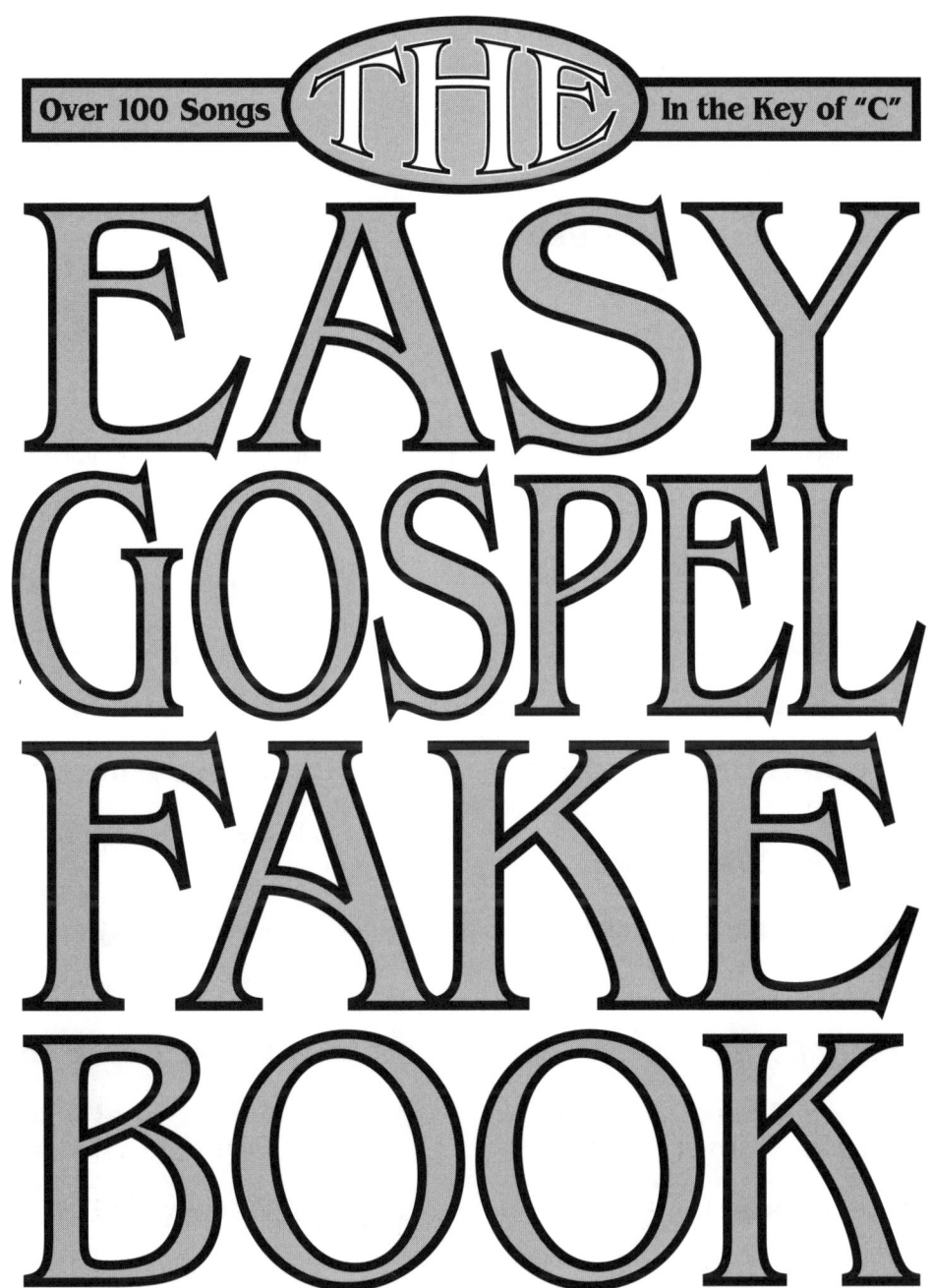

Over 100 Songs — In the Key of "C"

ISBN 0-634-02664-X

7777 W. BLUEMOUND RD. P.O. BOX 13819 MILWAUKEE, WI 53213

For all works contained herein:
Unauthorized copying, arranging, adapting, recording or public performance is an infringement of copyright.
Infringers are liable under the law.

Visit Hal Leonard Online at
www.halleonard.com

THE EASY GOSPEL FAKE BOOK

CONTENTS

4 INTRODUCTION	36 **God Will Take Care of You**
5 **Amazing Grace**	37 **Hallelujah, We Shall Rise**
6 **Are You Walkin' and A-Talkin' for the Lord**	38 **He Keeps Me Singing**
8 **Are You Washed in the Blood?**	40 **He Looked Beyond My Fault**
9 **At Calvary**	42 **He Loved Me with a Cross**
10 **At the Cross**	39 **He Touched Me**
12 **Because He Lives**	44 **He's Still Workin' on Me**
14 **Behold the Lamb**	46 **Heaven Came Down**
11 **Blessed Assurance**	45 **Higher Ground**
16 **Brighten the Corner Where You Are**	48 **His Eye Is on the Sparrow**
18 **Can He, Could He, Would He, Did He?**	50 **His Name Is Wonderful**
17 **Church in the Wildwood**	52 **Home Where I Belong**
20 **The Day He Wore My Crown**	51 **How Great Thou Art**
22 **Do Lord**	54 **I Bowed on My Knees and Cried Holy**
23 **Does Jesus Care?**	56 **I Feel Like Traveling On**
24 **Down at the Cross (Glory to His Name)**	57 **I Just Came to Praise the Lord**
25 **The Eastern Gate**	58 **I Just Feel Like Something Good Is About to Happen**
26 **The Family of God**	60 **I Love to Tell the Story**
28 **Fill My Cup, Lord**	61 **I Saw the Light**
29 **Footsteps of Jesus**	62 **I Stand Amazed in the Presence (My Savior's Love)**
30 **Get All Excited**	63 **I'd Rather Have Jesus**
32 **Give Me That Old Time Religion**	64 **I'll Fly Away**
34 **Give Them All to Jesus**	65 **In the Garden**
33 **God Said It, I Believe It, That Settles It!**	66 **In Times Like These**
	68 **It Took a Miracle**

70 It's Beginning to Rain	113 Shall We Gather at the River?
69 Jesus Paid It All	114 Sheltered in the Arms of God
72 Just a Closer Walk with Thee	116 Since Jesus Came into My Heart
73 Just a Little Talk with Jesus	118 Something Beautiful
74 Just Over in the Gloryland	117 Soon and Very Soon
76 The King Is Coming	120 Stepping on the Clouds
78 The King of Who I Am	122 Surely the Presence of the Lord Is in This Place
75 Lift Him Up	124 Sweet By and By
80 The Lily of the Valley	125 There Is Power in the Blood
81 Little Is Much When God Is in It	126 There's Something About That Name
82 The Longer I Serve Him	127 'Til the Storm Passes By
84 Love Lifted Me	128 Turn Your Radio On
83 The Love of God	130 The Unclouded Day
86 Mansion Over the Hilltop	131 Upon This Rock
88 Midnight Cry	134 Victory in Jesus
90 More Than Wonderful	136 We Shall Behold Him
92 Movin' Up to Gloryland	139 We'll Understand It Better By and By
87 My Savior First of All	140 When I Can Read My Title Clear
94 My Tribute	141 When the Roll Is Called Up Yonder
96 Now I Belong to Jesus	142 When We All Get to Heaven
97 The Old Rugged Cross	144 Whispering Hope
98 Part the Waters	143 Why Me? (Why Me, Lord?)
100 Peace in the Valley	146 Will the Circle Be Unbroken
102 Precious Lord, Take My Hand	148 Wings of a Dove
104 Precious Memories	150 Wonderful Grace of Jesus
106 Put Your Hand in the Hand	147 Written in Red
108 Ready to Go Home	
110 Rise Again	152 CHORD SPELLER
105 Rock of Ages	
112 Send the Light	

INTRODUCTION

What Is a Fake Book?

A fake book has one-line music notation consisting of melody, lyrics and chord symbols. This lead sheet format is a "musical shorthand" which is an invaluable resource for all musicians—hobbyists to professionals.

Here's how *The Easy Gospel Fake Book* differs from most standard fake books:

- All songs are in the key of C.

- Many of the melodies have been simplified.

- Only five basic chord types are used—major, minor, seventh, diminished and augmented.

- The music notation is larger for ease of reading.

In the event that you haven't used chord symbols to create accompaniment, or your experience is limited, a chord speller chart is included at the back of the book to help you get started.

Have fun!

ARE YOU WALKIN' AND A-TALKIN' FOR THE LORD

Copyright © 1952 (Renewed 1980) by Acuff-Rose Music, Inc. and Hiriam Music in the U.S.A.
All Rights for Hiriam Music Administered by Rightsong Music Inc.
All Rights outside the U.S.A. Controlled by Acuff-Rose Music, Inc.
All Rights Reserved   Used by Permission

Words and Music by
HANK WILLIAMS

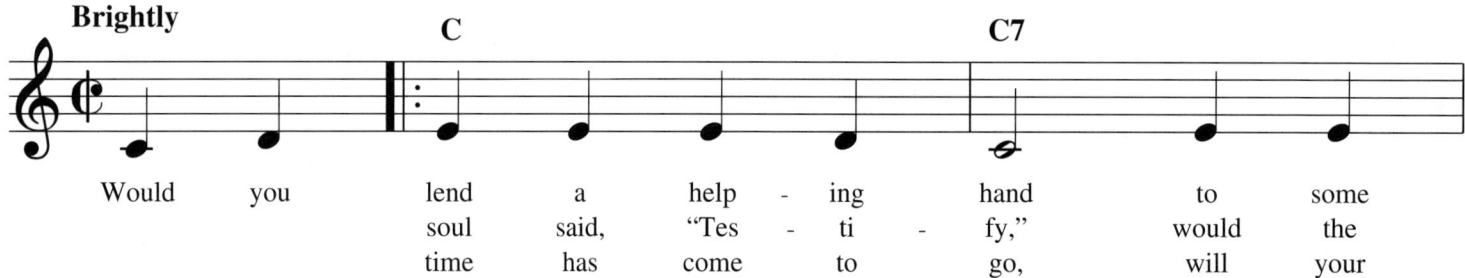

Would you lend a helping hand to some
soul said, "Tes - ti - fy," would the
time has come to go, will your

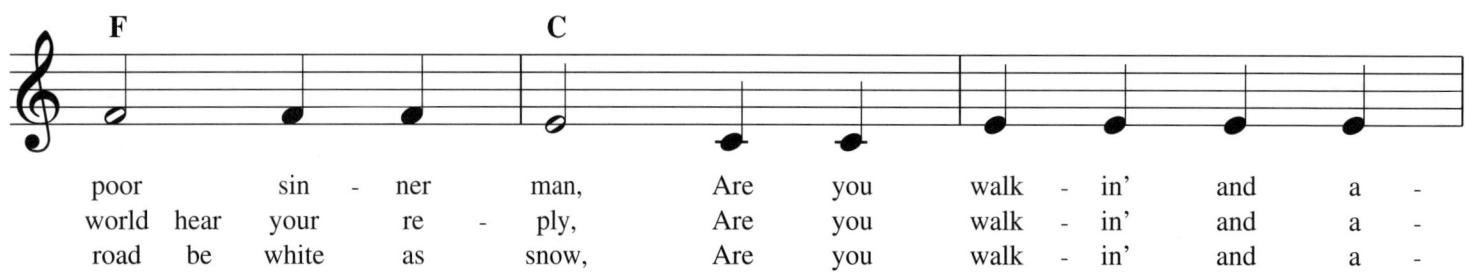

poor sin - ner man, Are you walk - in' and a -
world hear your re - ply, Are you walk - in' and a -
road be white as snow, Are you walk - in' and a -

talk - in' for the Lord? _____ Would you stop and try to
talk - in' for the Lord? _____ Would you stop and shout His
talk - in' for the Lord? _____ Will He take you by the

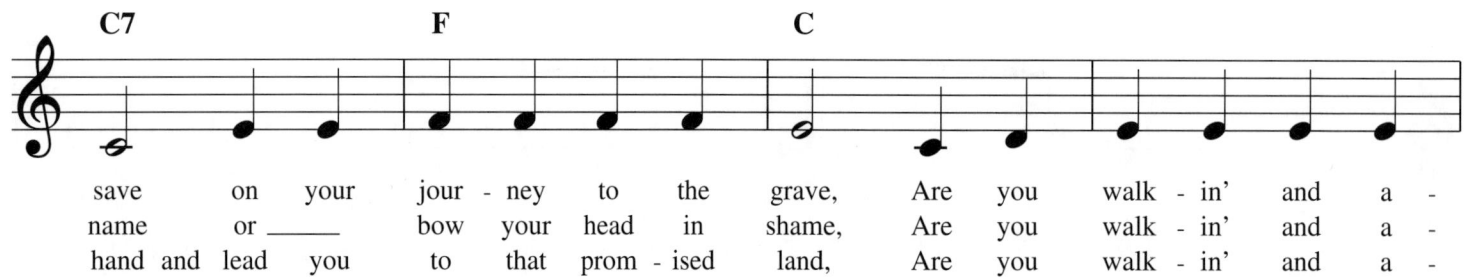

save on your jour - ney to the grave, Are you walk - in' and a -
name or _____ bow your head in shame, Are you walk - in' and a -
hand and lead you to that prom - ised land, Are you walk - in' and a -

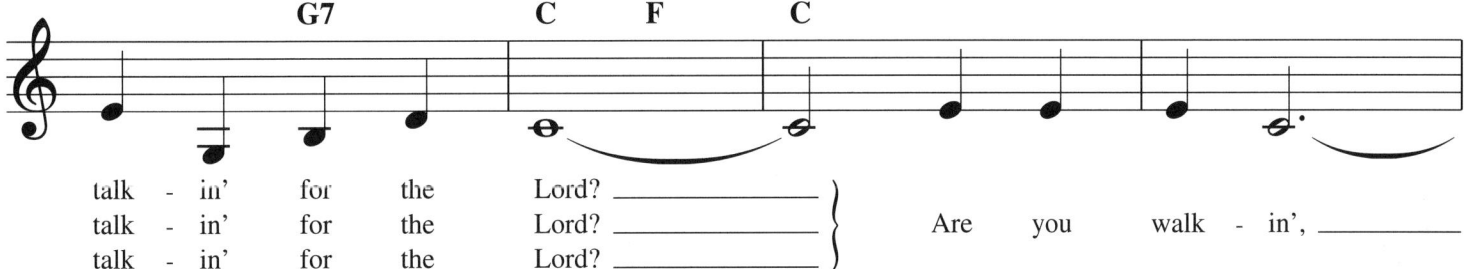
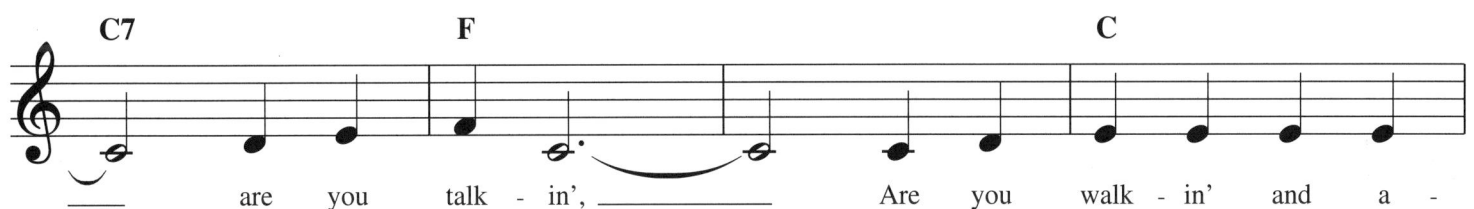
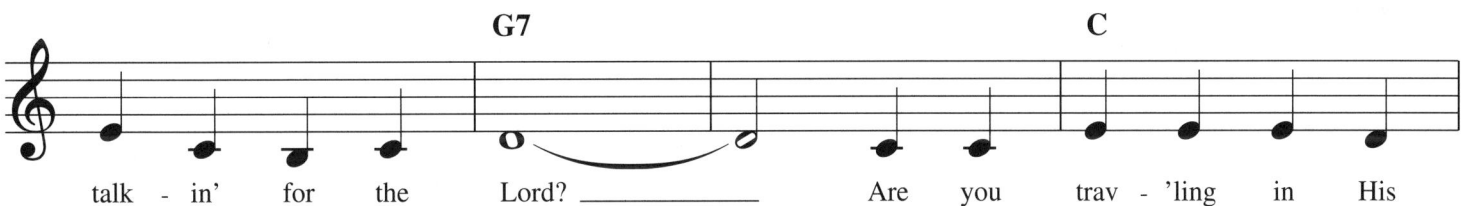
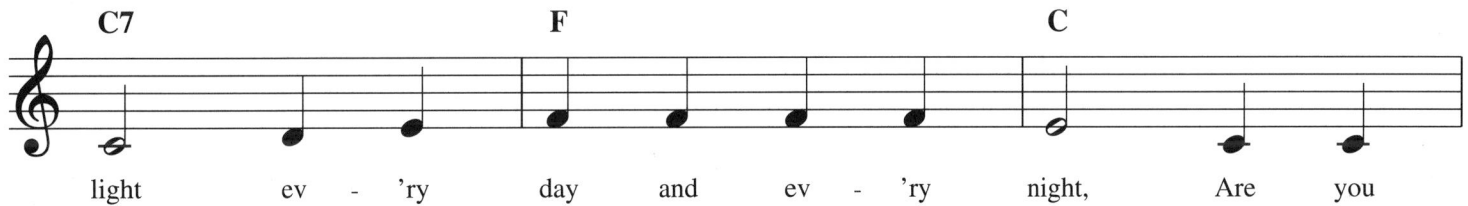

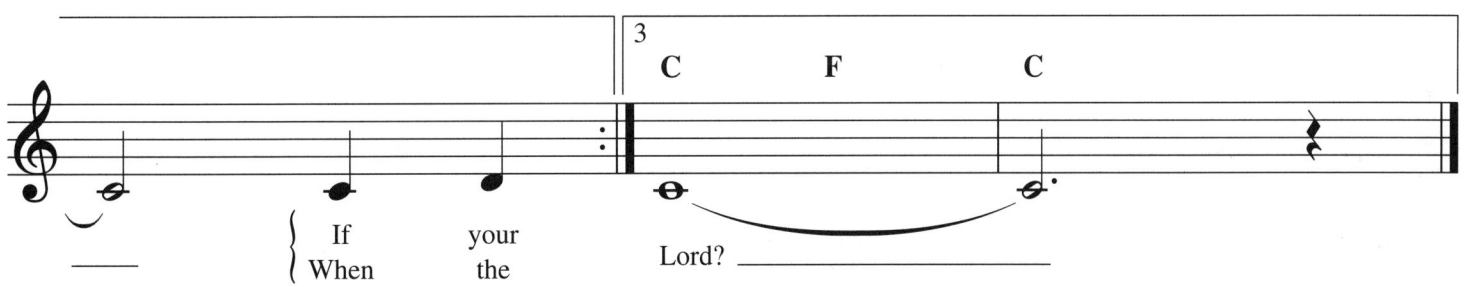

ARE YOU WASHED IN THE BLOOD?

Words and Music by
ELISHA A. HOFFMAN

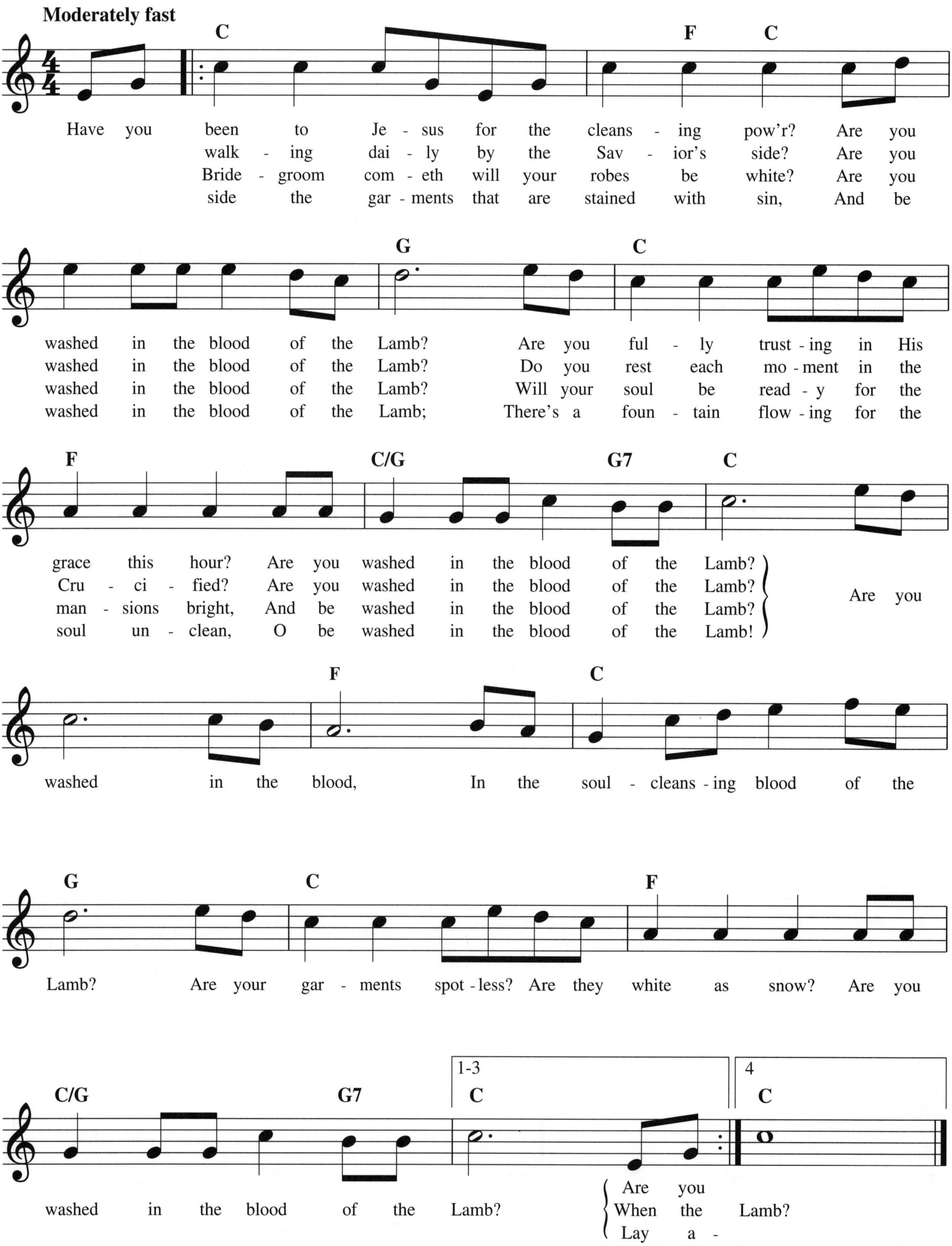
Moderately fast
C F C G C F C/G G7 C F C G C F C/G G7
Have you been to Je - sus for the cleans - ing pow'r? Are you washed in the blood of the Lamb? Are you ful - ly trust - ing in His grace this hour? Are you washed in the blood of the Lamb?
walk - ing dai - ly by the Sav - ior's side? Are you washed in the blood of the Lamb? Do you rest each mo - ment in the Cru - ci - fied? Are you washed in the blood of the Lamb?
Bride - groom com - eth will your robes be white? Are you washed in the blood of the Lamb? Will your soul be read - y for the man - sions bright, And be washed in the blood of the Lamb?
side the gar - ments that are stained with sin, And be washed in the blood of the Lamb; There's a foun - tain flow - ing for the soul un - clean, O be washed in the blood of the Lamb!
Are you washed in the blood, In the soul - cleans - ing blood of the Lamb? Are your gar - ments spot - less? Are they white as snow? Are you washed in the blood of the Lamb?
1-3
C
Are you
When the
Lay a -
4
C
Lamb?

AT CALVARY

Words by WILLIAM NEWELL
Music by DANIEL B. TOWNER

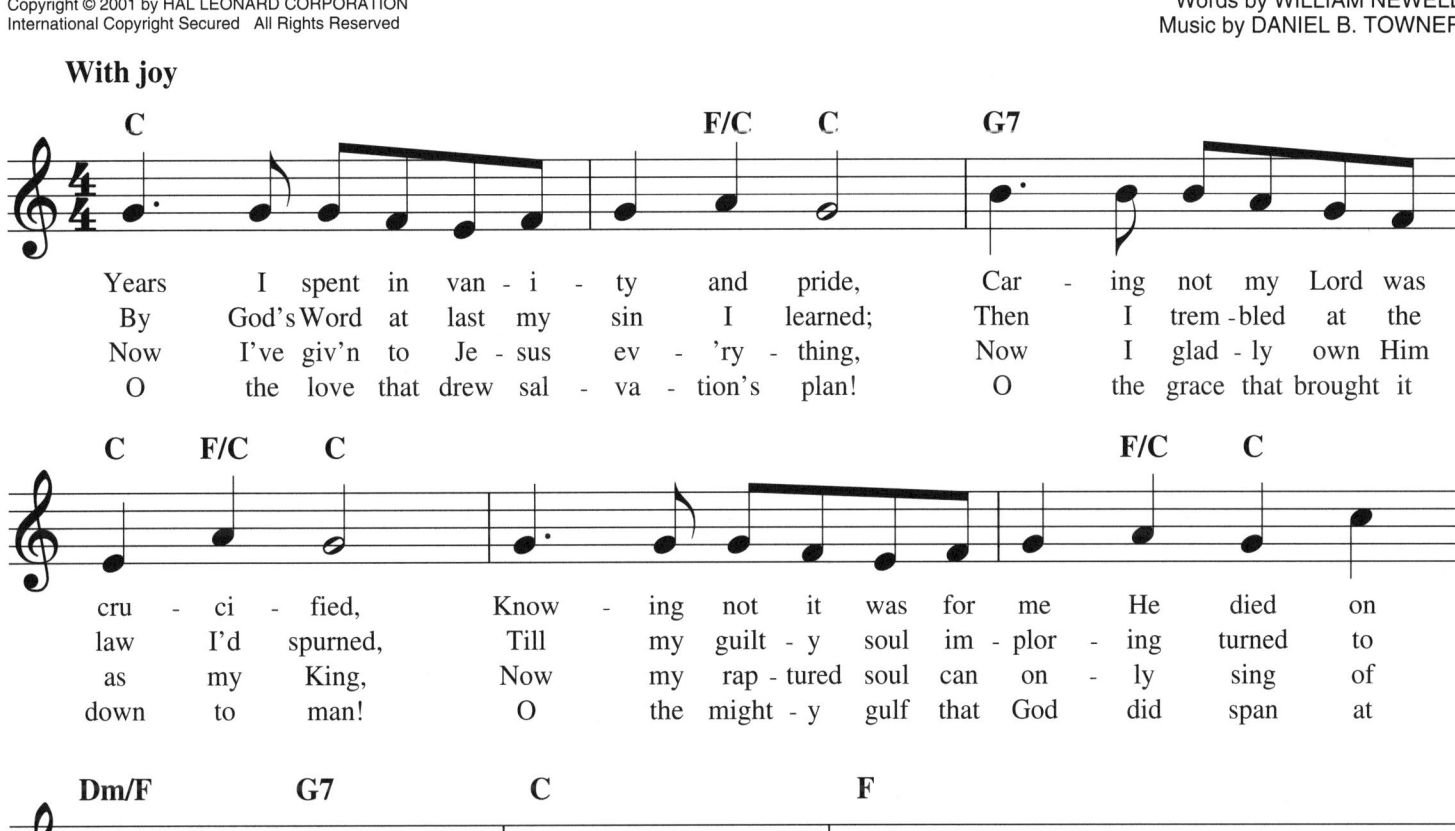
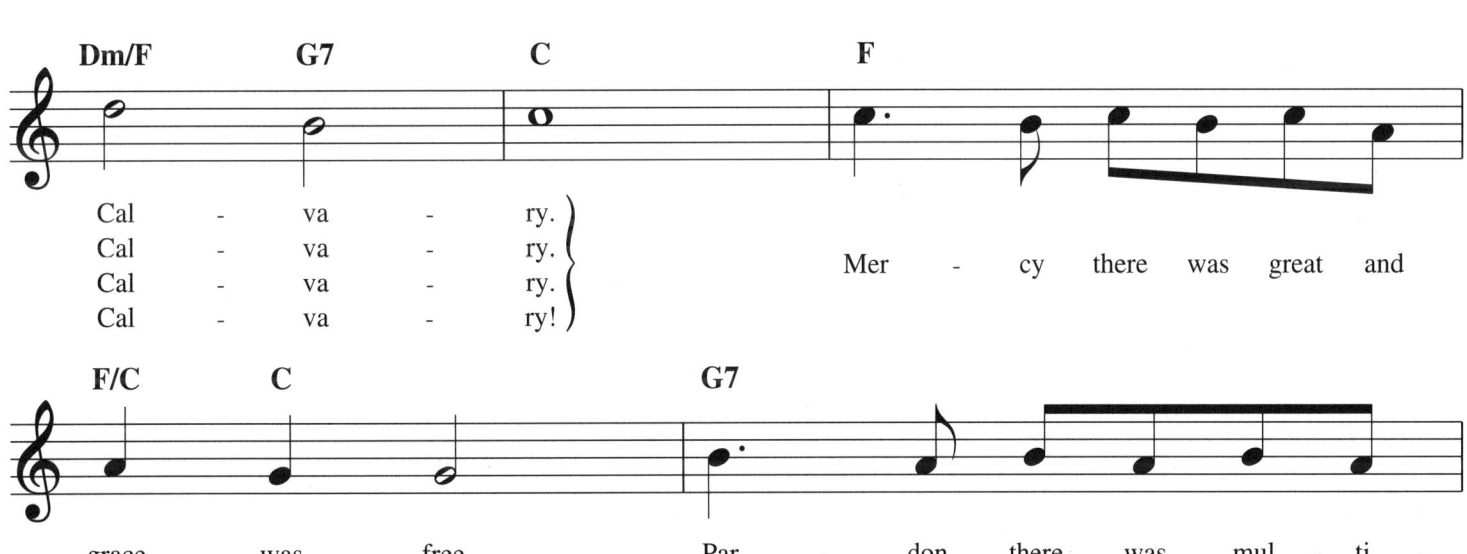
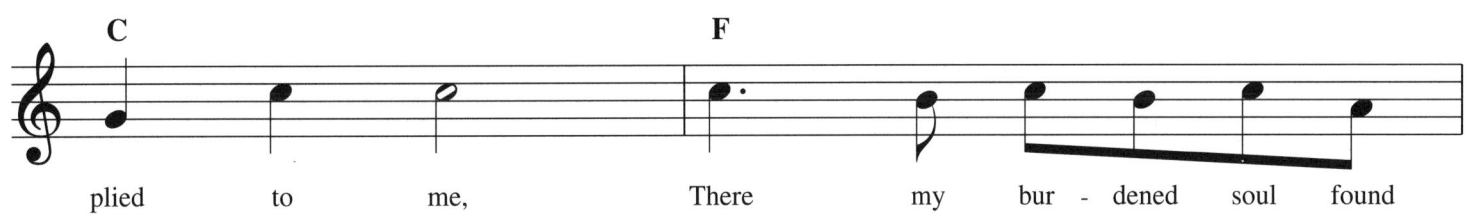
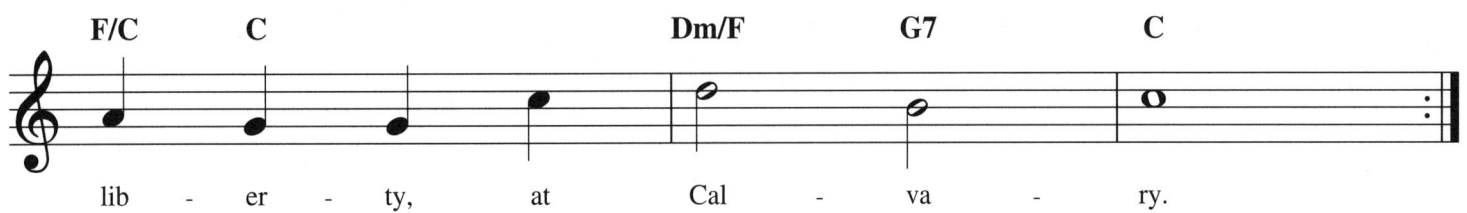

AT THE CROSS

Copyright © 2001 by HAL LEONARD CORPORATION
International Copyright Secured   All Rights Reserved

Words by ISAAC WATTS and RALPH E. HUDSON
Music by RALPH E. HUDSON

Moderately

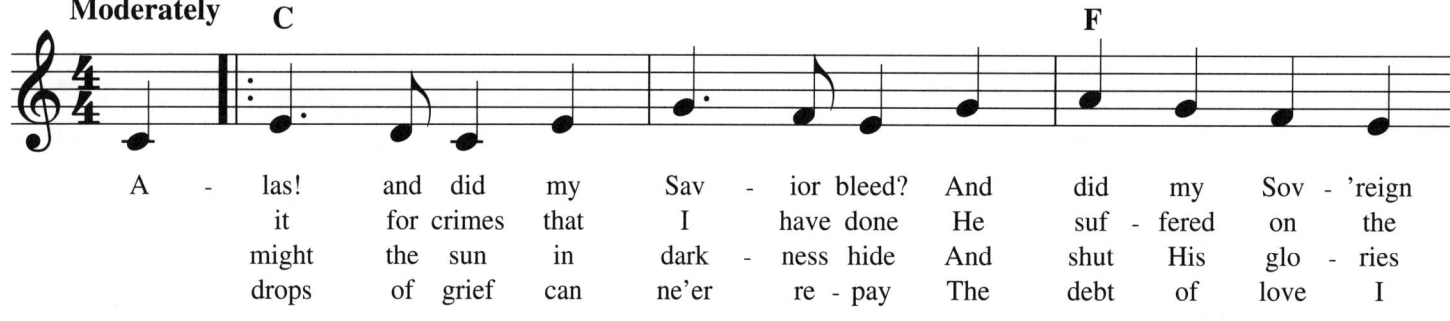

A- las! and did my Sav- ior bleed? And did my Sov- 'reign
it for crimes that I have done He suf- fered on the
might the sun in dark- ness hide And shut His glo- ries
drops of grief can ne'er re- pay The debt of love I

die? Would He de- vote that sa- cred head For
tree? A- maz- ing pit- y! grace un- known! And
in, When Christ, the might- y Mak- er, died For
owe. Here, Lord, I give my- self a- way; 'Tis

sin- ners such as I?
love be- yond de- gree!
man, the crea- ture's sin.
all that I can do!

At the cross, at the cross where I

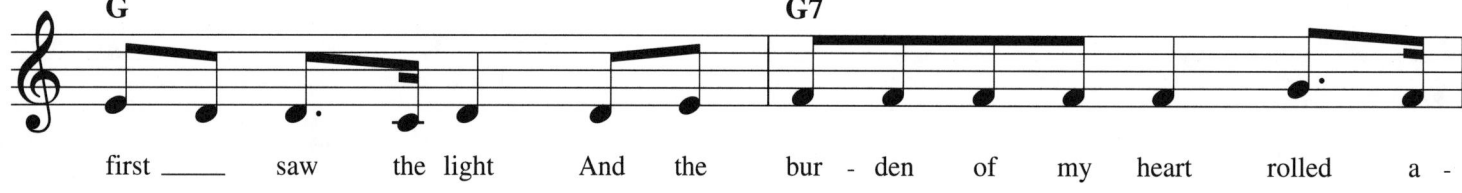

first ___ saw the light And the bur- den of my heart rolled a-

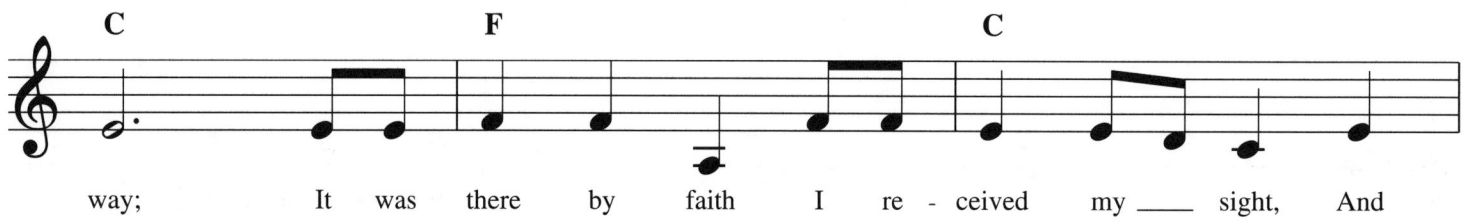

way; It was there by faith I re- ceived my ___ sight, And

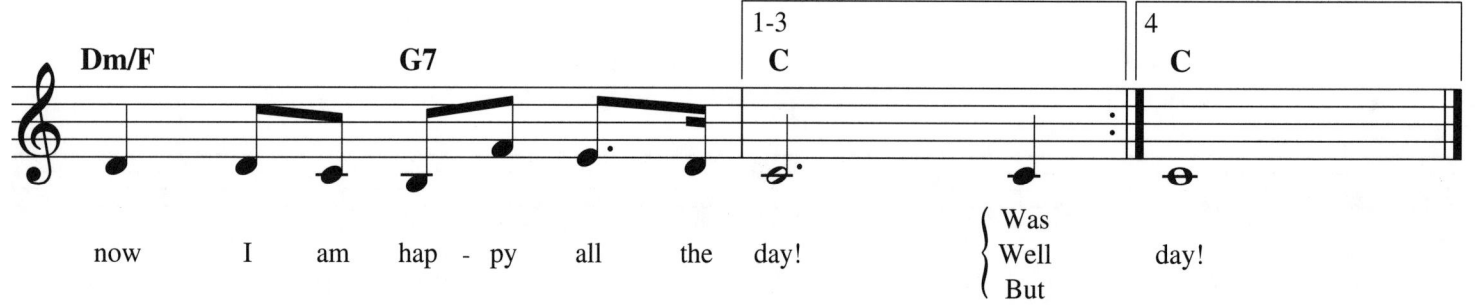

now I am hap- py all the day!

{ Was
  Well   day!
  But

BLESSED ASSURANCE

Lyrics by FANNY J. CROSBY
Music by PHOEBE PALMER KNAPP

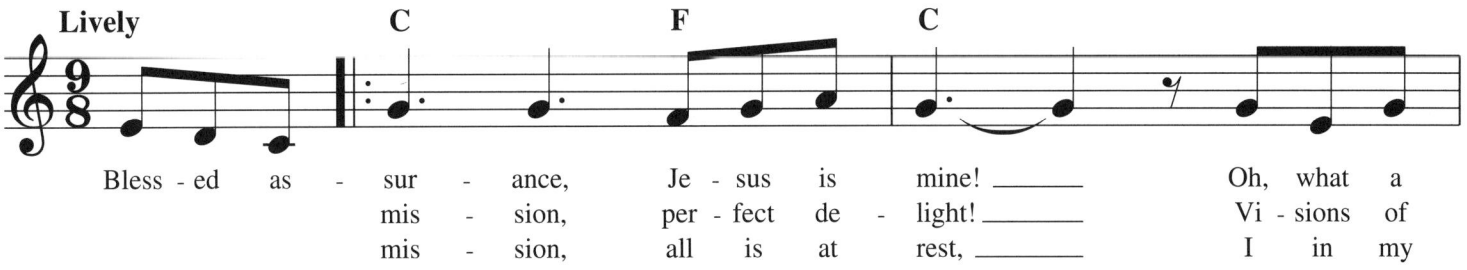

Bless-ed as-sur-ance, Je-sus is mine! Oh, what a
mis-sion, per-fect de-light! Vi-sions of
mis-sion, all is at rest, I in my

fore-taste of glo-ry di-vine! Heir of sal-va-tion, pur-chase of
rap-ture now burst on my sight. An-gels de-scend-ing bring from a-
Sav-ior am hap-py and blest. Watch-ing and wait-ing look-ing a-

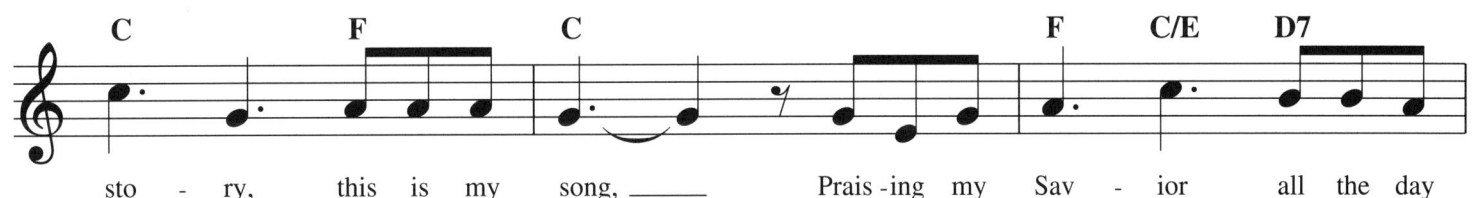

God, Born of His Spir-it, washed in His blood.
bove, Ech-oes of mer-cy, whis-pers of love.
bove, Filled with His good-ness, lost in His love.

This is my

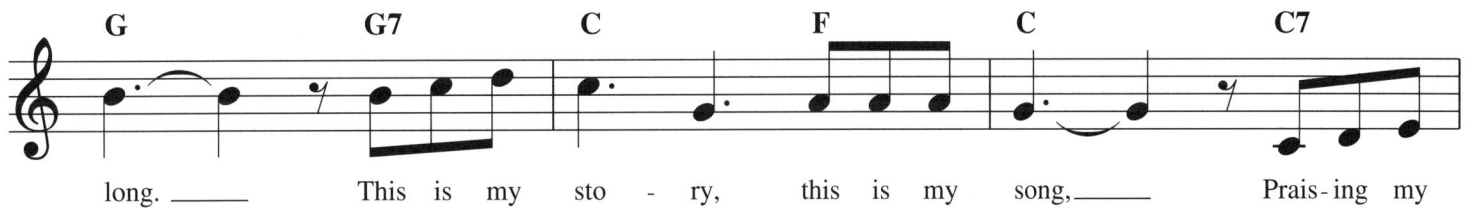

sto-ry, this is my song, Prais-ing my Sav-ior all the day

long. This is my sto-ry, this is my song, Prais-ing my

Sav-ior all the day long. Per-fect sub- long.

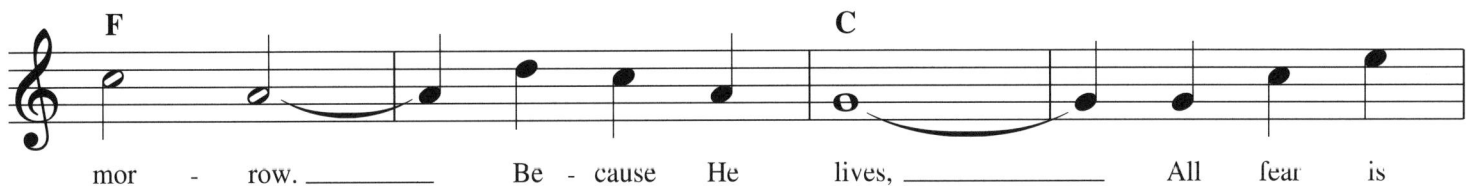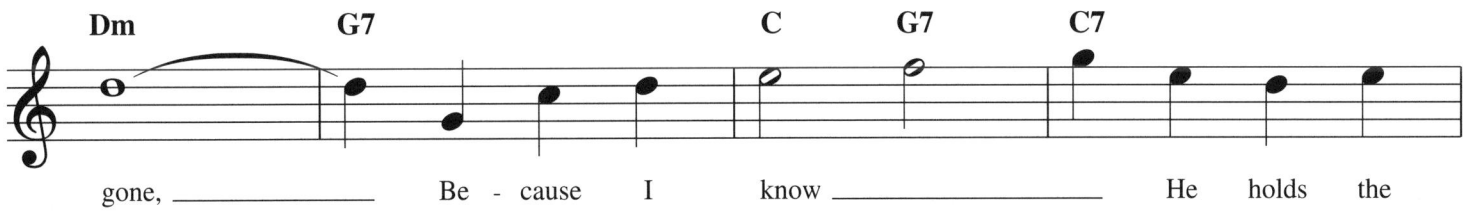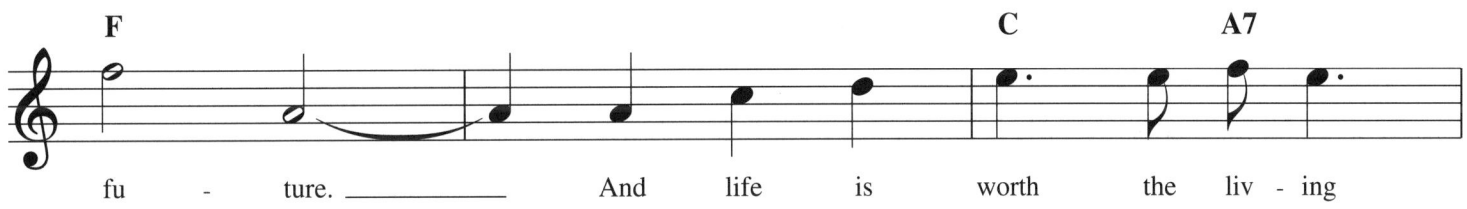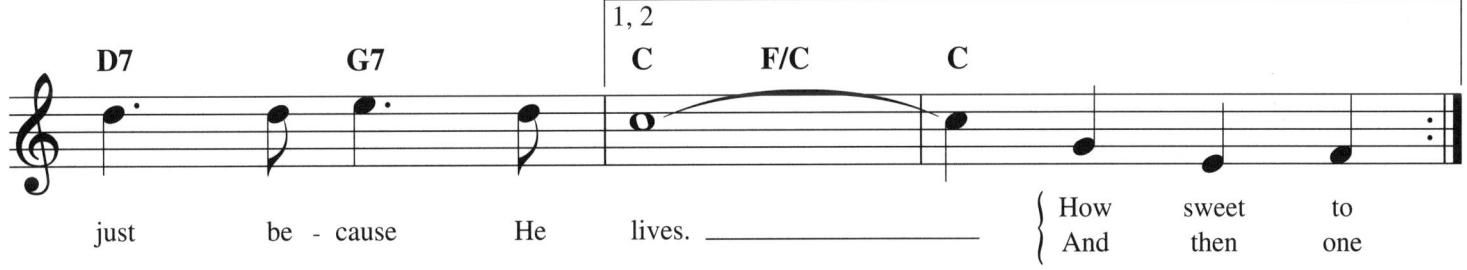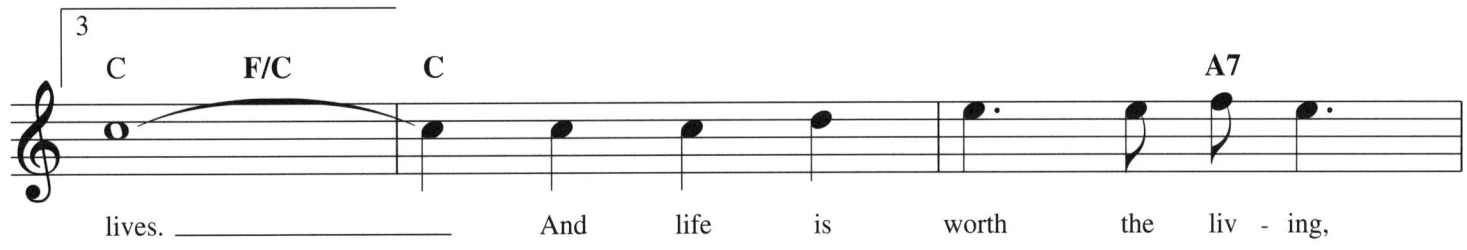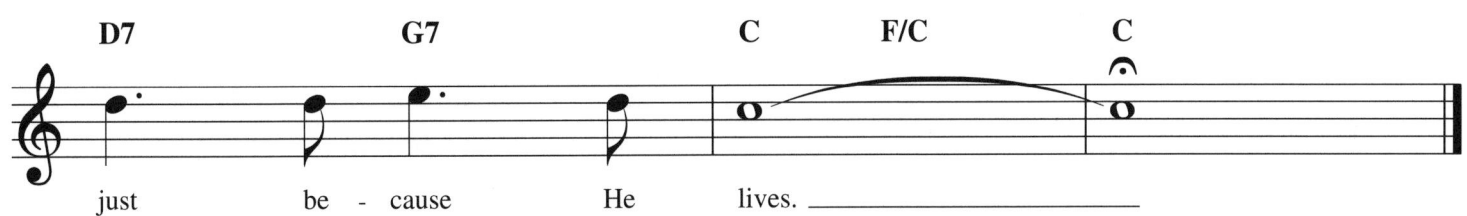

BEHOLD THE LAMB

Words and Music by
DOTTIE RAMBO

© 1979 John T. Benson Publishing Co. (ASCAP)
(a div. of Brentwood-Benson Music Publishing, Inc.)
All Rights Reserved   Used by Permission

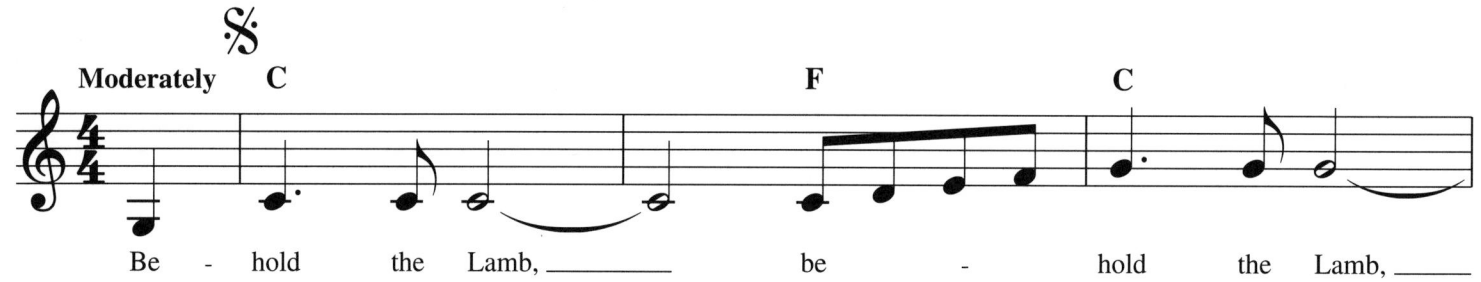

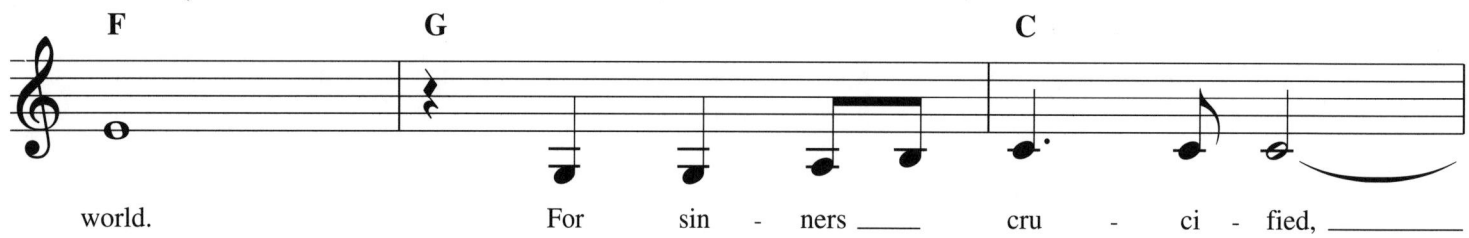
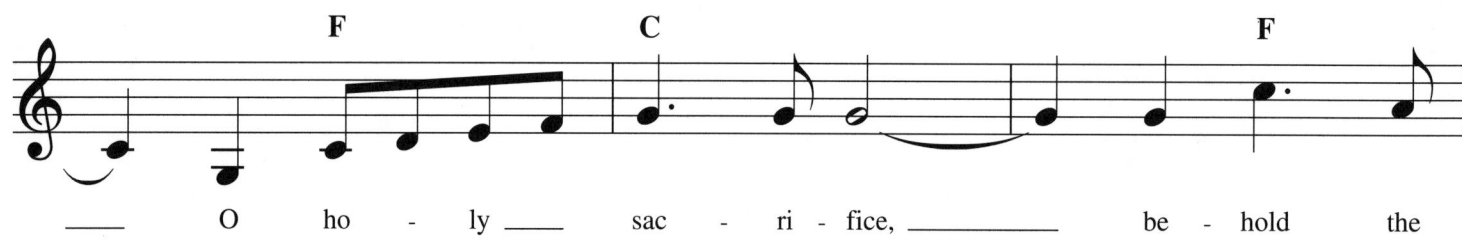
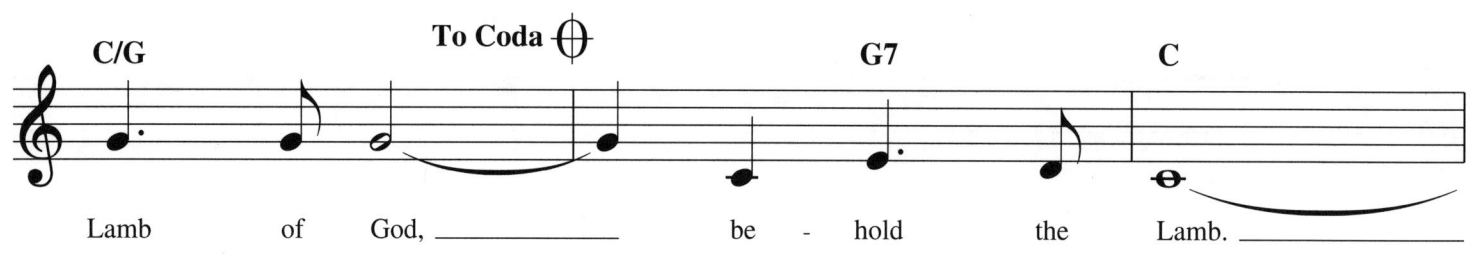

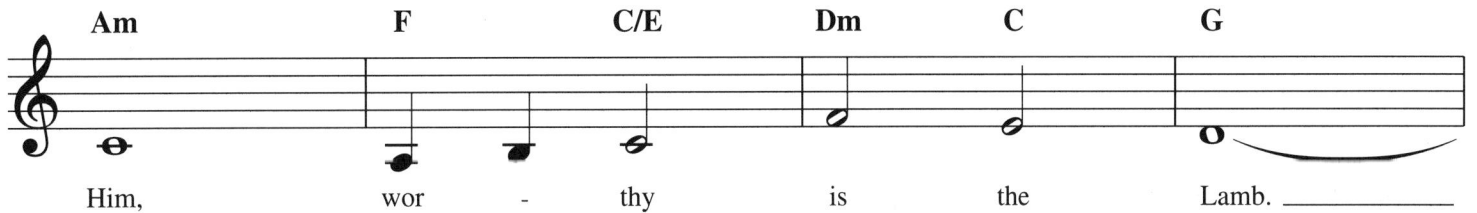
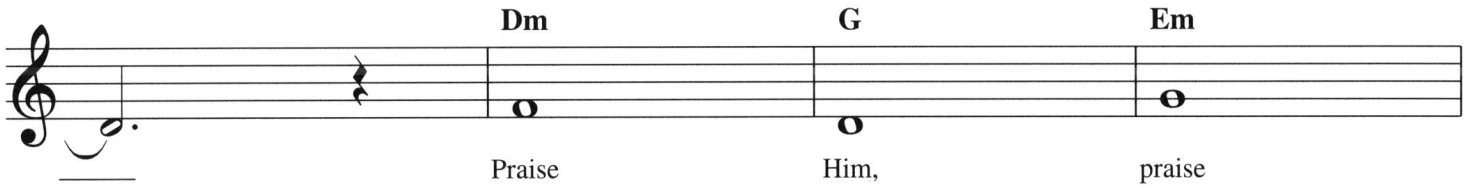
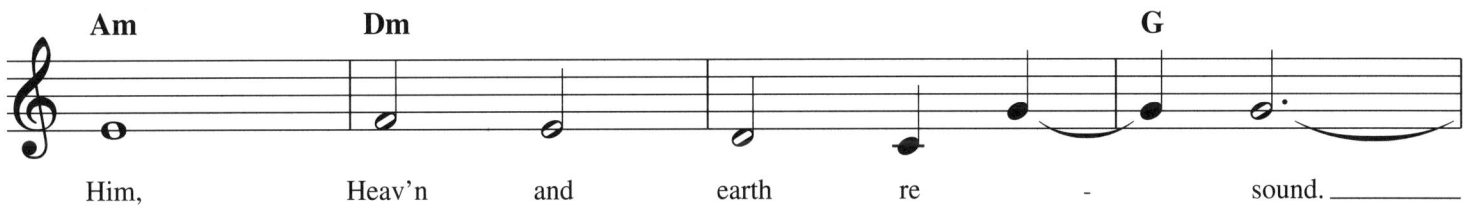
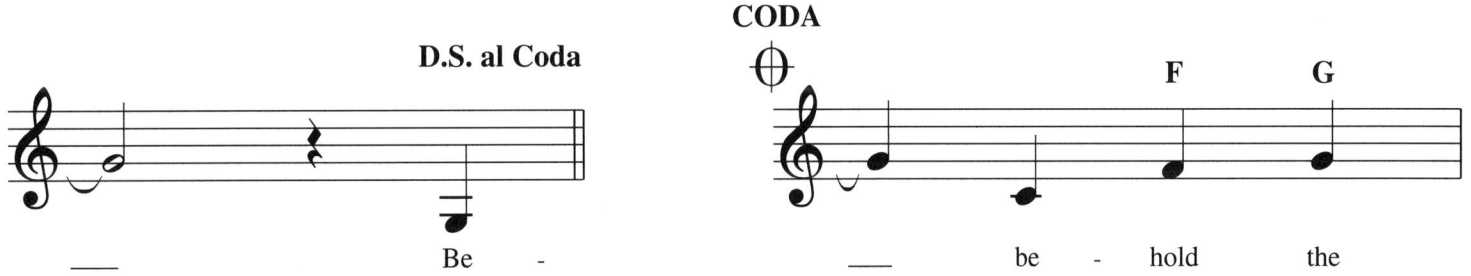
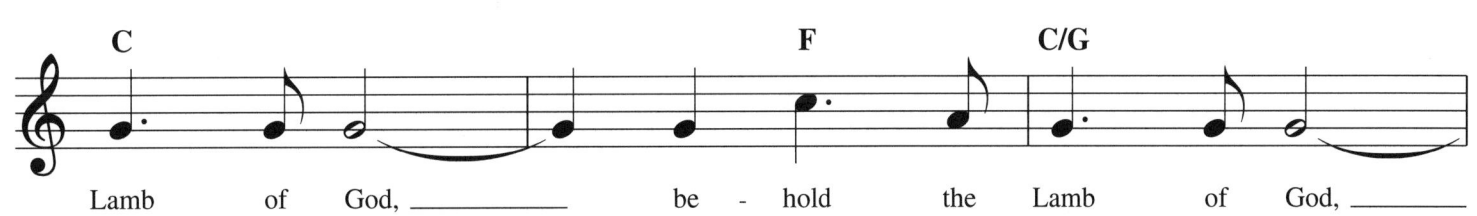
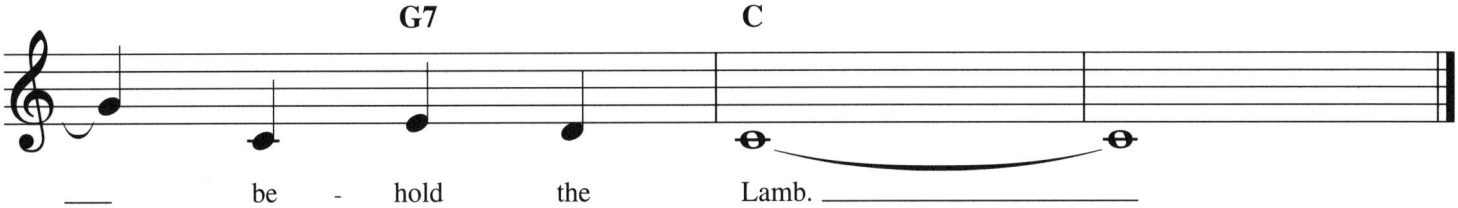

BRIGHTEN THE CORNER WHERE YOU ARE

Words by INA DULEY OGDON
Music by CHARLES H. GABRIEL

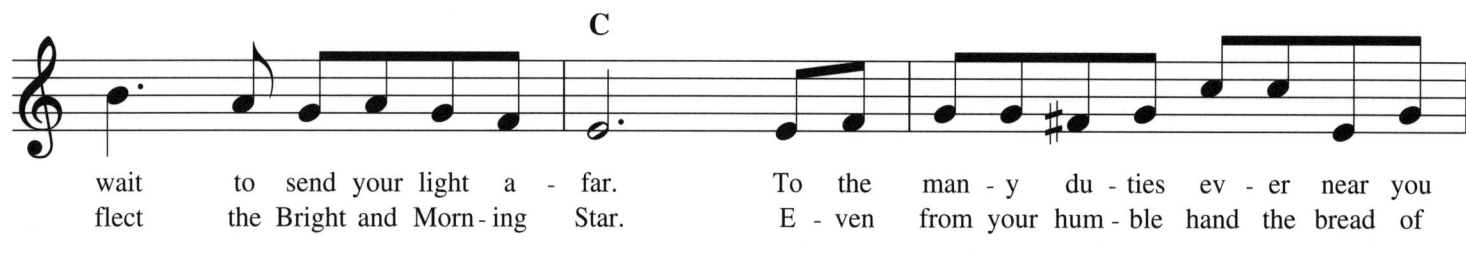

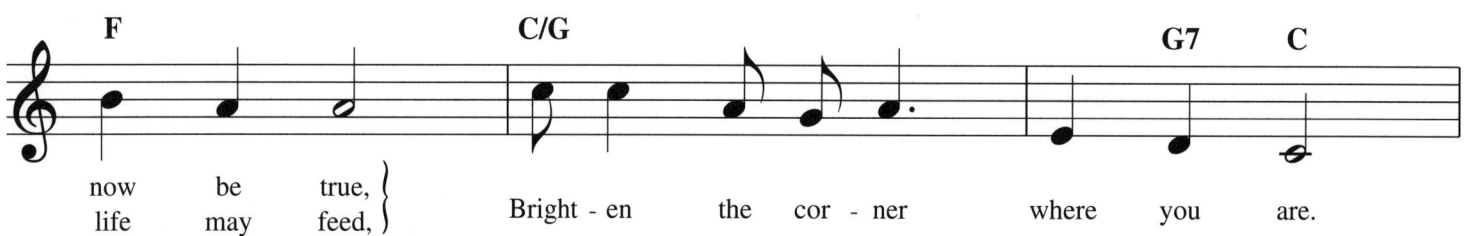

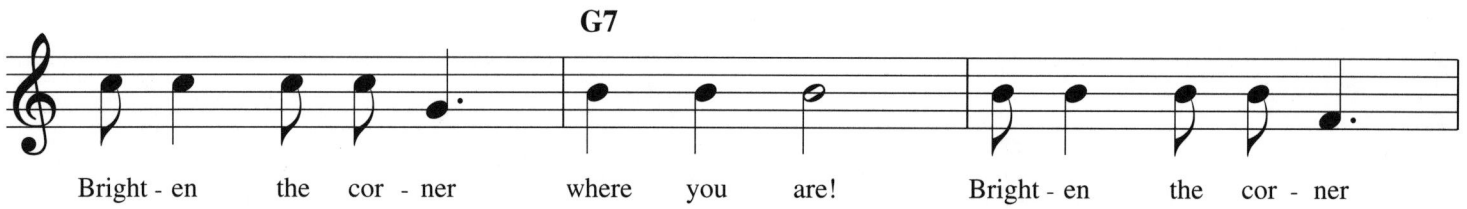

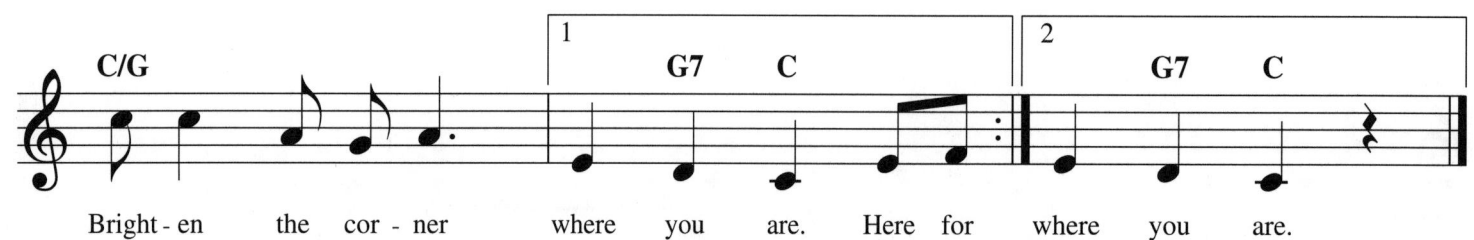

CAN HE, COULD HE, WOULD HE, DID HE?

© 1986, 1988 Word Music, Inc. and Ariose Music
Ariose Music Admin. by EMI Christian Music Publishing
All Rights Reserved   Used by Permission

Words and Music by DWIGHT LILES
and JOHN CHISUM

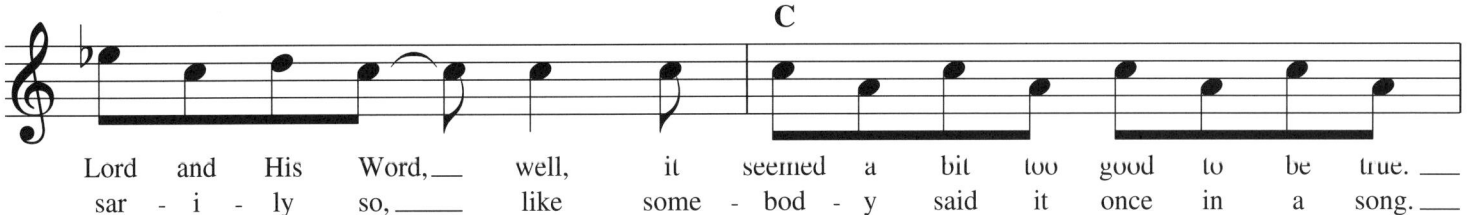

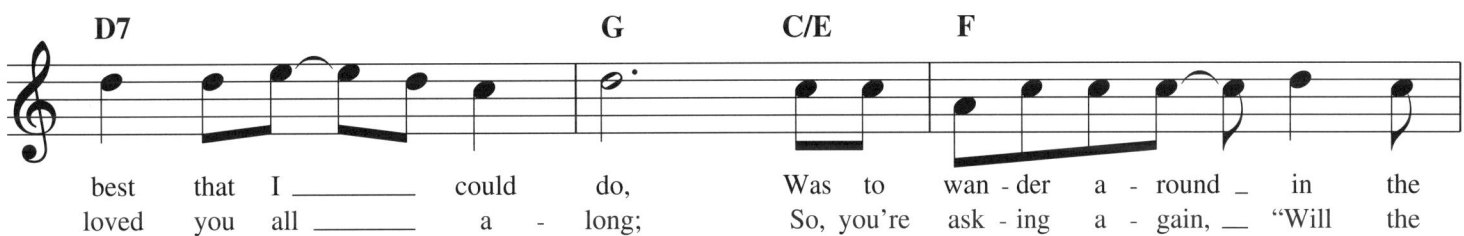
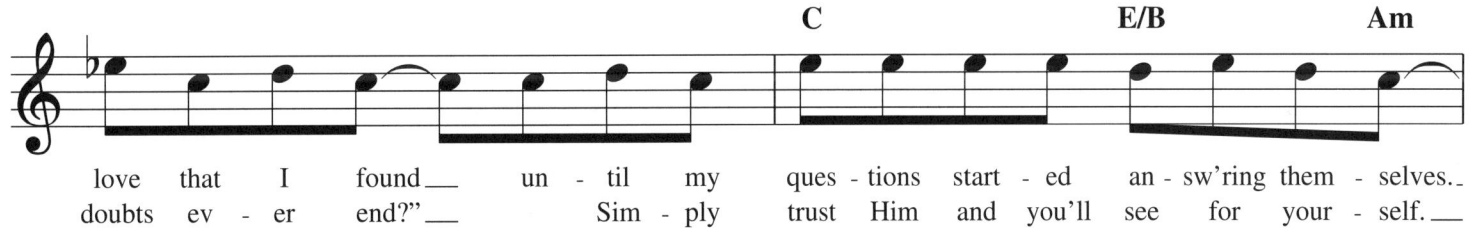
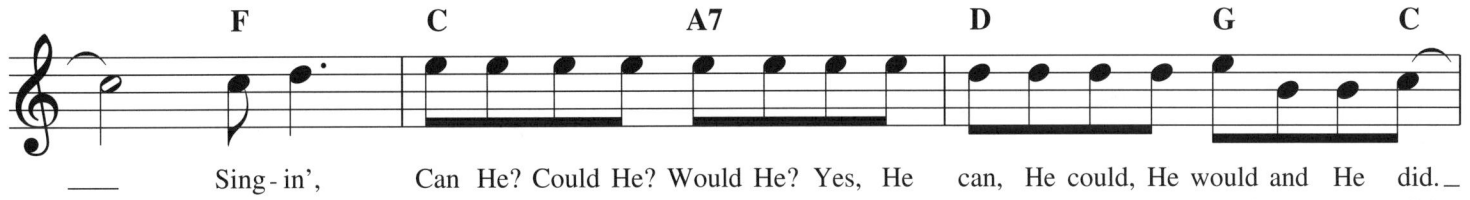
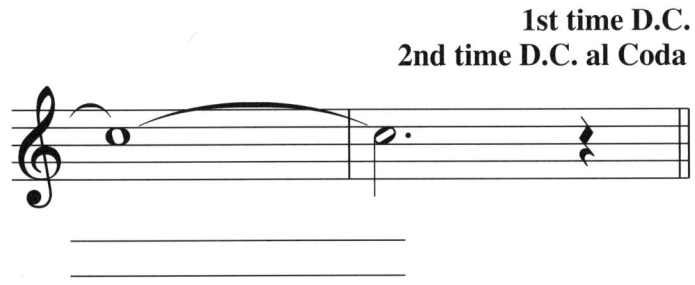
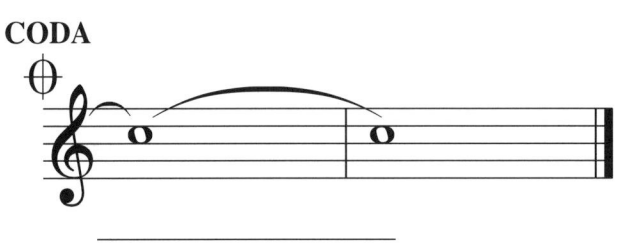

THE DAY HE WORE MY CROWN

Copyright © 1978 by Multisongs, Inc.
International Copyright Secured   All Rights Reserved

Words and Music by
PHIL JOHNSON

Reflectively

The cit - y was Je - ru - sa - lem,
He brought me love that on - ly He could give.
But he walked right through the gate

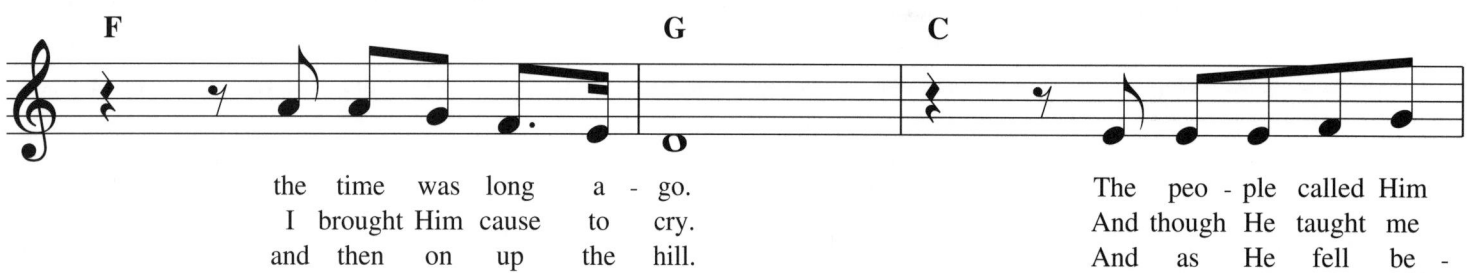

the time was long a - go.
I brought Him cause to cry.
and then on up the hill.

The peo - ple called Him
And though He taught me
And as He fell be -

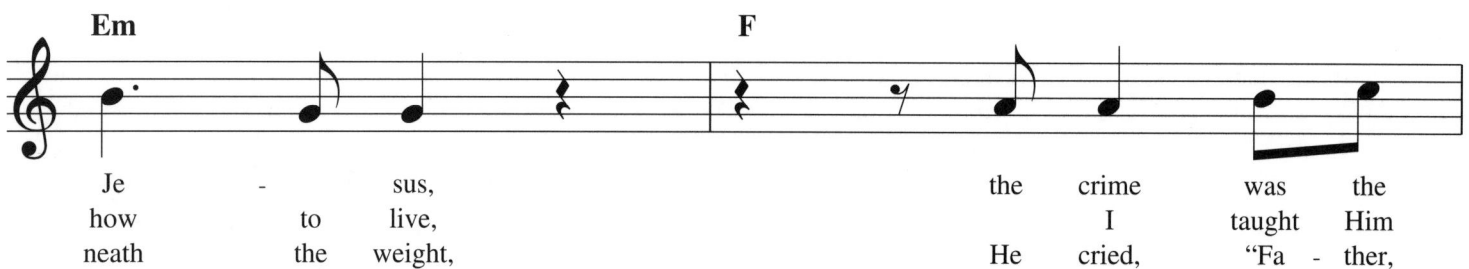

Je - sus,
how to live,
neath the weight,

the crime was the
I taught Him
He cried, "Fa - ther,

love He showed.
how to die.
not my will."

And I'm the one to blame;

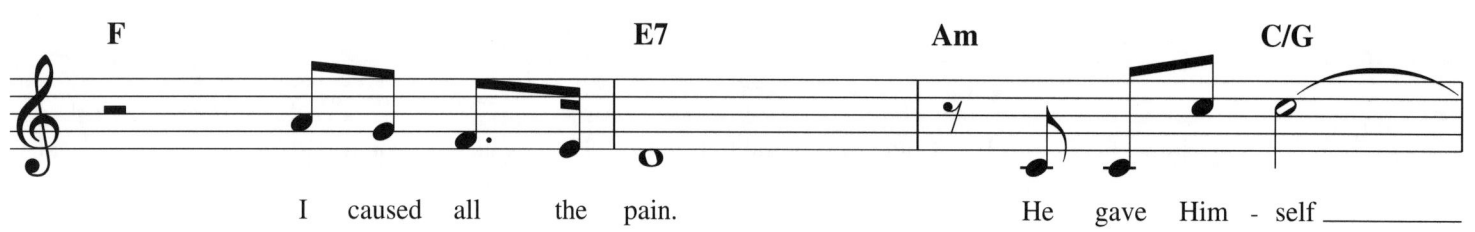

I caused all the pain.   He gave Him - self

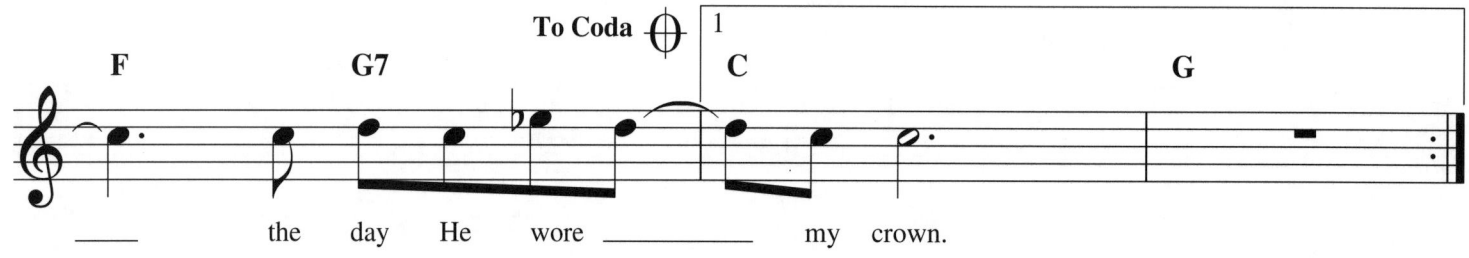

the day He wore my crown.

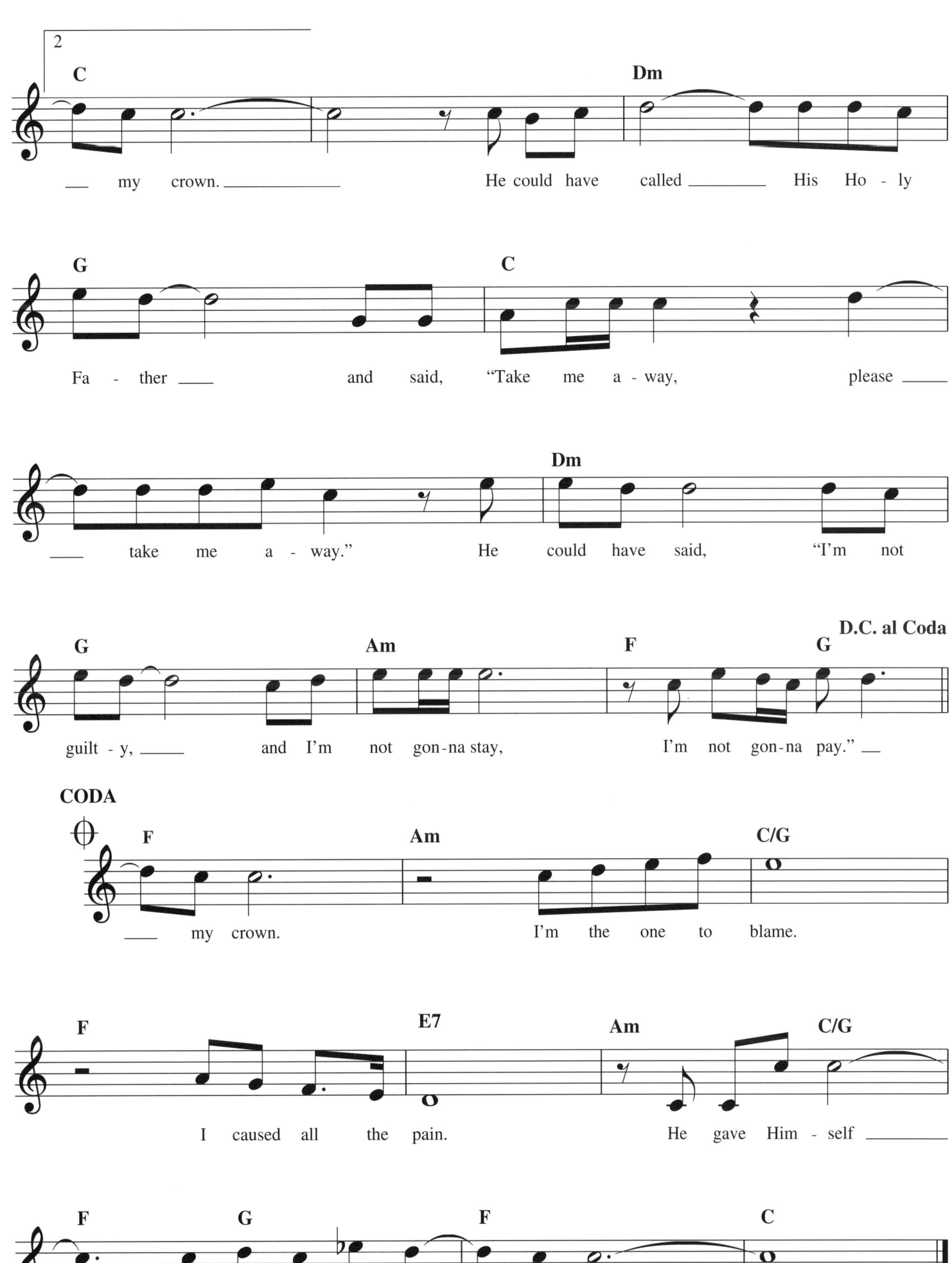

DO LORD

Traditional

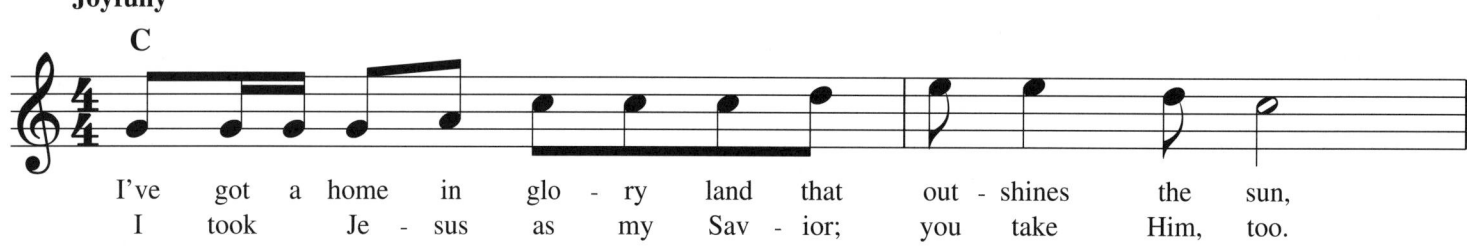
I've got a home in glory land that out-shines the sun,
I took Jesus as my Savior; you take Him, too.

I've got a home in glory land that out-shines the sun,
I took Jesus as my Savior; you take Him, too.

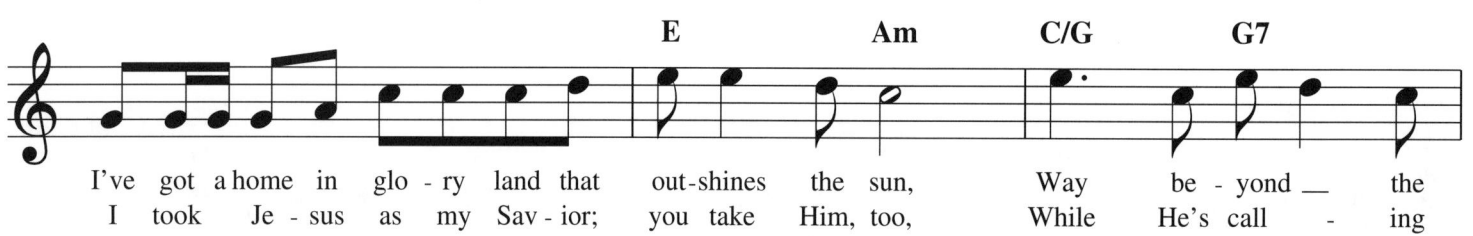
I've got a home in glory land that out-shines the sun, Way beyond ___ the
I took Jesus as my Savior; you take Him, too, While He's call - ing

blue.
you. Do Lord, O do Lord, O do re-mem-ber me.

Do Lord, O do Lord, O do re-mem-ber me. Do Lord, O do Lord, O

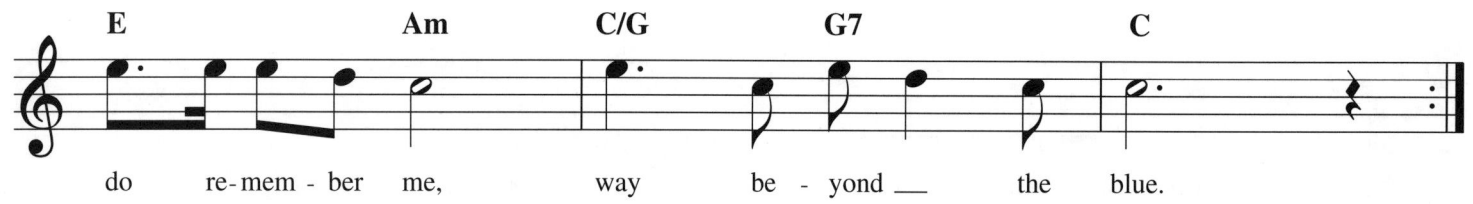
do re-mem-ber me, way be-yond ___ the blue.

DOES JESUS CARE?

Words by FRANK E. GRAEFF
Music by J. LINCOLN HALL

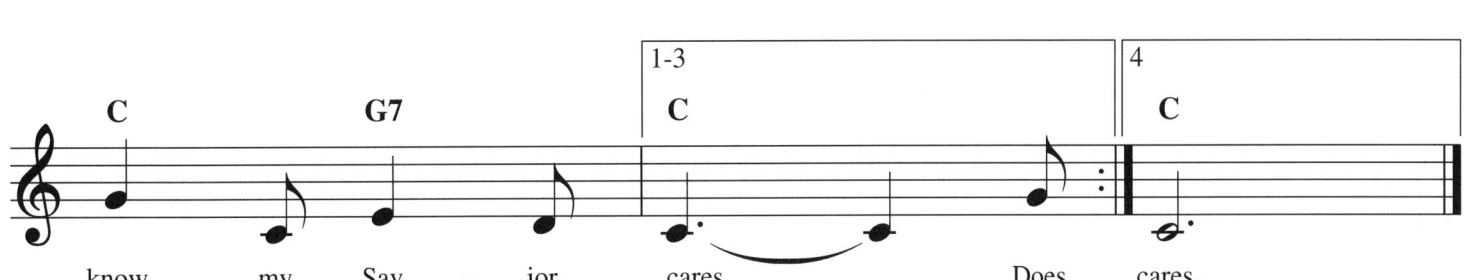

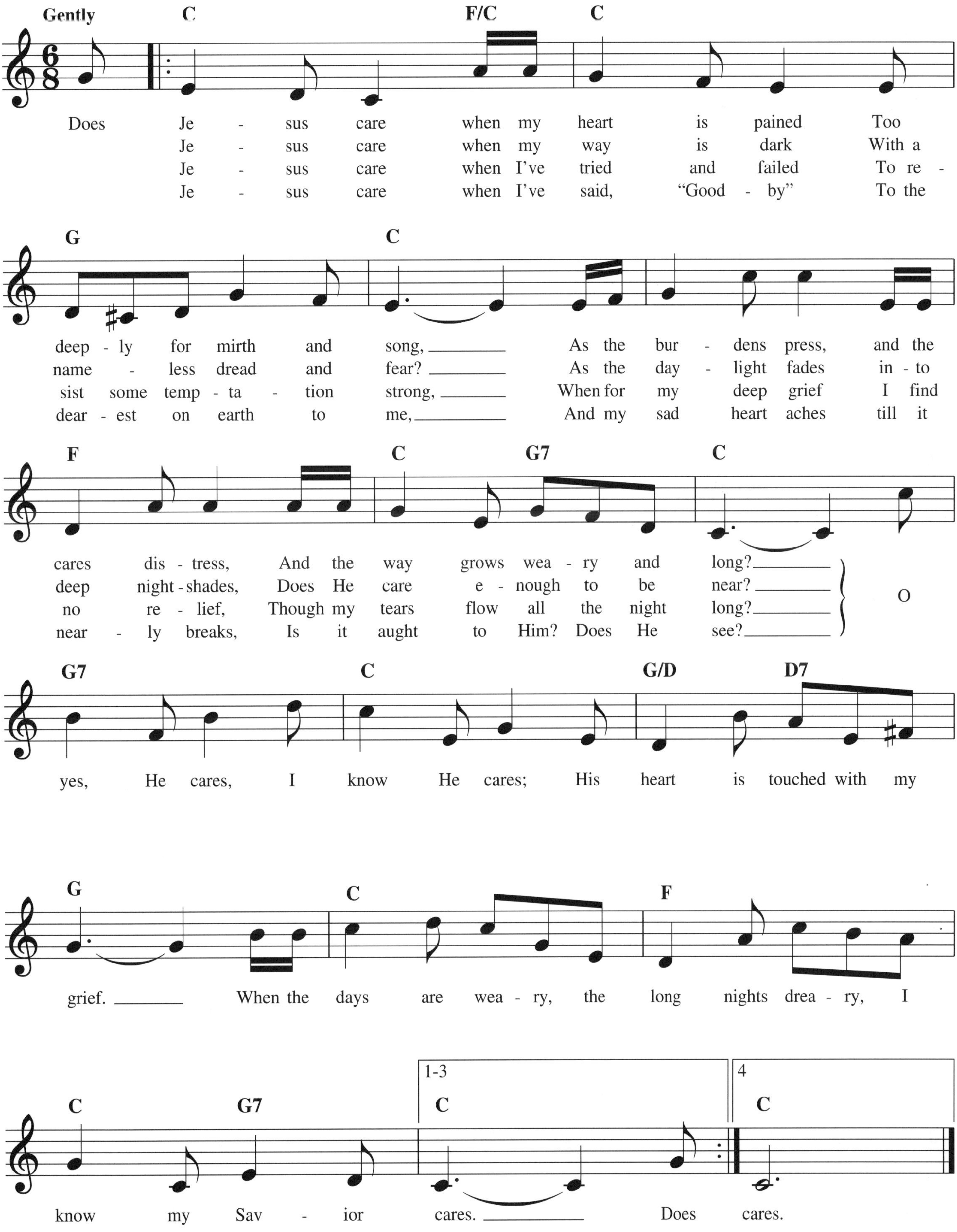

DOWN AT THE CROSS

(Glory to His Name)

Words by ELISHA A. HOFFMAN
Music by JOHN H. STOCKTON

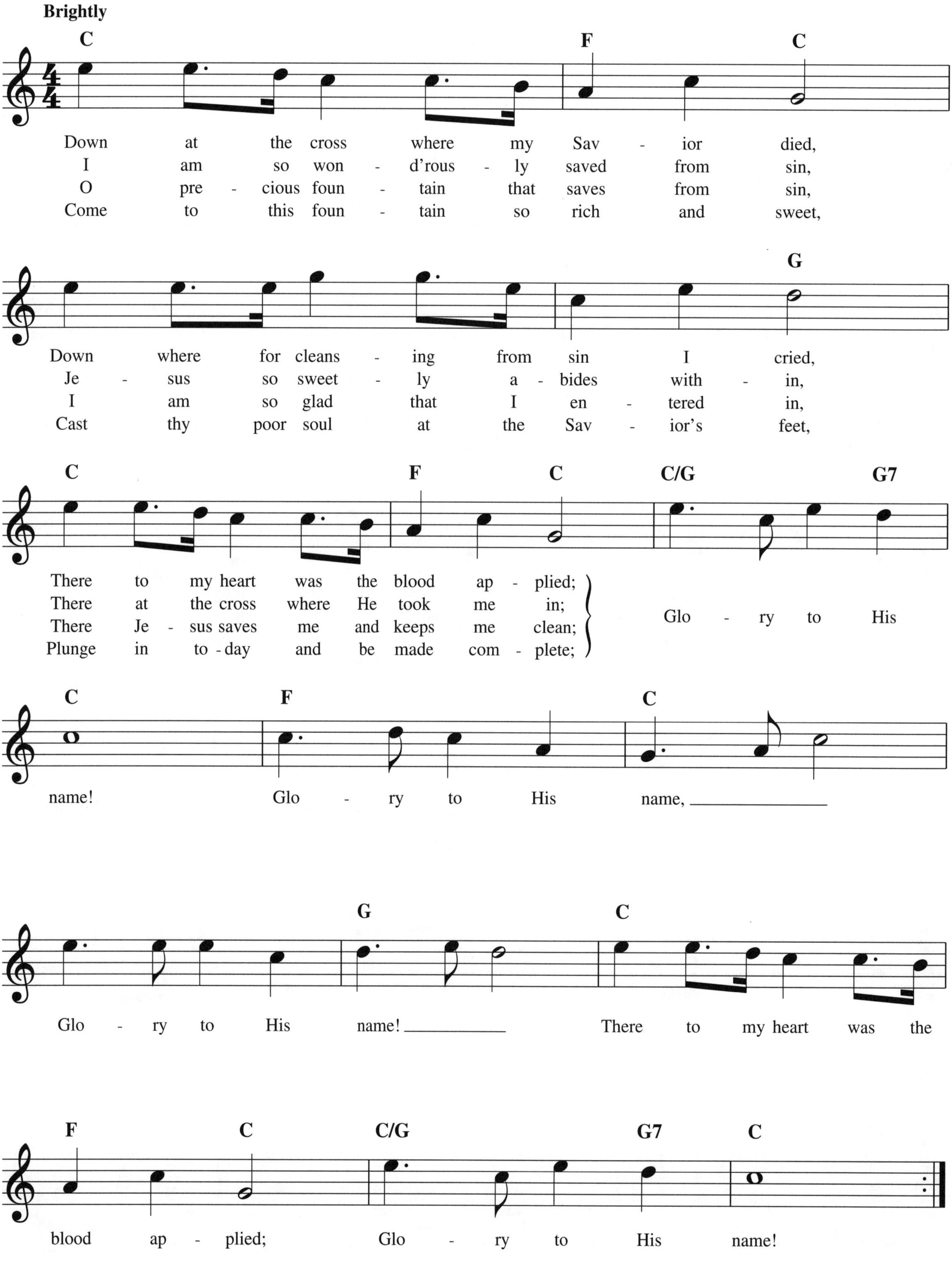
Brightly
C F C
Down at the cross where my Sav - ior died,
I am so won - d'rous - ly saved from sin,
O pre - cious foun - tain that saves from sin,
Come to this foun - tain so rich and sweet,
G
Down where for cleans - ing from sin I cried,
Je - sus so sweet - ly a - bides with - in,
I am so glad that I en - tered in,
Cast thy poor soul at the Sav - ior's feet,
C F C C/G G7
There to my heart was the blood ap - plied;
There at the cross where He took me in;
There Je - sus saves me and keeps me clean;
Plunge in to - day and be made com - plete;
Glo - ry to His
C F C
name! Glo - ry to His name,
G C
Glo - ry to His name! There to my heart was the
F C C/G G7 C
blood ap - plied; Glo - ry to His name!

THE EASTERN GATE

Words and Music by
ISAIAH G. MARTIN

Copyright © 2001 by HAL LEONARD CORPORATION
International Copyright Secured   All Rights Reserved

Moderately fast

I will meet you in the morn-ing, Just in-side the East-ern
If you has-ten off to glo-ry, Lin-ger near the East-ern
Keep your lamps all trimmed and burn-ing, For the Bride-groom watch and
O the joys of that glad meet-ing With the saints who for us

Gate.   Then be read-y, faith-ful pil-grim,
Gate;   For I'm com-ing in the morn-ing,
wait;   He'll be with us at the meet-ing
wait!   What a bless-ed, hap-py meet-ing

Lest with you it be too late.
So you'll not have long to wait.
Just in-side the East-ern Gate.
Just in-side the East-ern Gate!

I will meet you in the morn-ing, I will meet you in the morn-ing Just in-side the East-ern Gate o-ver there. I will meet you in the morn-ing, I will meet you in the morn-ing, I will meet you in the morn-ing o-ver there.

THE FAMILY OF GOD

Words and Music by WILLIAM J. and GLORIA GAITHER
Music by WILLIAM J. GAITHER

Copyright © 1970 (Renewed) William J. Gaither, Inc. (ASCAP)
All Rights Controlled by Gaither Copyright Management
All Rights Reserved   Used by Permission

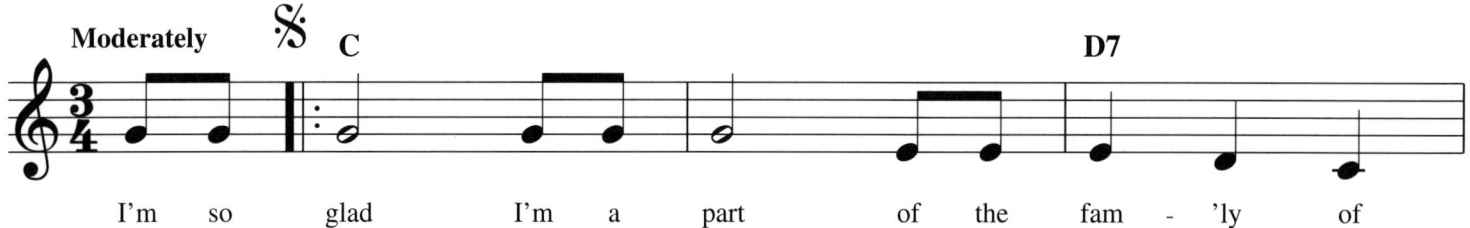

I'm so glad I'm a part of the fam-'ly of

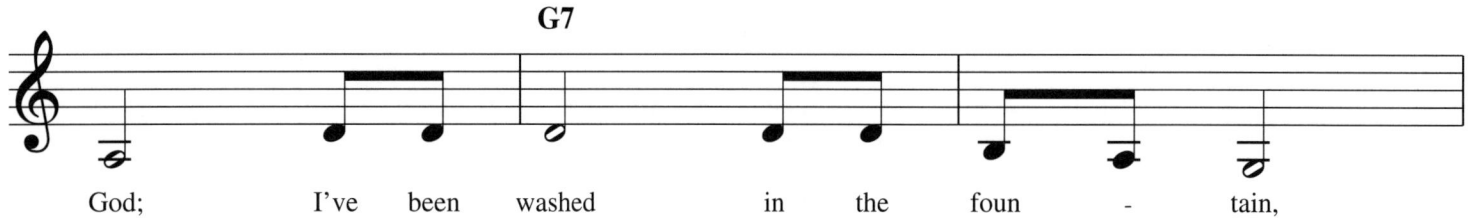

God; I've been washed in the foun - tain,

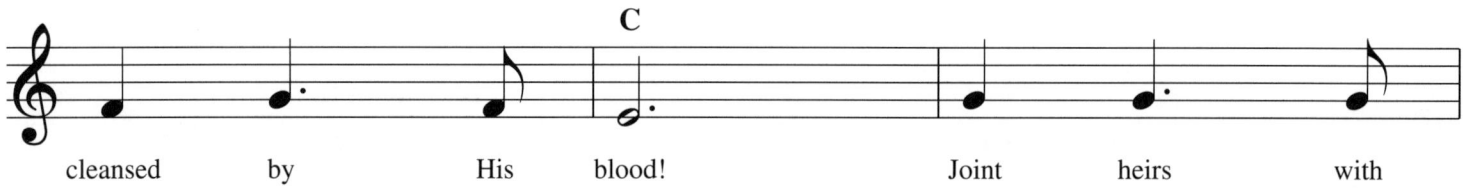

cleansed by His blood! Joint heirs with

Je - sus as we trav - el this sod, For I'm

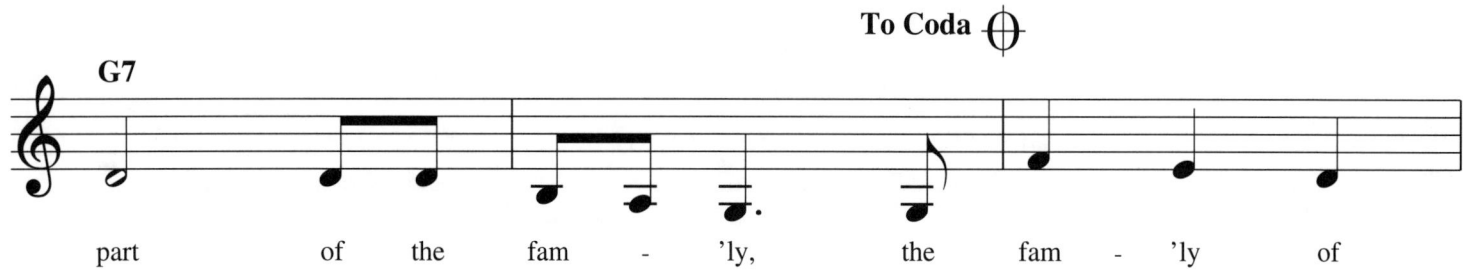

part of the fam - 'ly, the fam - 'ly of

God. / You will no - tice we say
    \ From the door of an

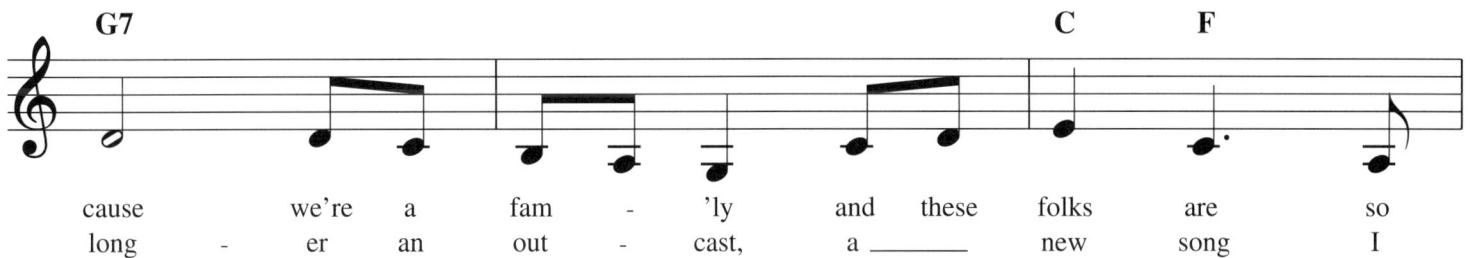

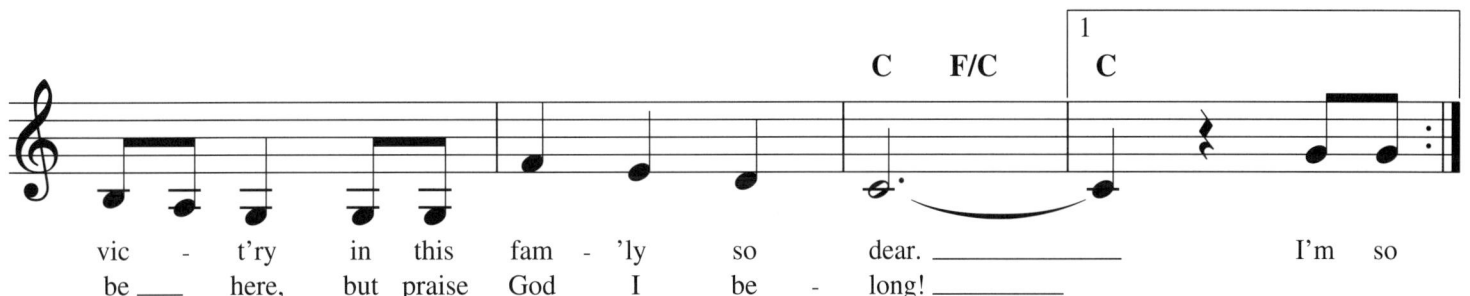

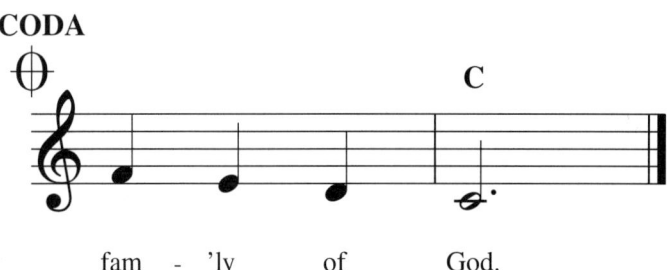

FILL MY CUP, LORD

© 1959 (Renewed 1988) Word Music, Inc.
All Rights Reserved   Used by Permission

Words and Music by
RICHARD BLANCHARD

Like the wom-an at the well I was seek-ing ___ for
mil-lions in this world who are crav-ing ___ the
broth-er, if the things this world gave you ___ leave

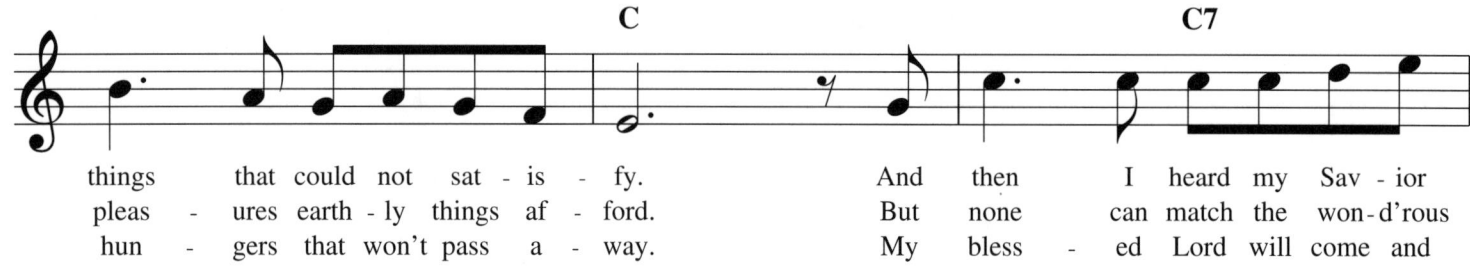

things that could not sat-is-fy. And then I heard my Sav-ior
pleas-ures earth-ly things af-ford. But none can match the won-d'rous
hun-gers that won't pass a-way. My bless-ed Lord will come and

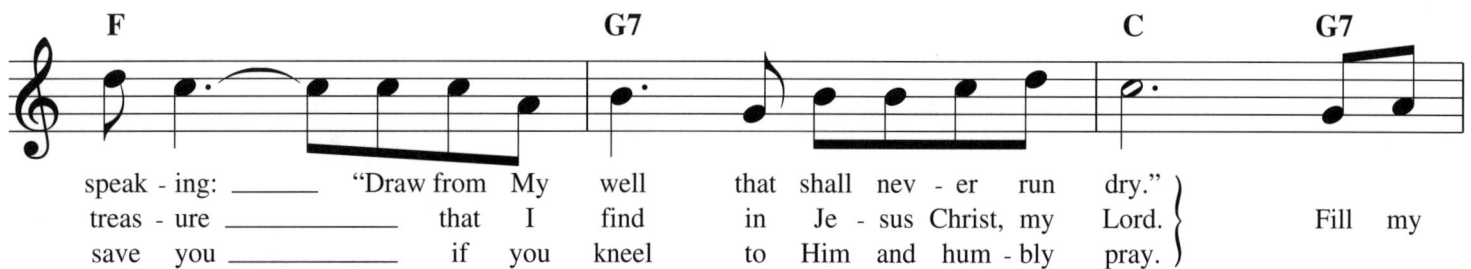

speak-ing: ___ "Draw from My well that shall nev-er run dry."
treas-ure ___ that I find in Je-sus Christ, my Lord.   Fill my
save you ___ if you kneel to Him and hum-bly pray.

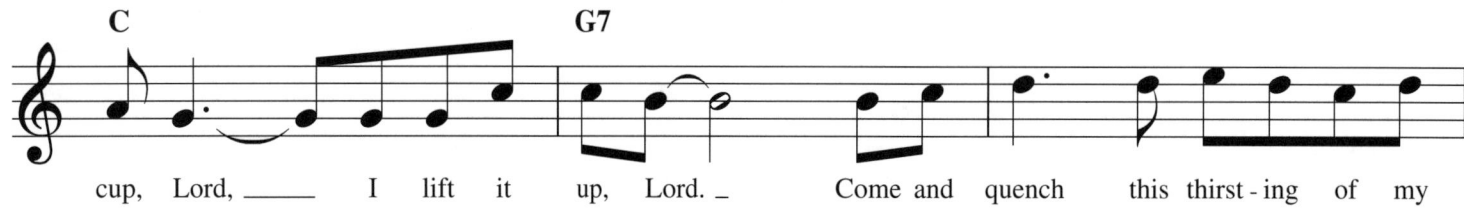

cup, Lord, ___ I lift it up, Lord. ___ Come and quench this thirst-ing of my

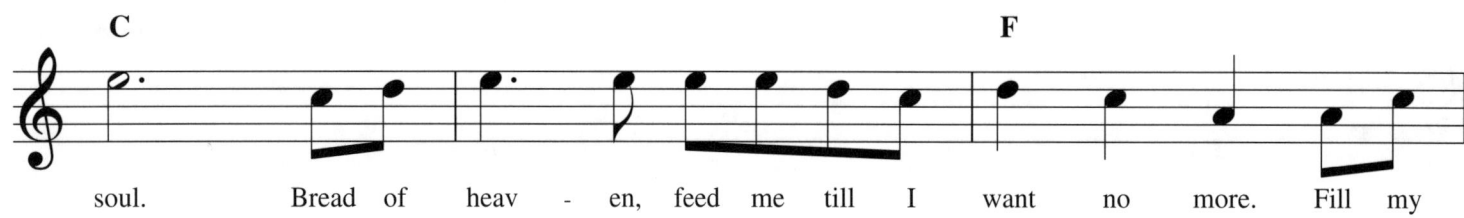

soul. Bread of heav-en, feed me till I want no more. Fill my

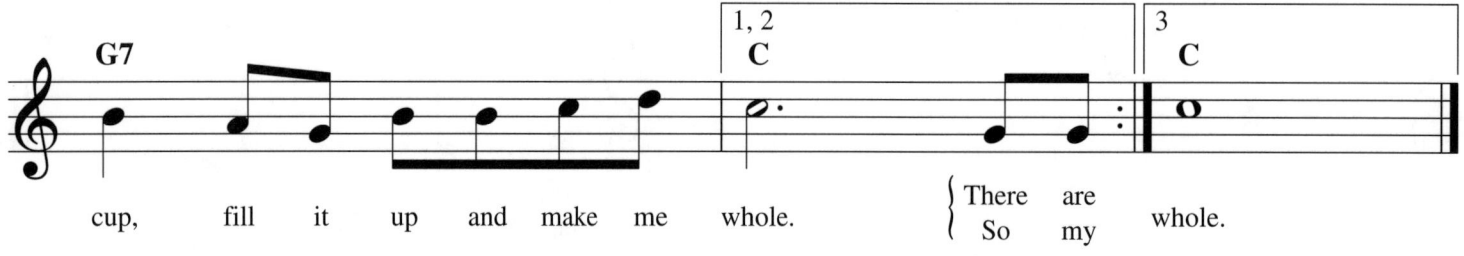

cup, fill it up and make me whole.   There are
So my   whole.

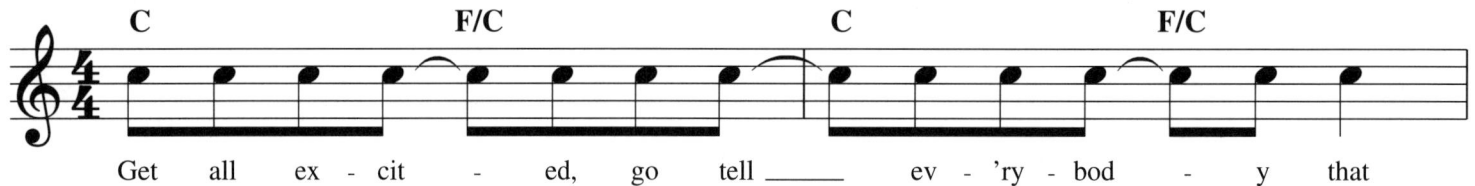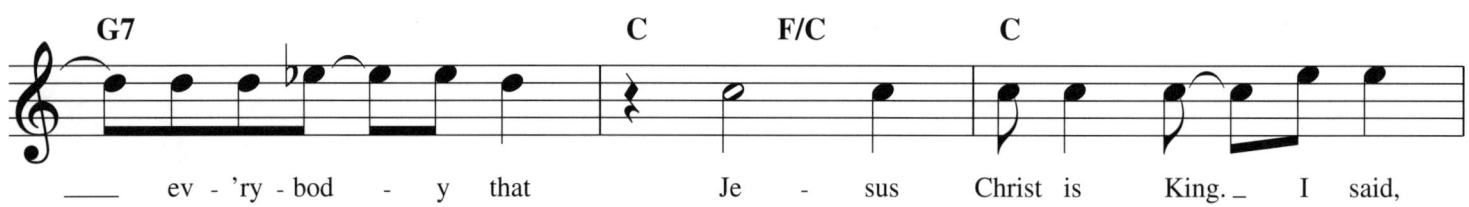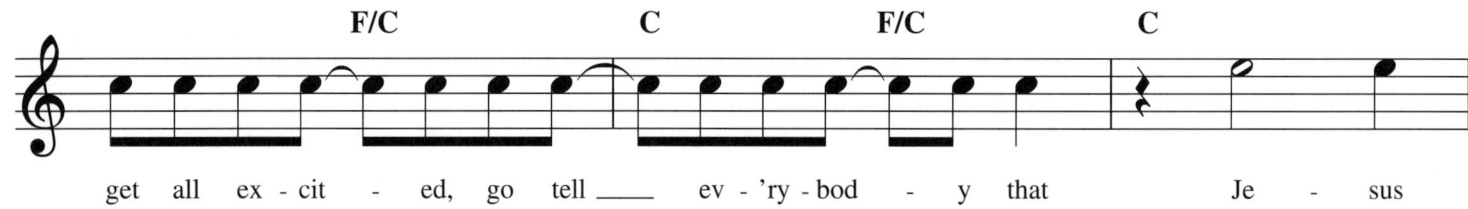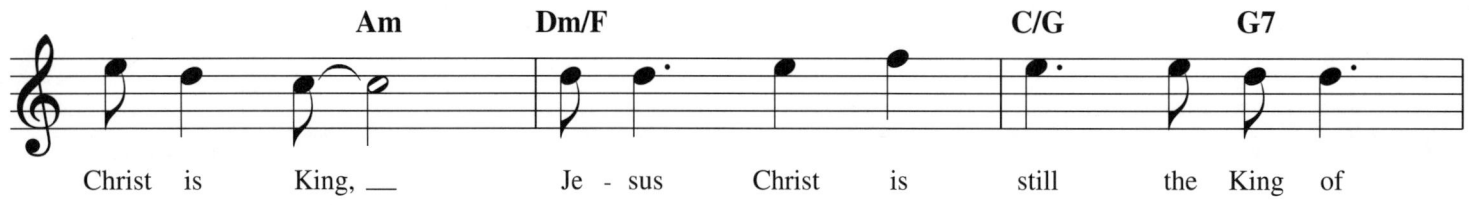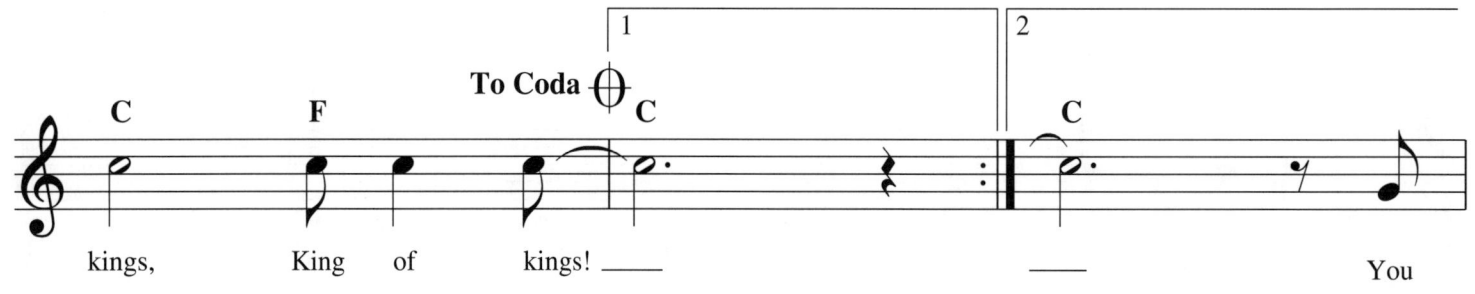

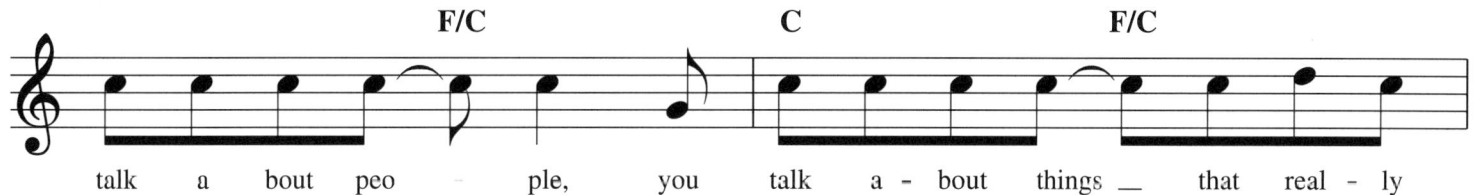
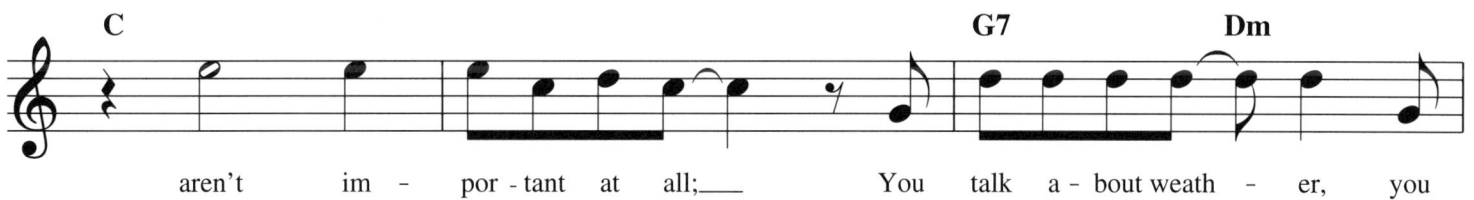
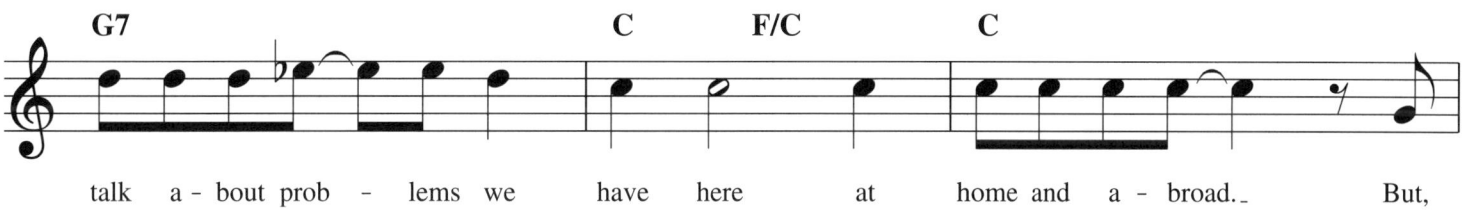

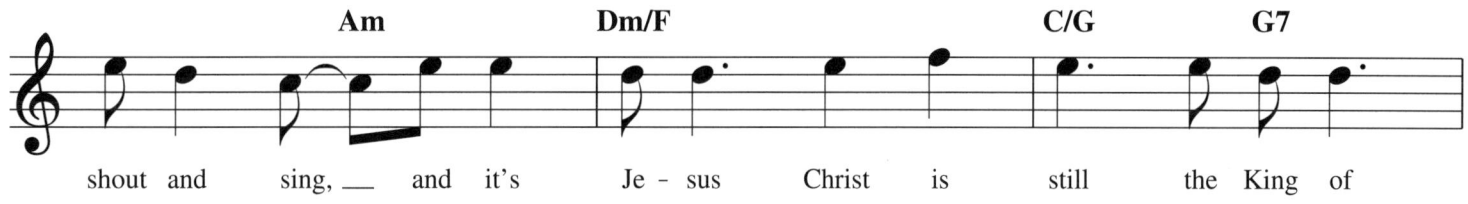
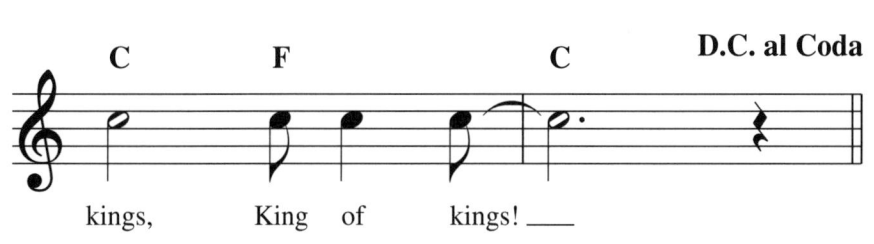
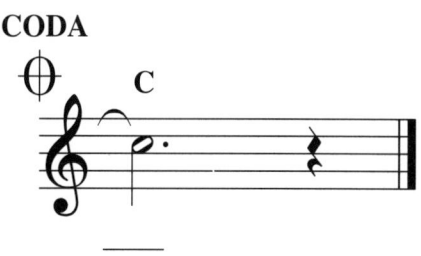

GIVE ME THAT OLD TIME RELIGION

Traditional

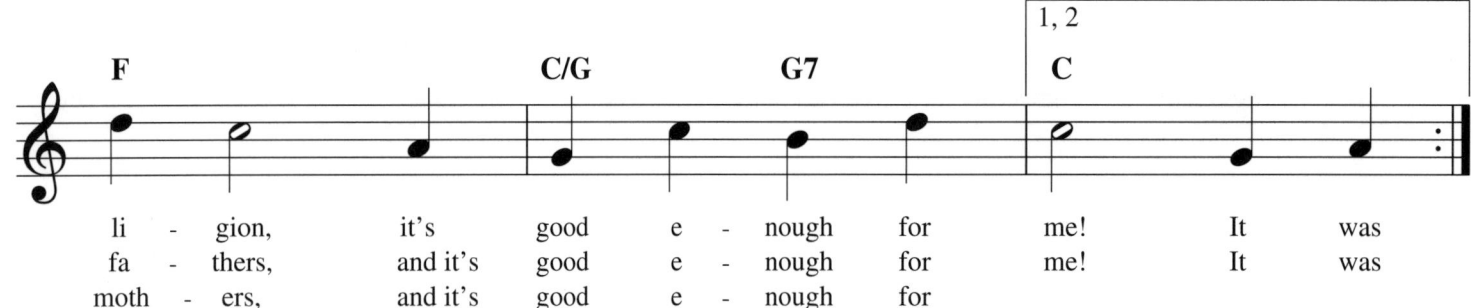
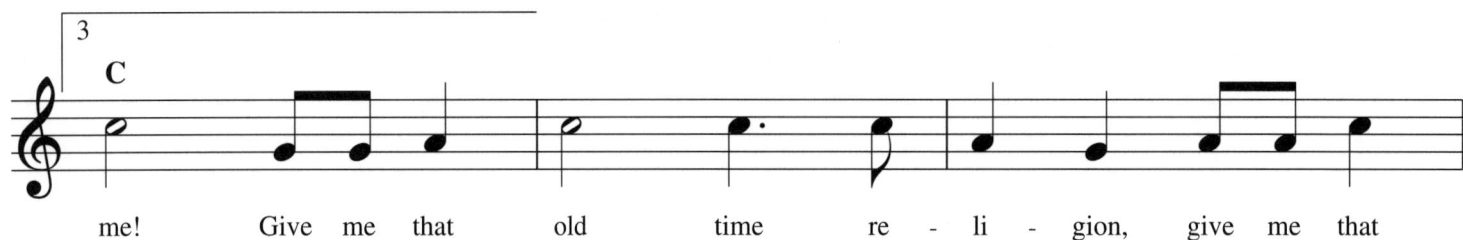

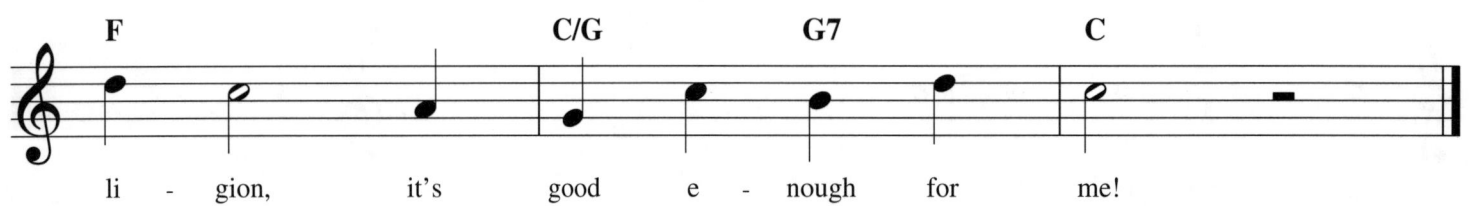

GOD SAID IT, I BELIEVE IT, THAT SETTLES IT!

Words and Music by STEPHEN R. ADAMS and GENE BRAUN

God said it and I be-lieve it, and that

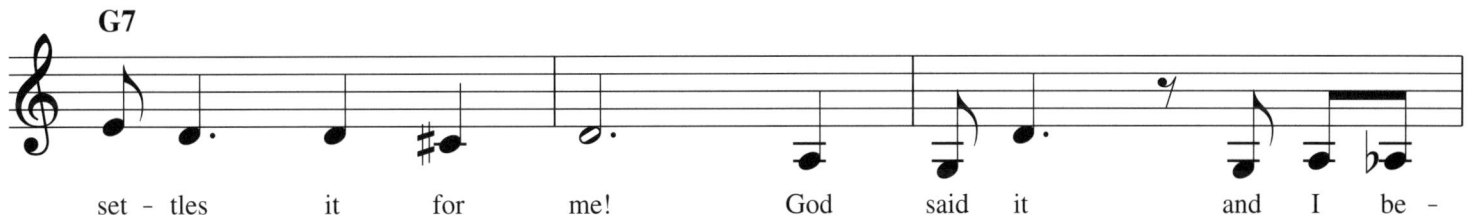
set-tles it for me! God said it and I be-

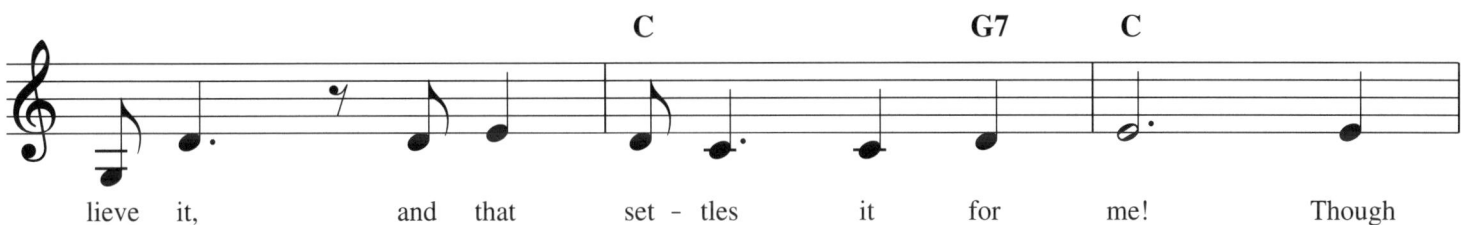
lieve it, and that set-tles it for me! Though

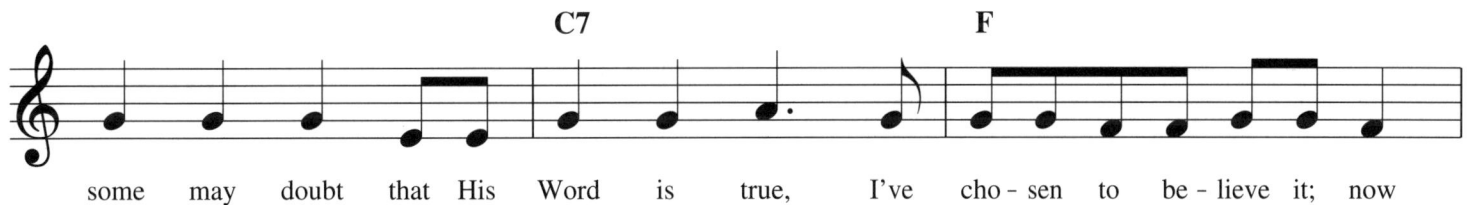
some may doubt that His Word is true, I've cho-sen to be-lieve it; now

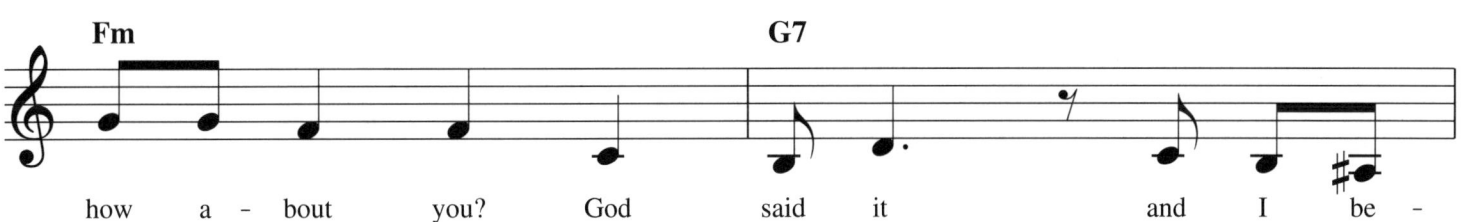
how a-bout you? God said it and I be-

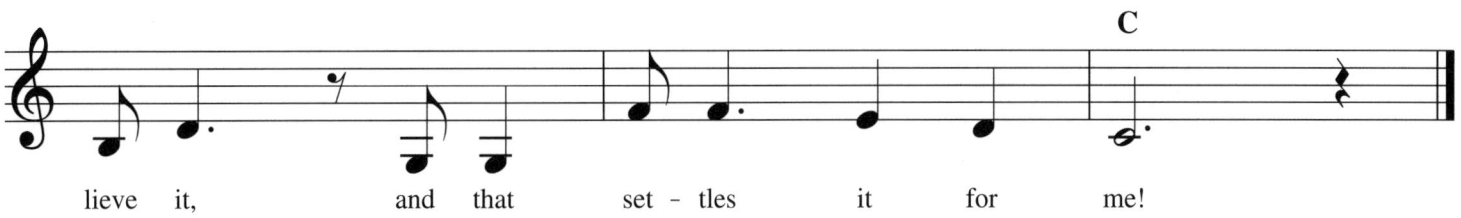
lieve it, and that set-tles it for me!

GIVE THEM ALL TO JESUS

Copyright © 1975 by Multisongs, Inc.
International Copyright Secured   All Rights Reserved

Words and Music by BOB BENSON SR.
and PHIL JOHNSON

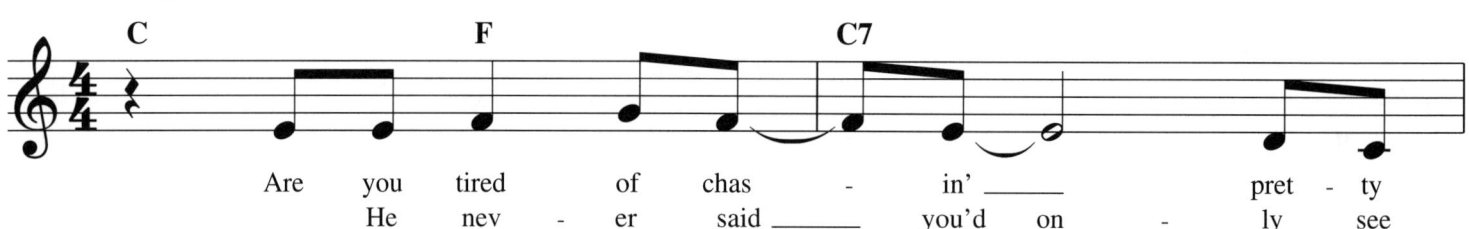
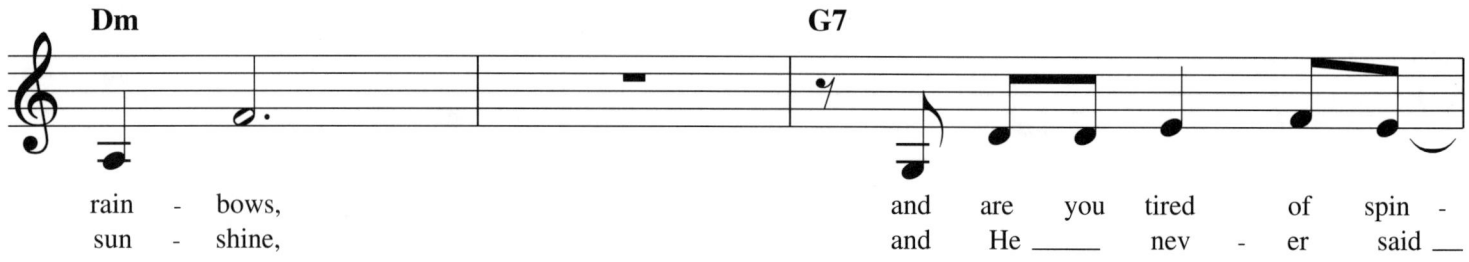
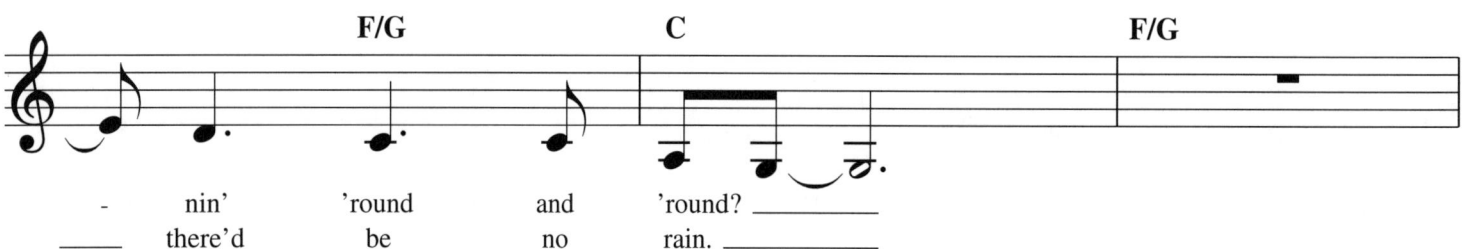
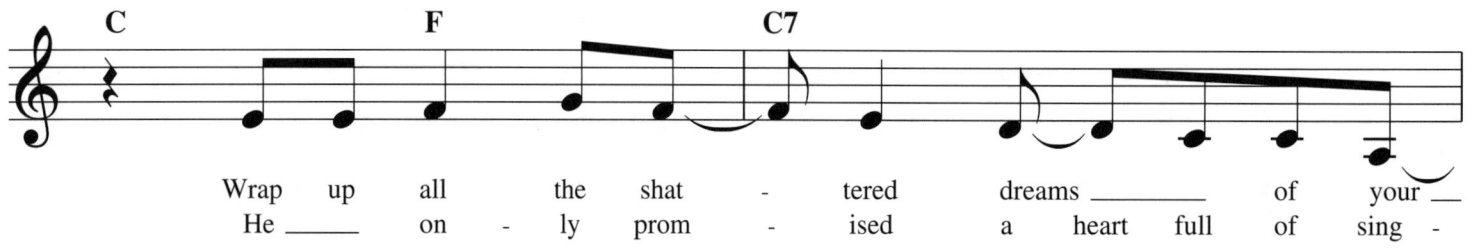
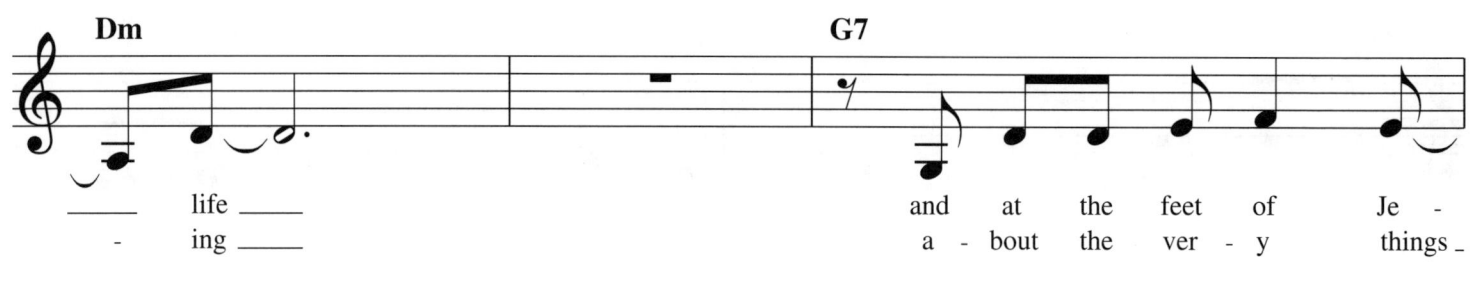
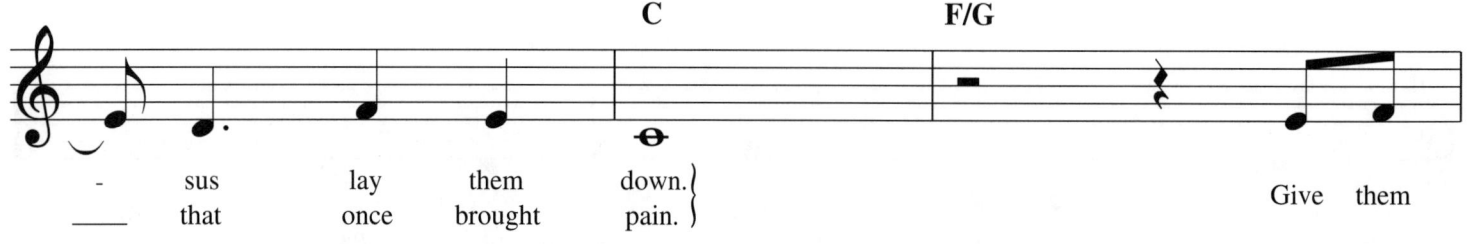

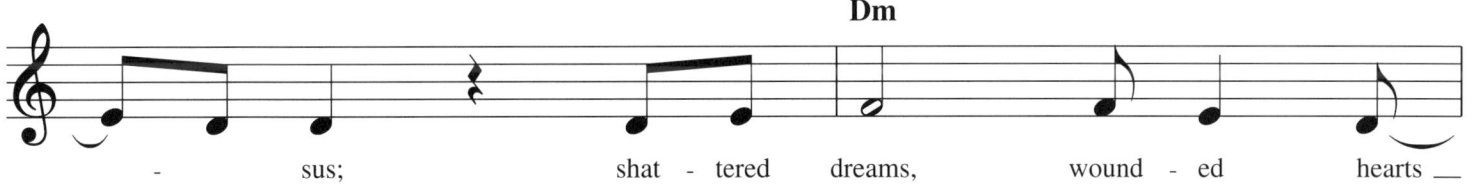
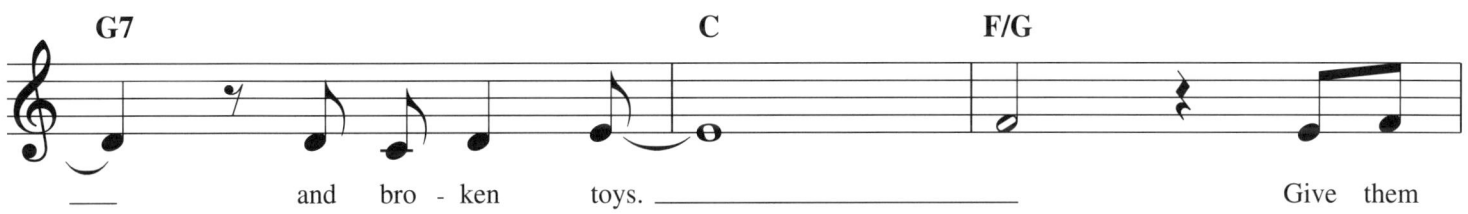
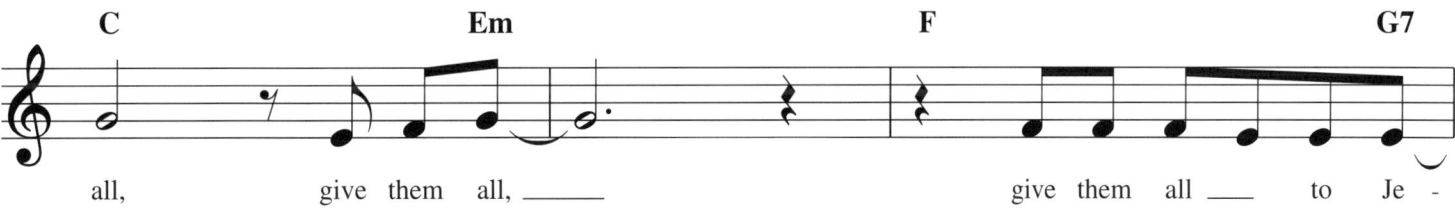
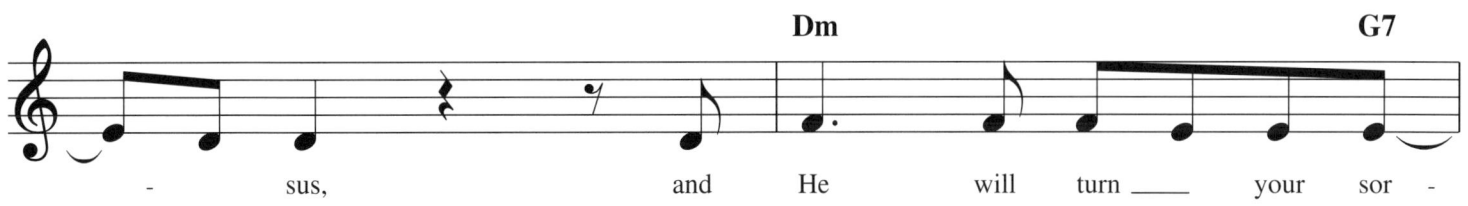
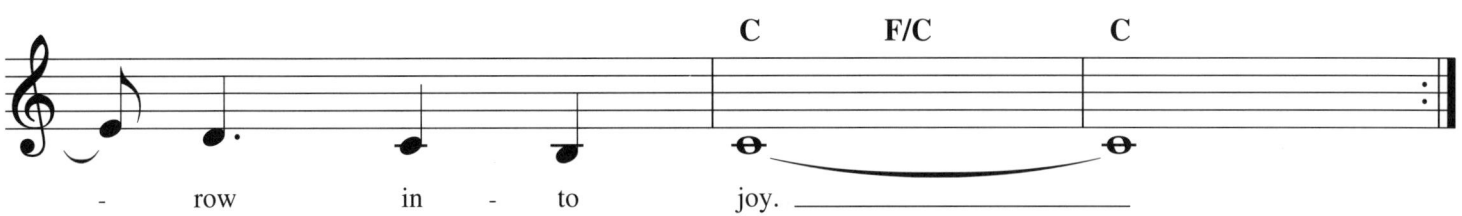

GOD WILL TAKE CARE OF YOU

Words by CIVILLA D. MARTIN
Music by W. STILLMAN MARTIN

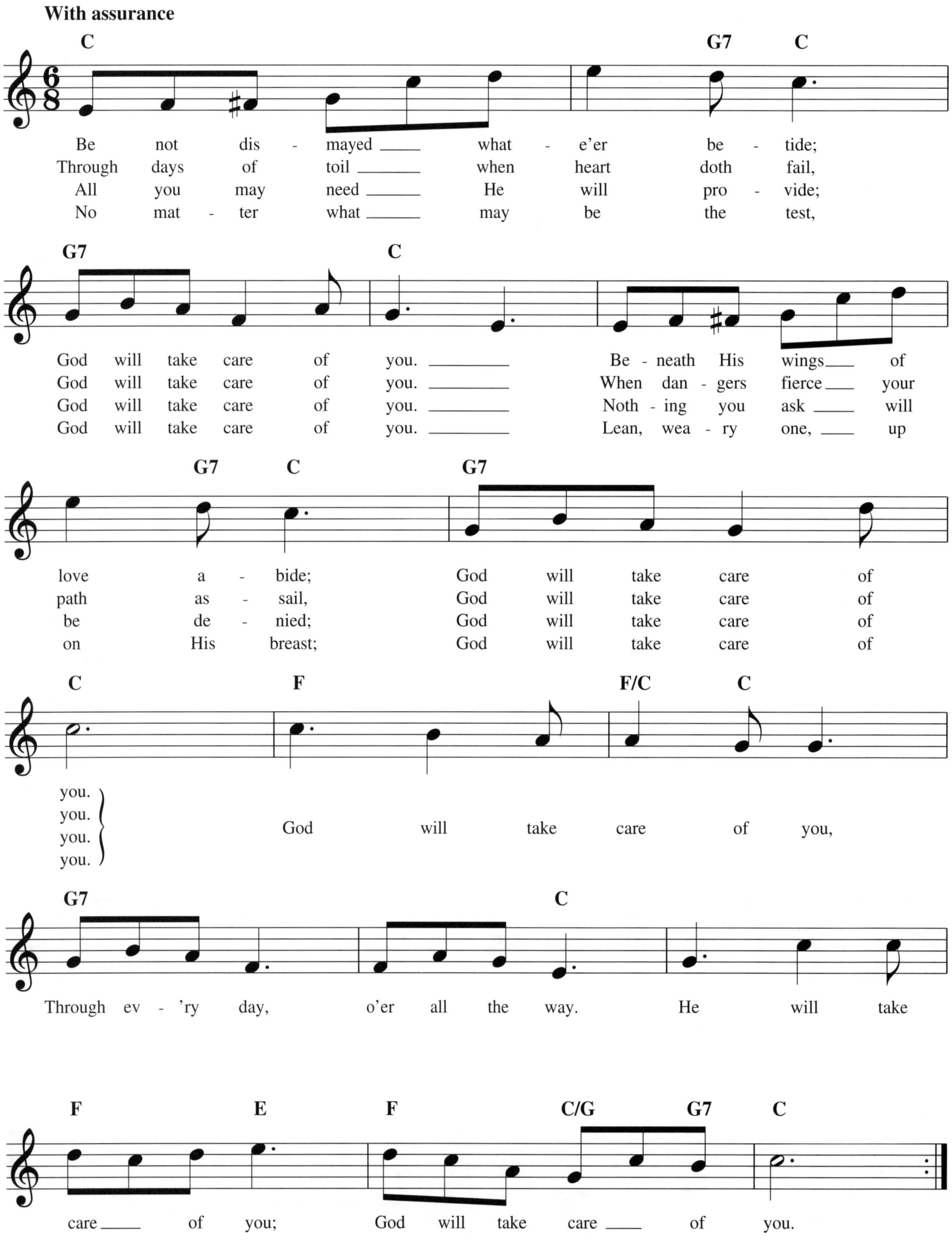
With assurance
C G7 C
Be not dis - mayed what - e'er be - tide;
Through days of toil when heart doth fail,
All you may need He will pro - vide;
No mat - ter what may be the test,
G7 C
God will take care of you. Be - neath His wings of
God will take care of you. When dan - gers fierce your
God will take care of you. Noth - ing you ask will
God will take care of you. Lean, wea - ry one, up
G7 C G7
love a - bide; God will take care of
path as - sail, God will take care of
be de - nied; God will take care of
on His breast; God will take care of
C F F/C C
you. you. you. you.
God will take care of you,
G7 C
Through ev - 'ry day, o'er all the way. He will take
F E F C/G G7 C
care of you; God will take care of you.

HE KEEPS ME SINGING

Copyright © 2001 by HAL LEONARD CORPORATION
International Copyright Secured   All Rights Reserved

Words and Music by
LUTHER B. BRIDGERS

Joyfully

| C | F/C C | D7 | G |

There's with-in my heart a mel - o - dy, Je - sus whis-pers sweet and
All my life was wrecked by sin and strife; Dis - cord filled my heart with
Feast - ing on the rich - es of His grace, Rest - ing 'neath His shel - t'ring
Though some-times He leads through wa - ters deep, Tri - als fall a - cross the
Soon He's com - ing back to wel - come me, Far be - yond the star - ry

| C/G | G7 | C | F/C C | D7 |

low: "Fear not, I am with thee; peace, be still,"
pain. Je - sus swept a - cross the bro - ken strings,
wing, Al - ways look - ing on His smil - ing face;
way, Though some - times the path seems rough and steep,
sky; I shall wing my flight to worlds un - known,

| G | C/G G7 | C |

In all of life's ebb and flow.
Stirred the slum - b'ring chords a - gain.
That is why I shout and sing.   Je - sus, Je - sus,
See His foot - prints all the way.
I shall reign with Him on high.

| G7 | | | C |

Je - sus, sweet - est name I know,

| | F | G | C/G G7 | C |

Fills my ev - 'ry long - ing, keeps me sing - ing as I go.

HE TOUCHED ME

Copyright © 1963 (Renewed) William J. Gaither, Inc. (ASCAP)
All Rights Controlled by Gaither Copyright Management
All Rights Reserved   Used by Permission

Words and Music by
WILLIAM J. GAITHER

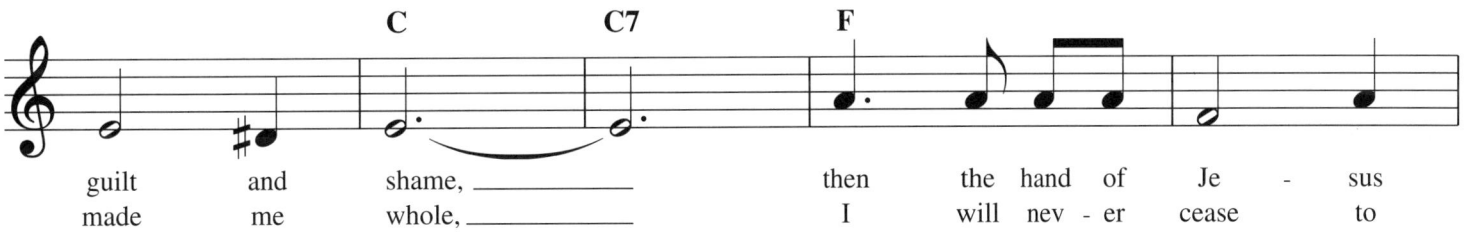

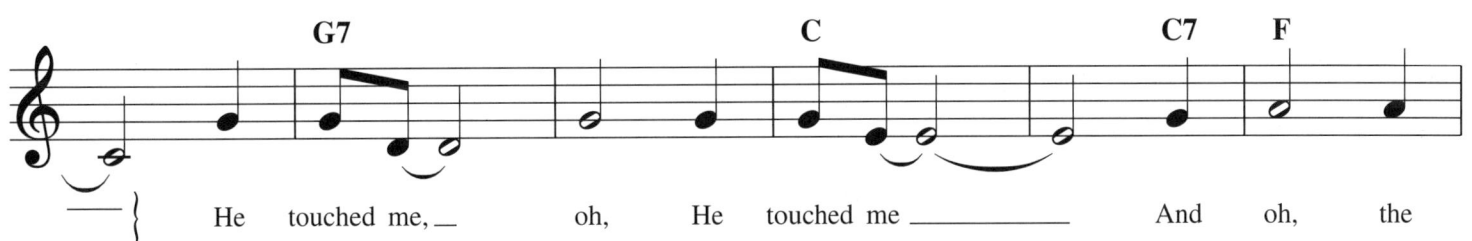
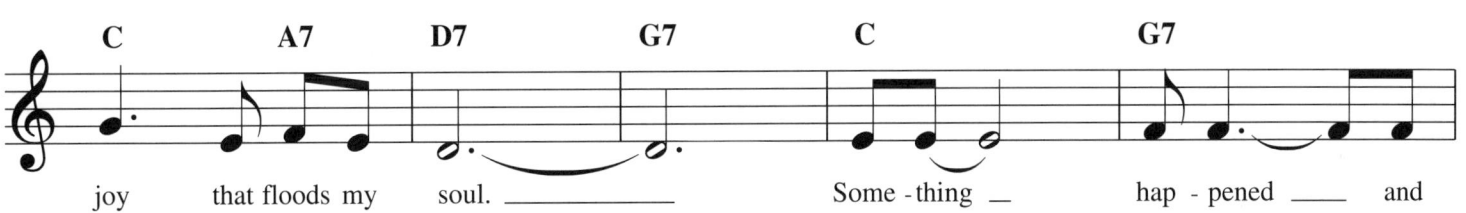
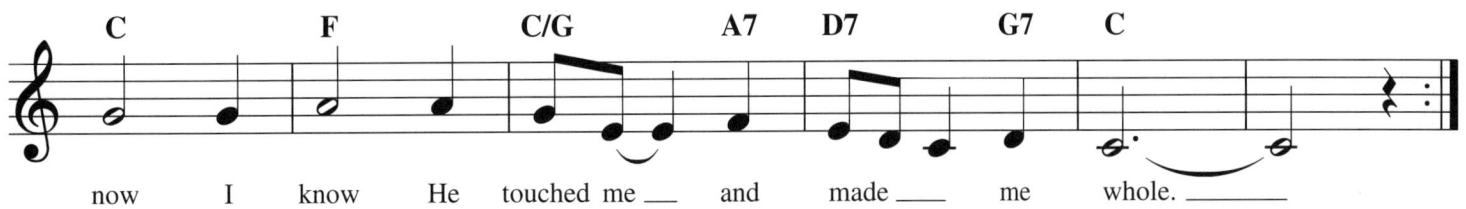

HE LOOKED BEYOND MY FAULT

© 1968 John T. Benson Publishing Co. (ASCAP) (admin. by Brentwood-Benson Music Publishing, Inc.)
Copyright Renewed
All Rights Reserved   Used by Permission

Words and Music by
DOTTIE RAMBO

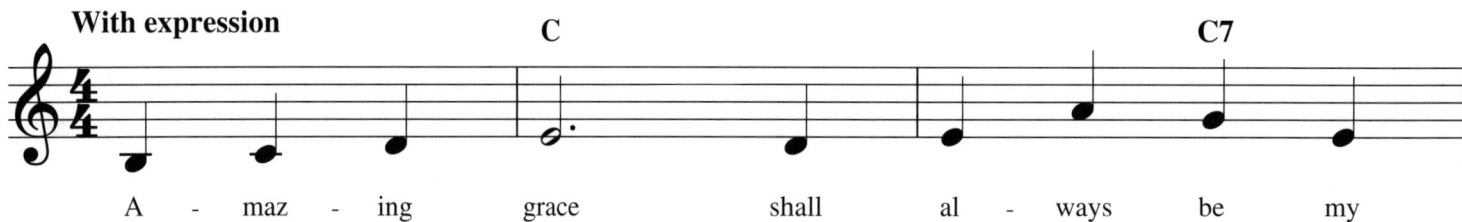
A - maz - ing grace shall al - ways be my

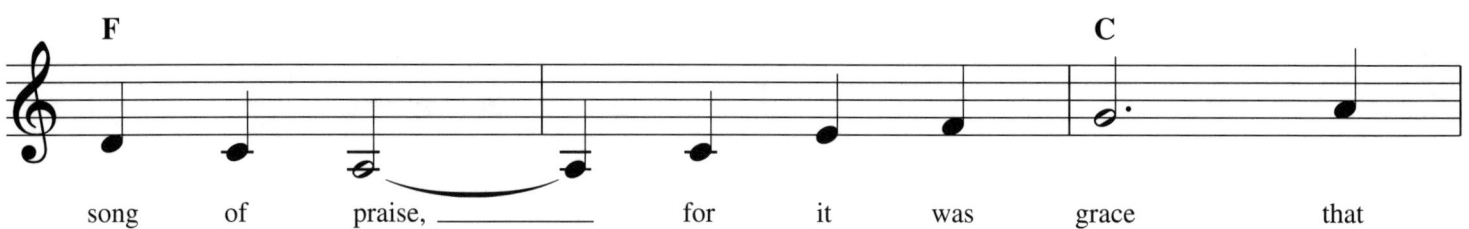
song of praise, _____ for it was grace that

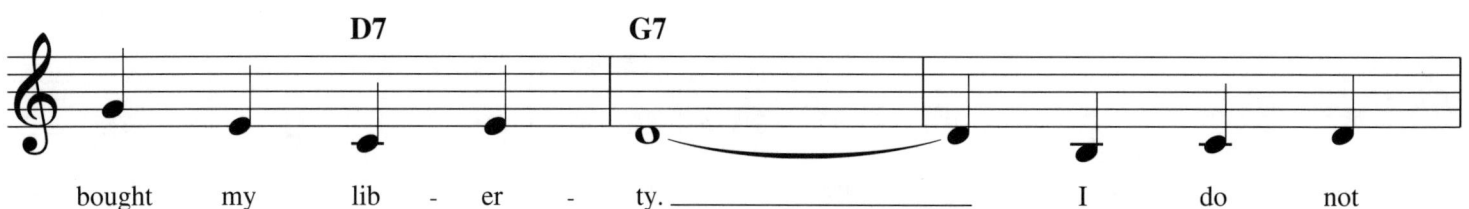
bought my lib - er - ty. _____ I do not

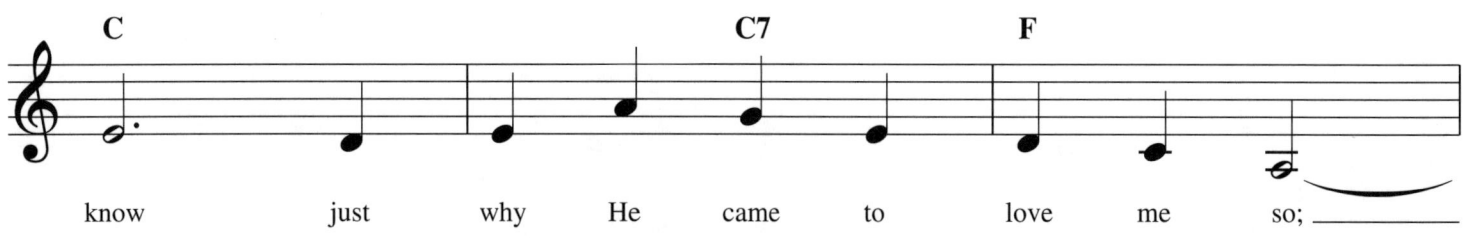
know just why He came to love me so; _____

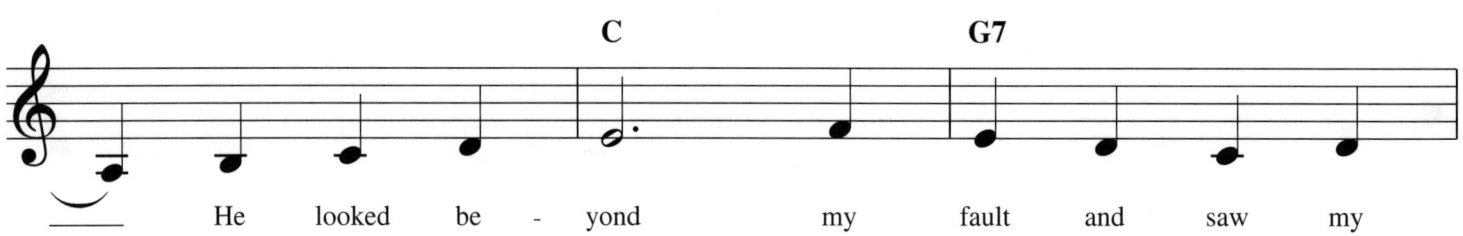
_____ He looked be - yond my fault and saw my

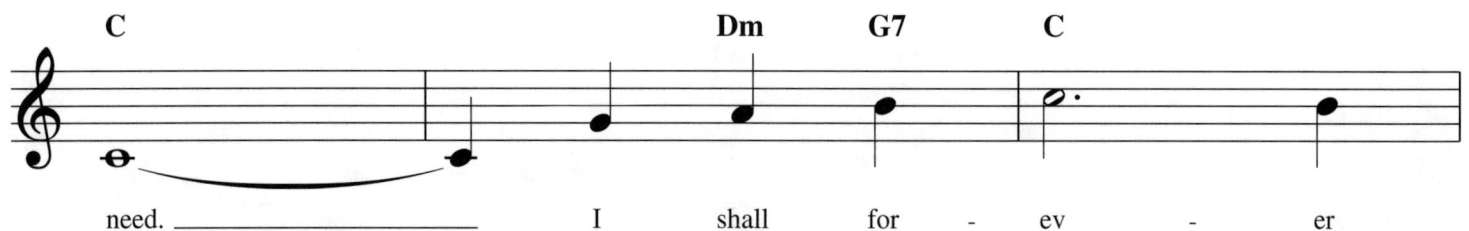
need. _____ I shall for - ev - er

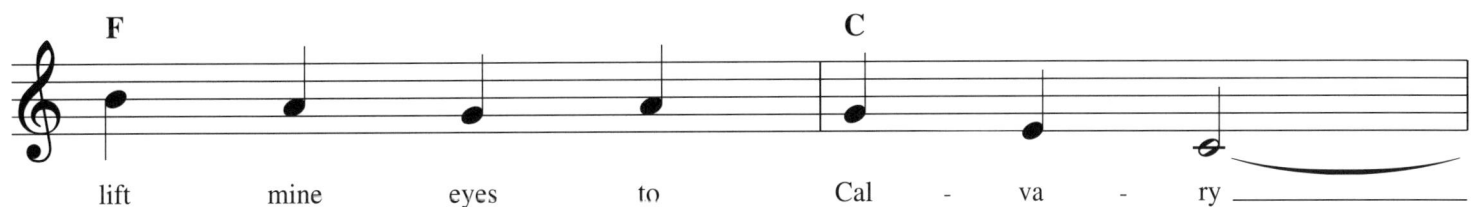
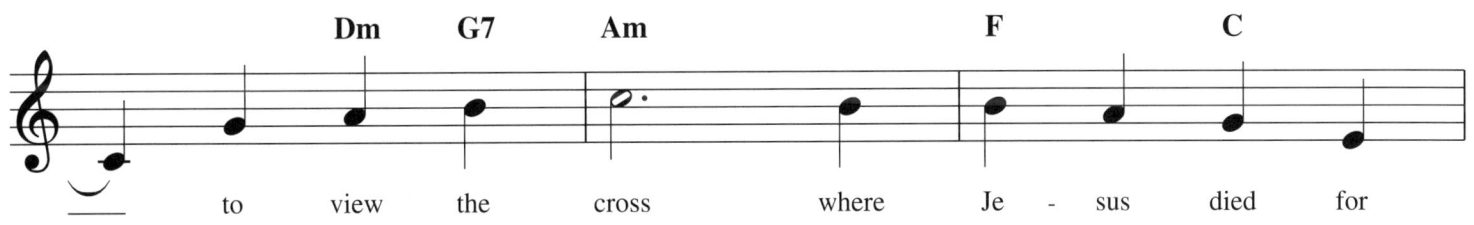
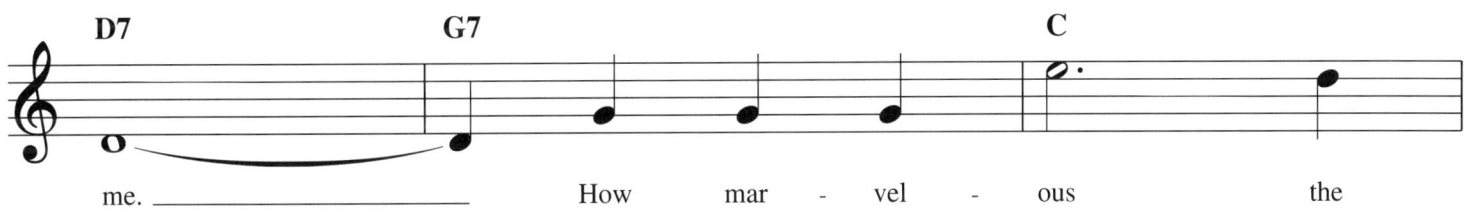
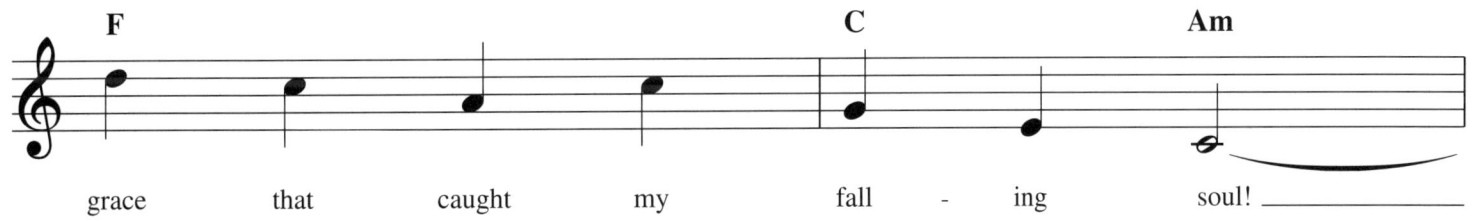
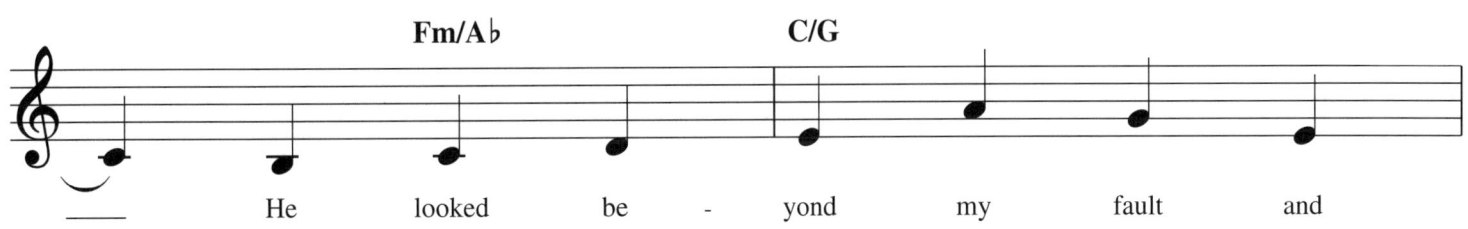
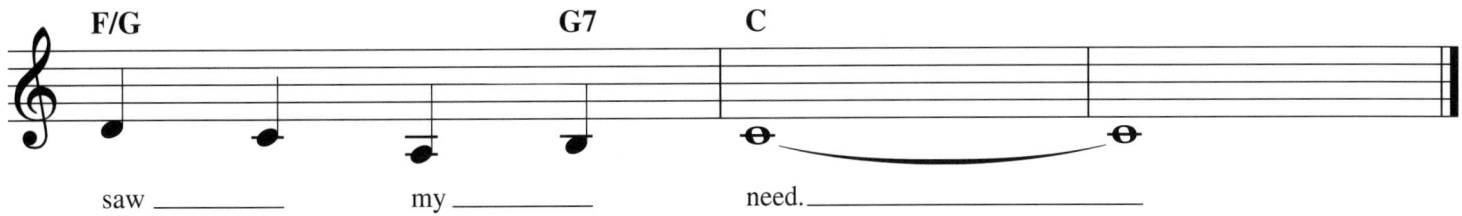

HE LOVED ME WITH A CROSS

Words and Music by JOEL LINDSEY and SUE SMITH

© 1994 Paragon Music Corp. (ASCAP), John T. Benson Publishing Co. (ASCAP) and First Verse Music (ASCAP) (admin. by Brentwood-Benson Music Publishing, Inc.)
All Rights Reserved   Used by Permission

Tenderly

You left a throne in heav - en to come to Beth - le -
He knew from the be - gin - ning the price He'd have to

hem, I will not for - get the way He
pay, for my heart had gone so far be - yond what

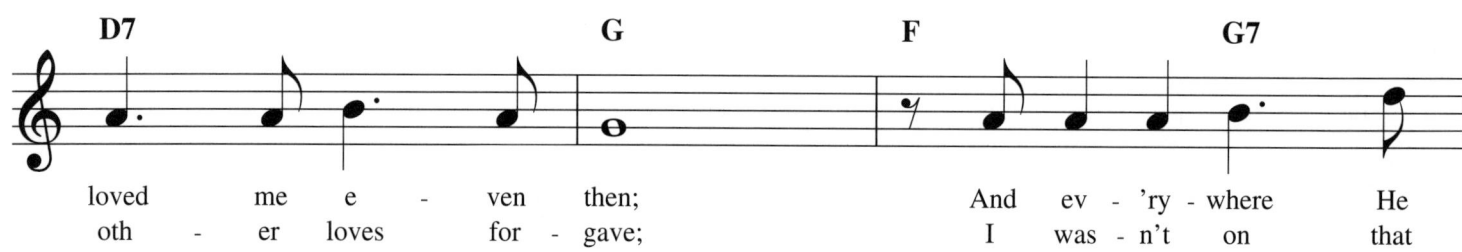
loved me e - ven then; And ev - 'ry - where He
oth - er loves for - gave; I was - n't on that

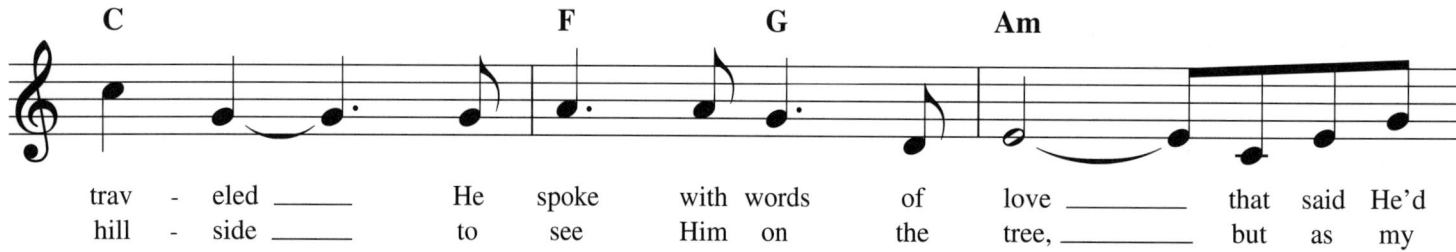
trav - eled He spoke with words of love that said He'd
hill - side to see Him on the tree, but as my

go to an - y dis - tance to show what I was wor - thy of.
guilt was placed up - on Him I know that some - how He saw me.

And when at last the dust - y road had turned to Cal - va -
And I would be a sin - ner en - slaved by all my

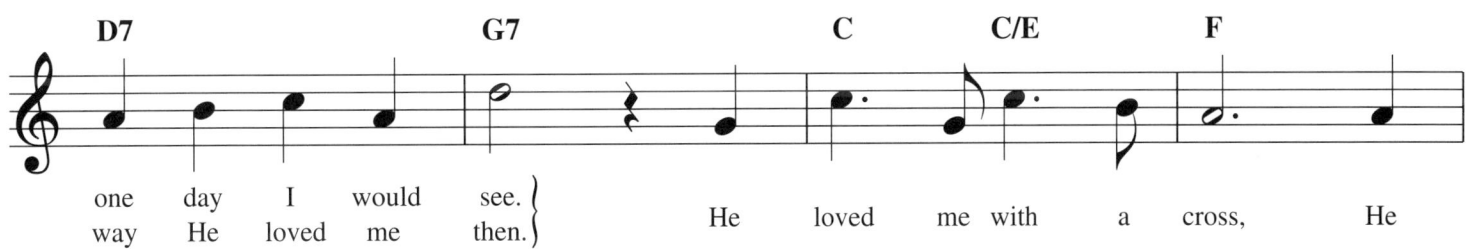
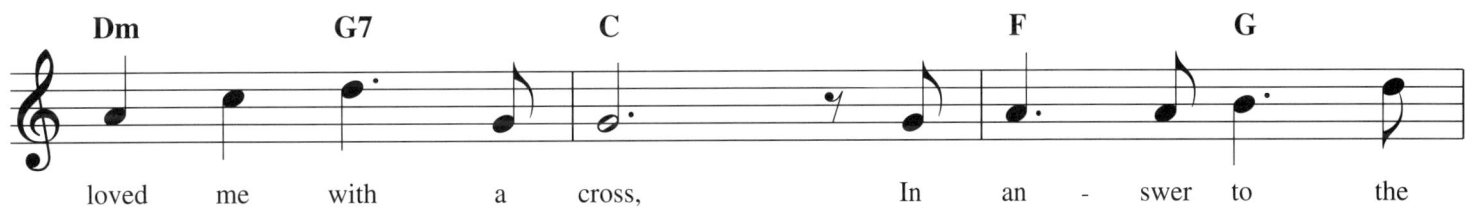
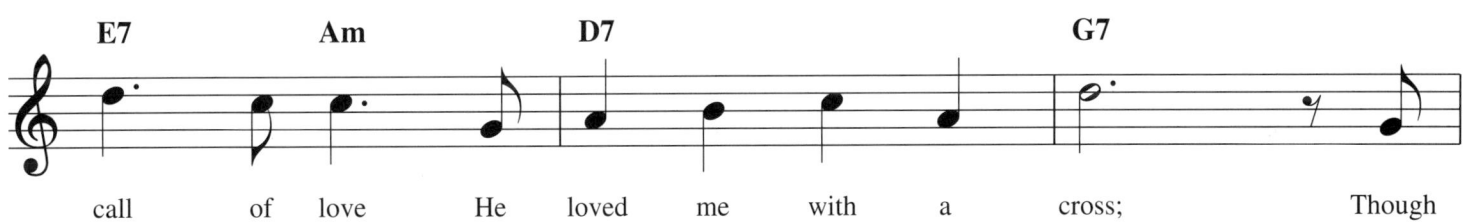

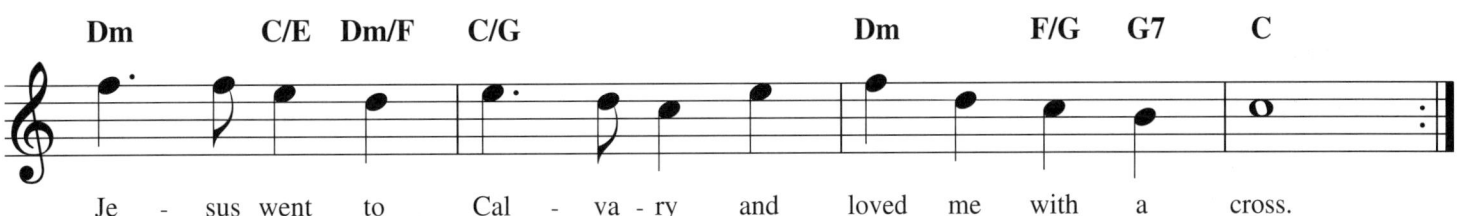

HE'S STILL WORKIN' ON ME

© 1980 Bridge Building Music (BMI) and Family & Friends Music (BMI)
(both admin. by Brentwood-Benson Music Publishing, Inc.)
All Rights Reserved   Used by Permission

Words and Music by
JOEL HEMPHILL

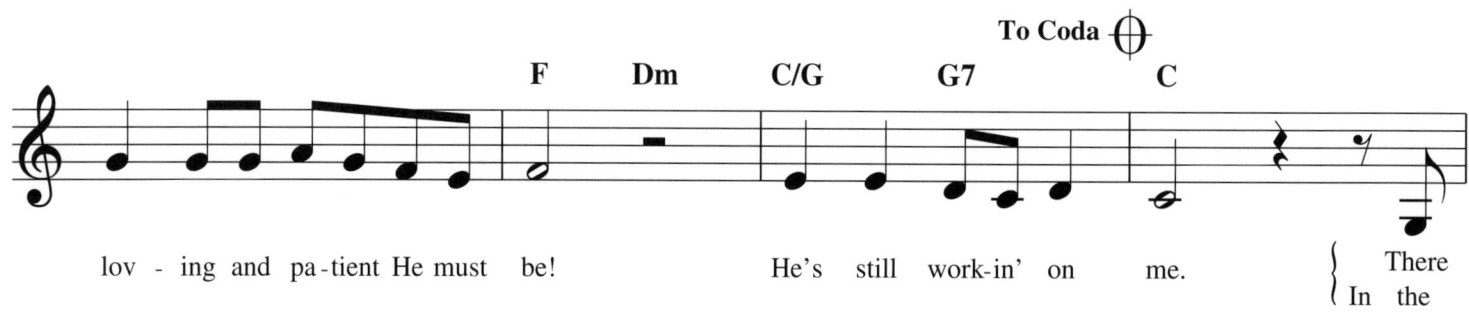

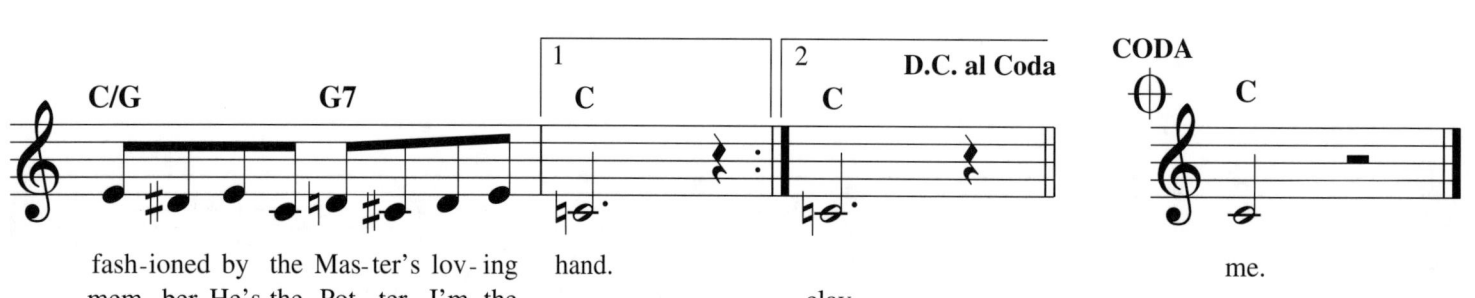

HEAVEN CAME DOWN

Copyright © 1961, Renewed 1989 by John W. Peterson Music Company (ASCAP)
All Rights Reserved   International Copyright Secured   Used by Permission

Words and Music by
JOHN W. PETERSON

Brightly

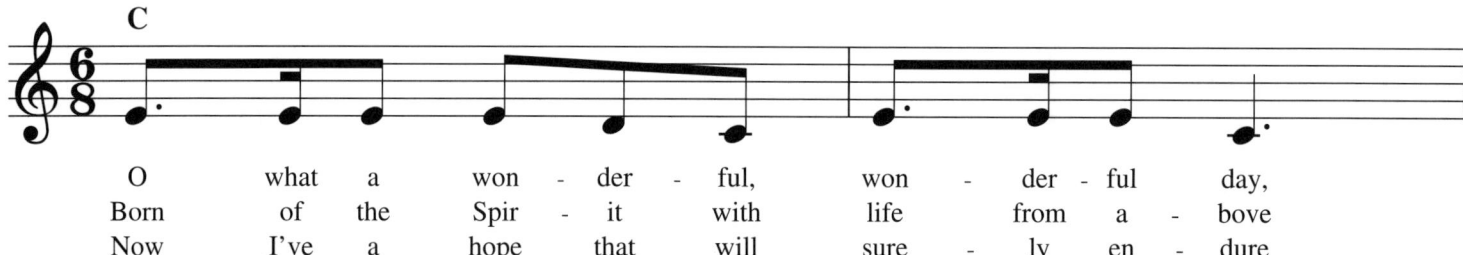

O what a won - der - ful, won - der - ful day,
Born of the Spir - it with life from a - bove
Now I've a hope that will sure - ly en - dure

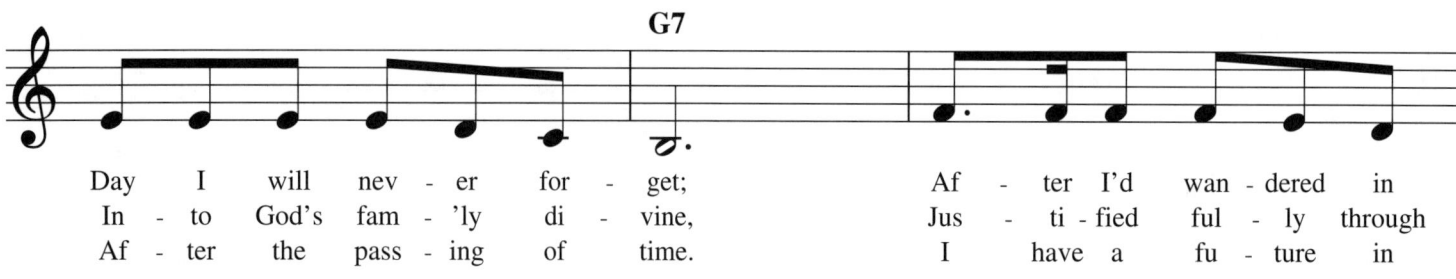

Day I will nev - er for - get;   Af - ter I'd wan - dered in
In - to God's fam - 'ly di - vine,   Jus - ti - fied ful - ly through
Af - ter the pass - ing of time.   I have a fu - ture in

dark - ness a - way,   Je - sus my Sav - ior I met.
Cal - va - ry's love,   O what a stand - ing is mine.
heav - en for sure   There in those man - sions sub - lime.

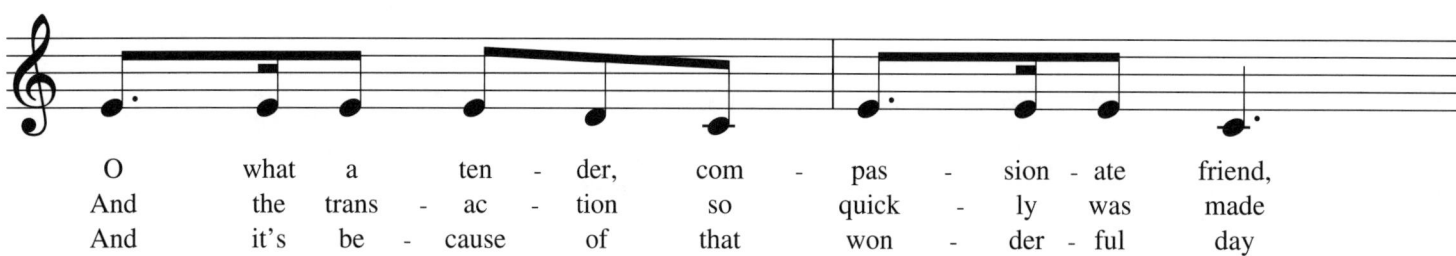

O what a ten - der, com - pas - sion - ate friend,
And the trans - ac - tion so quick - ly was made
And it's be - cause of that won - der - ful day

He met the need of my heart;   Shad - ows dis - pel - ling, with
When as a sin - ner I came;   Took of the of - fer of
When at the cross I be - lieved;   Rich - es e - ter - nal and

joy I am tell - ing, He made all the dark - ness de -
grace He did prof - fer. He saved me, O praise His dear
bless - ings su - per - nal From His pre - cious hand I re -

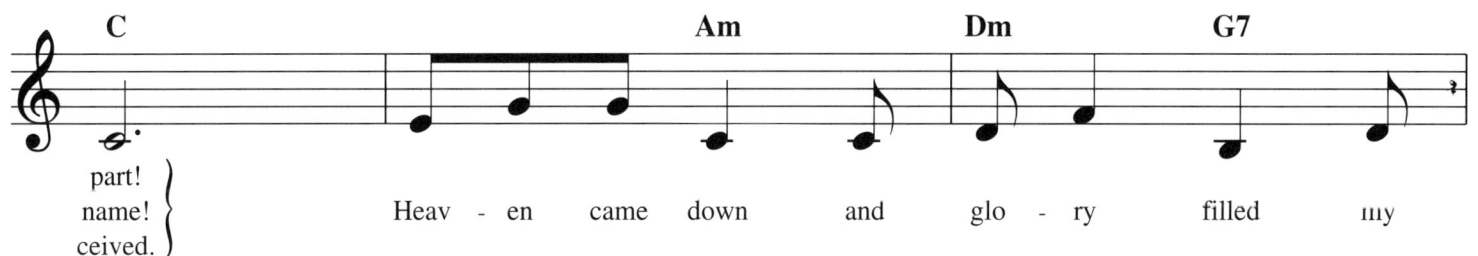
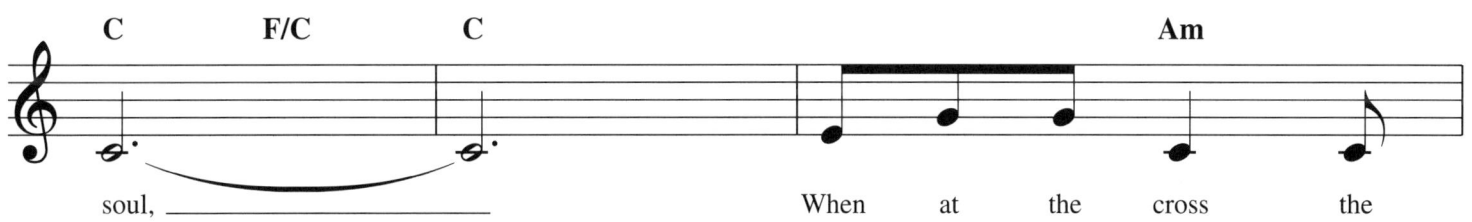
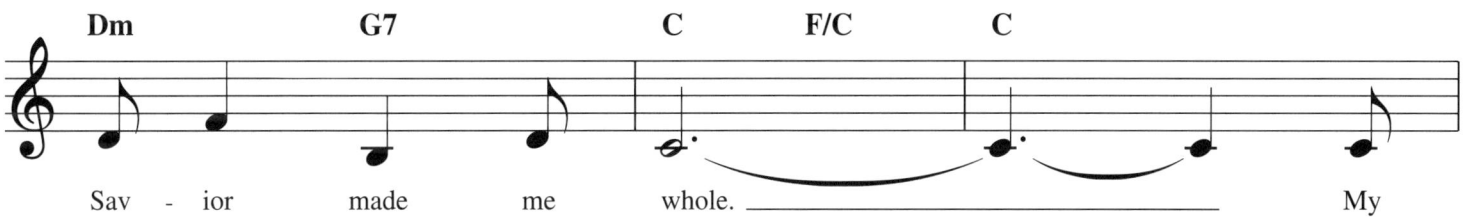

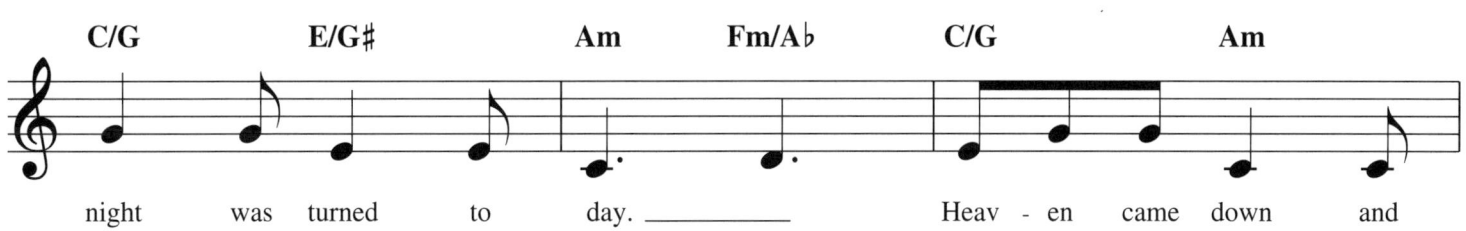
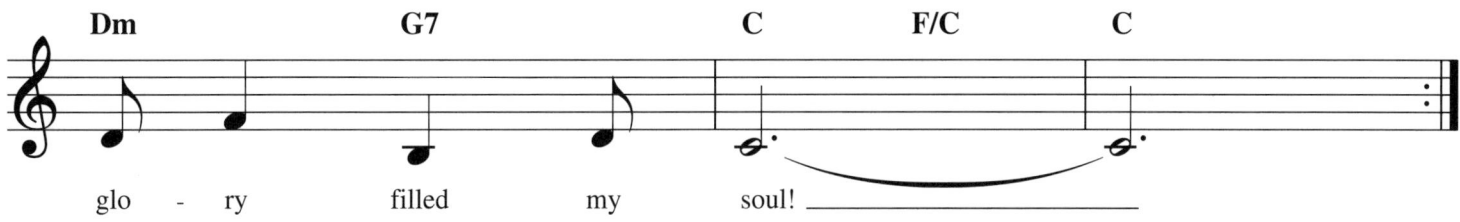

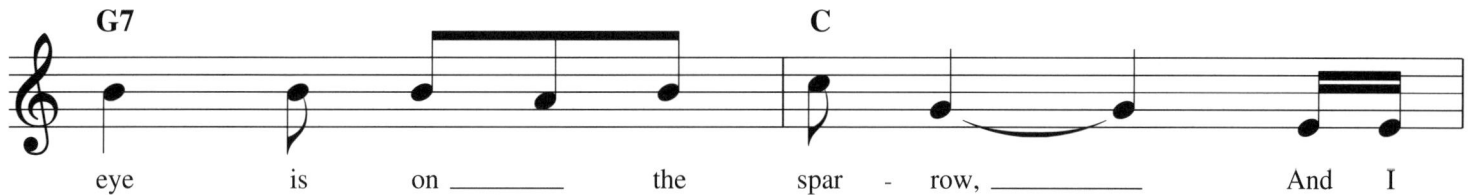
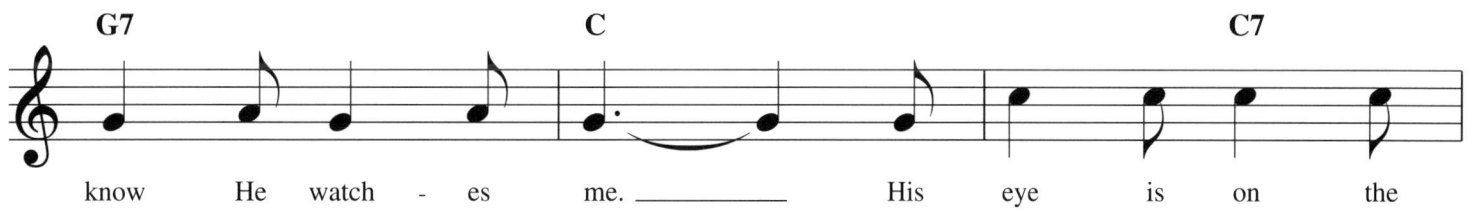
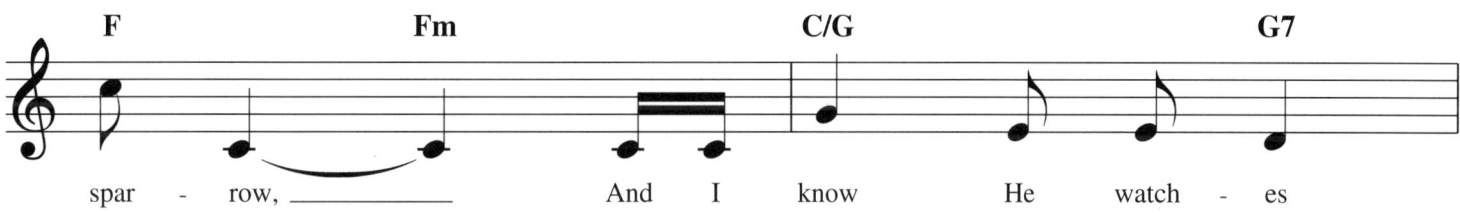

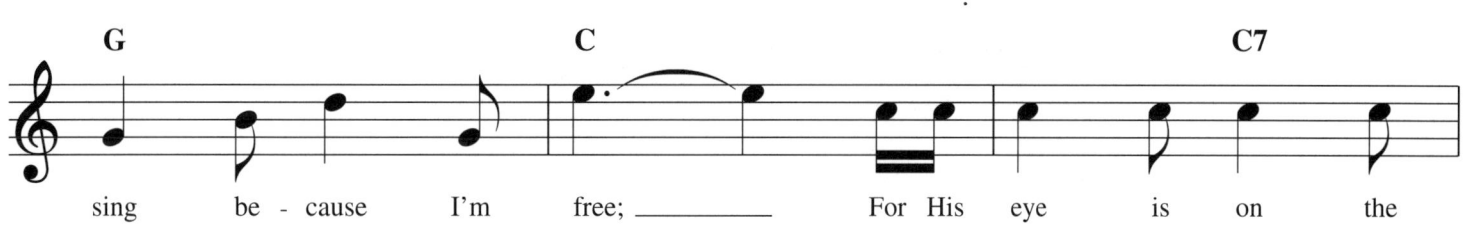
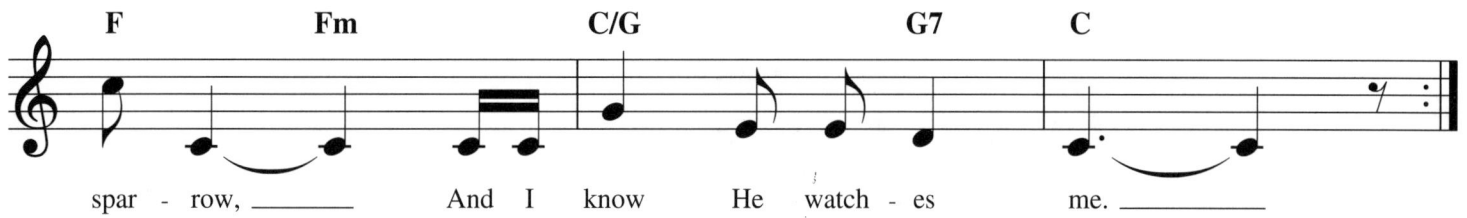

HIS NAME IS WONDERFUL

© Copyright 1959 (Renewed 1987) by MANNA MUSIC, INC., 35255 Brooten Road, Pacific City, OR 97135
All Rights Reserved   Used by Permission

Words and Music by
AUDREY MIEIR

Prayerfully

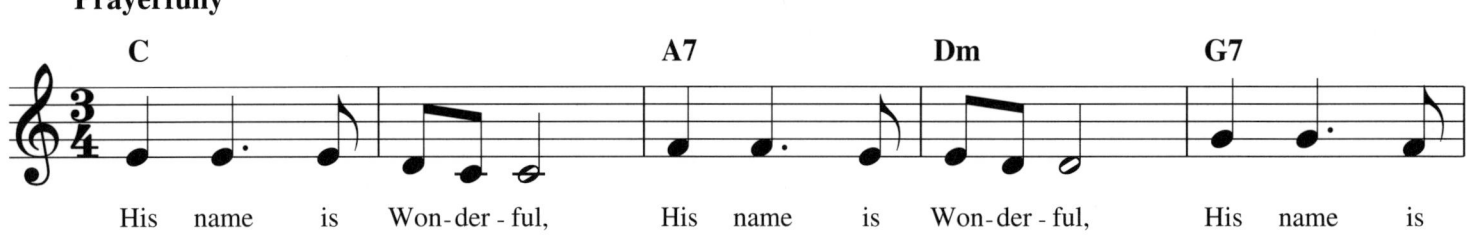

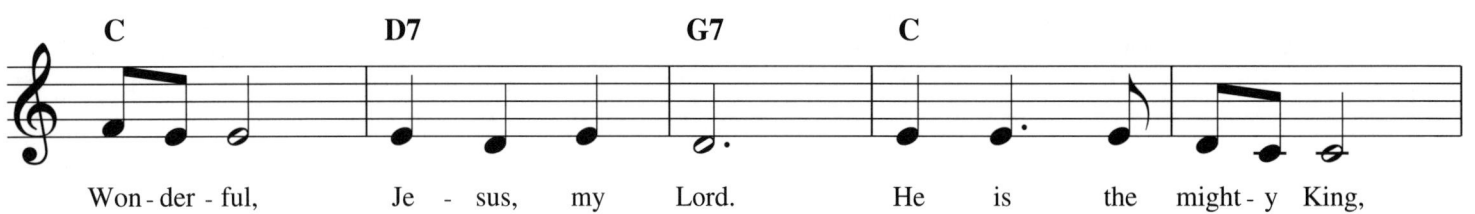

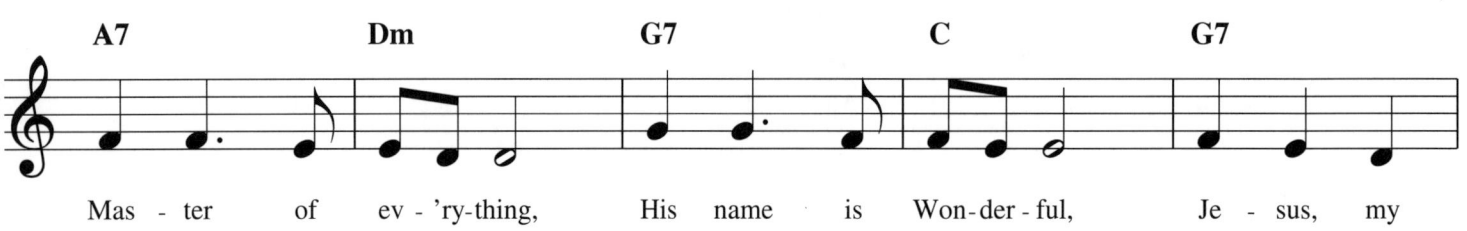

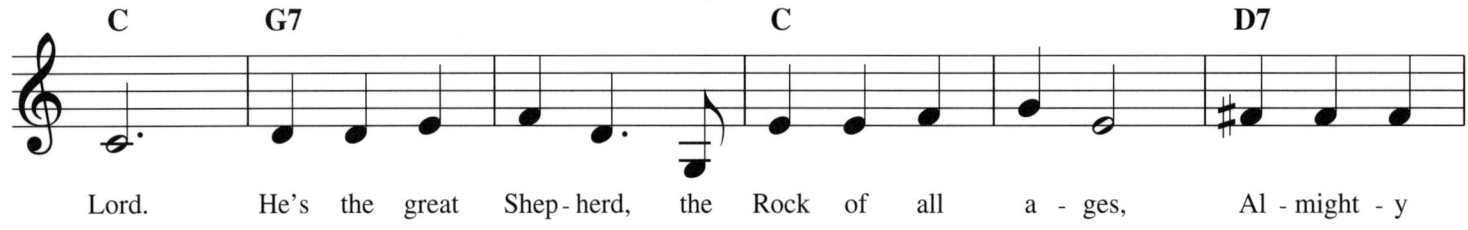

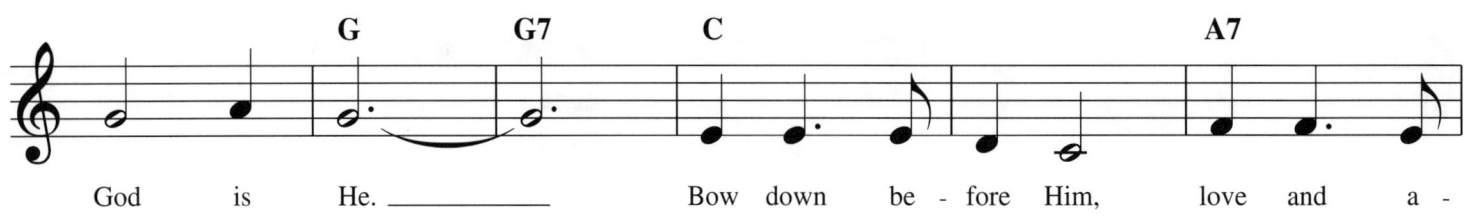

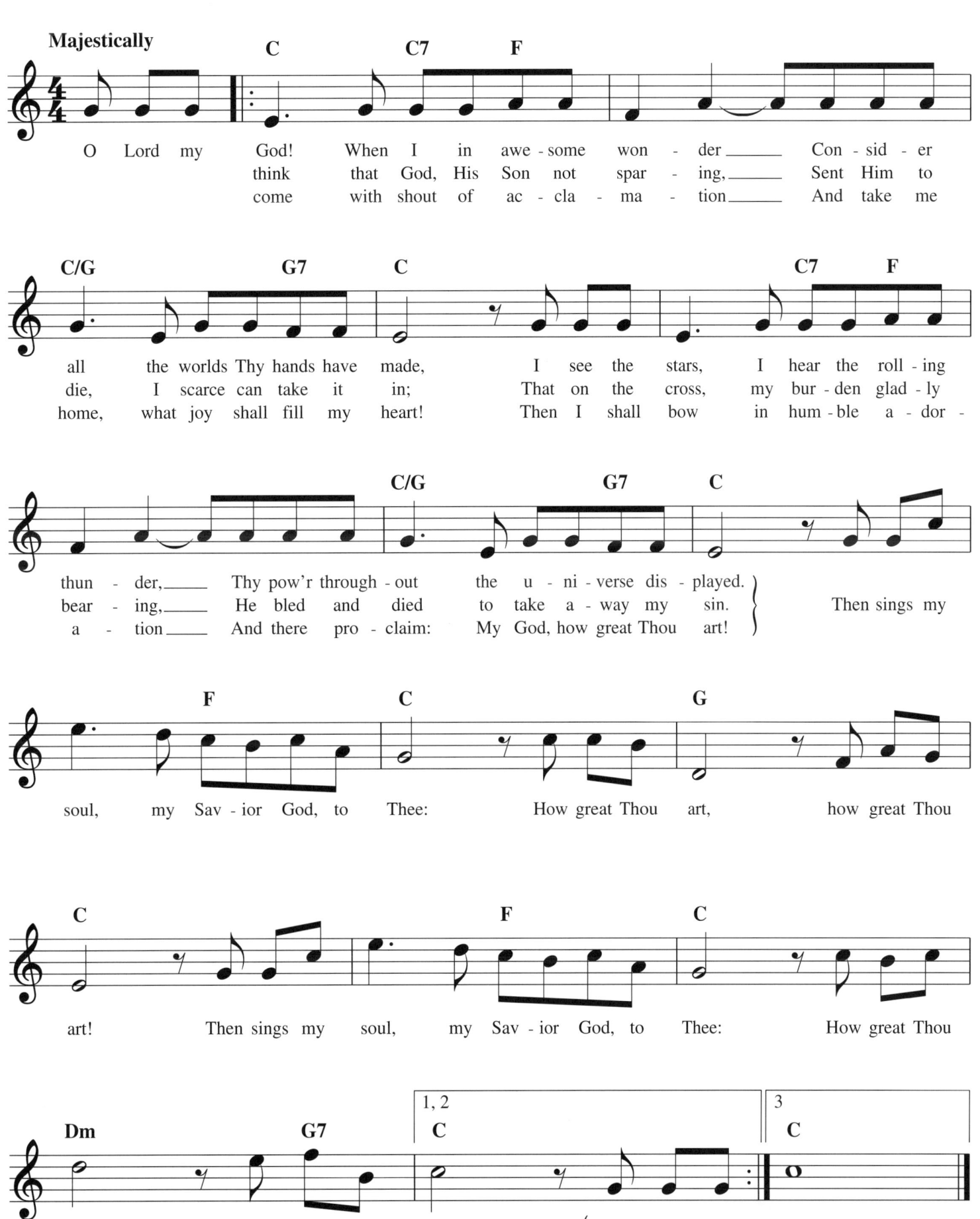

HOME WHERE I BELONG

© 1976 Word Music, Inc.
All Rights Reserved Used by Permission

Words and Music by
PAT TERRY

Moderately fast

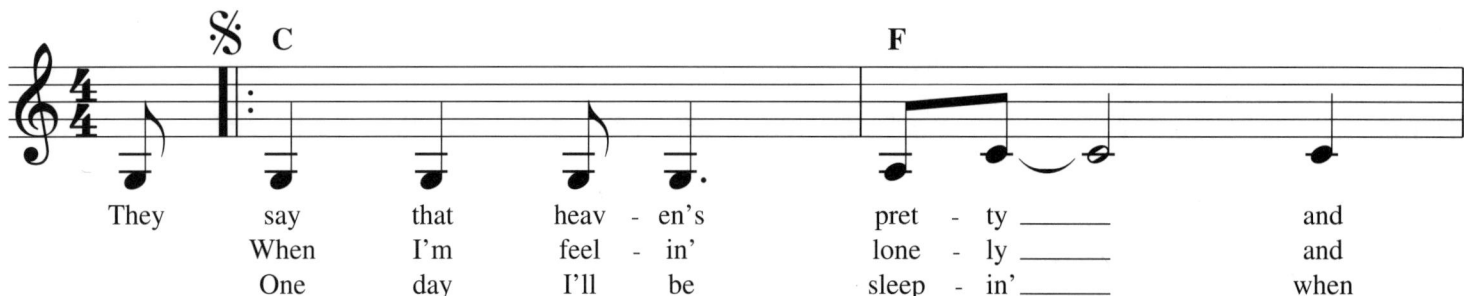

They say that heav - en's pret - ty liv - in' here is too; but
When I'm feel - in' lone - ly and when I'm feel - in' blue, it's
One day I'll be sleep - in' when death knocks at my door, and

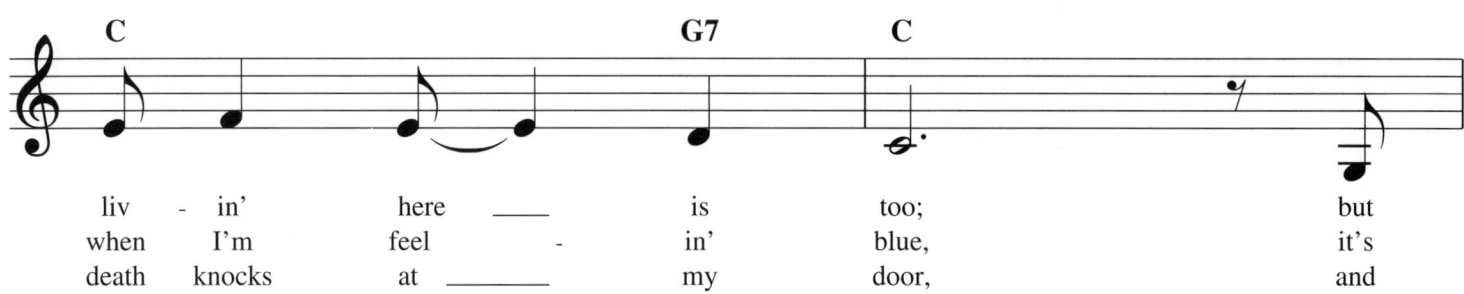

if they said that I would have to choose be - tween the two, I'd go home.
such a joy to know that I am on - ly pass - in' through. I'm head - ed home,
I'll a - wake to find that I'm not home - sick an - y - more, 'cause I'll be home,

Go - in' home
I'm go - in' home
I'll be home

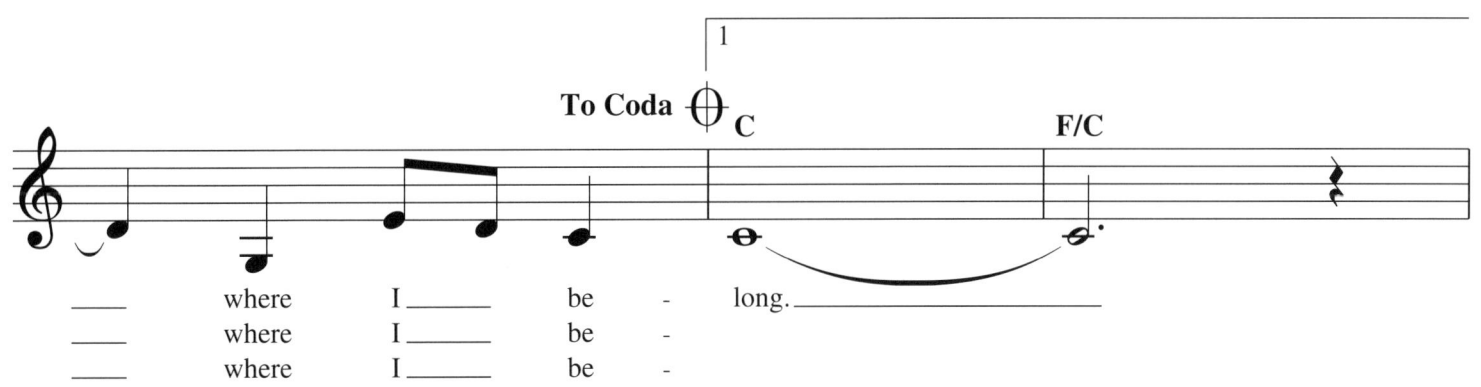
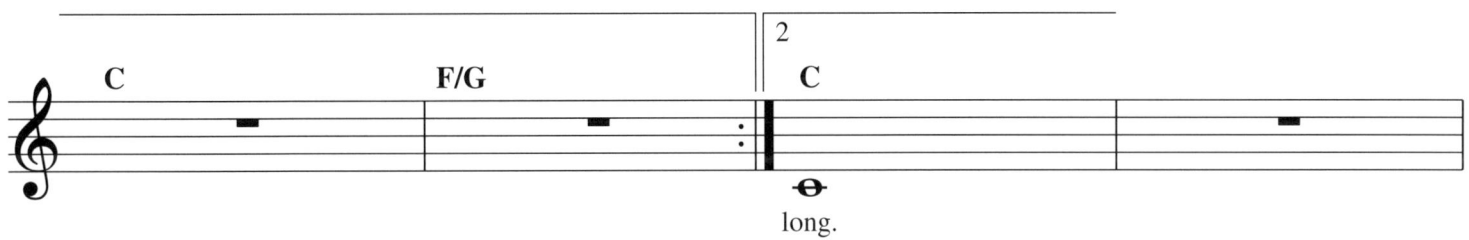

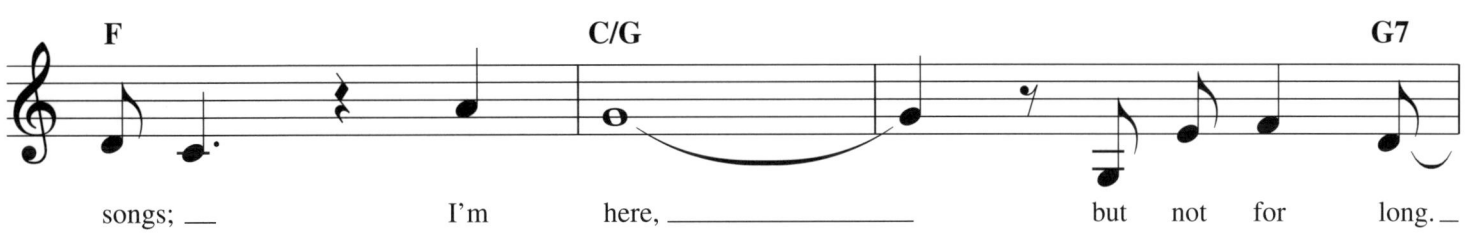
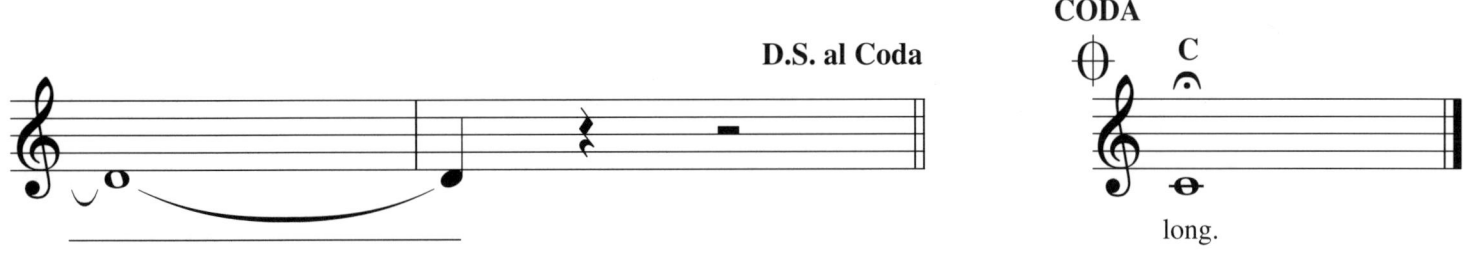

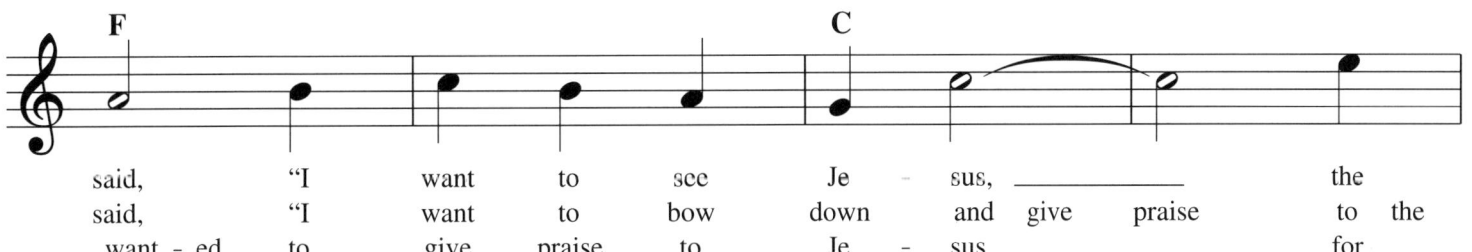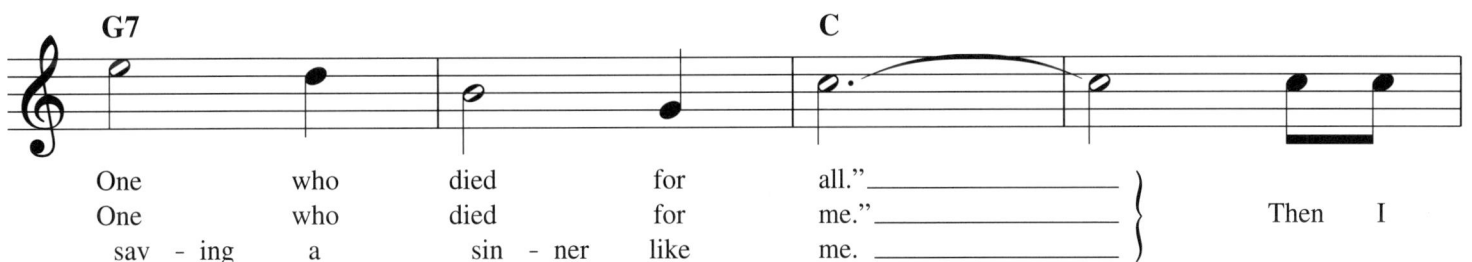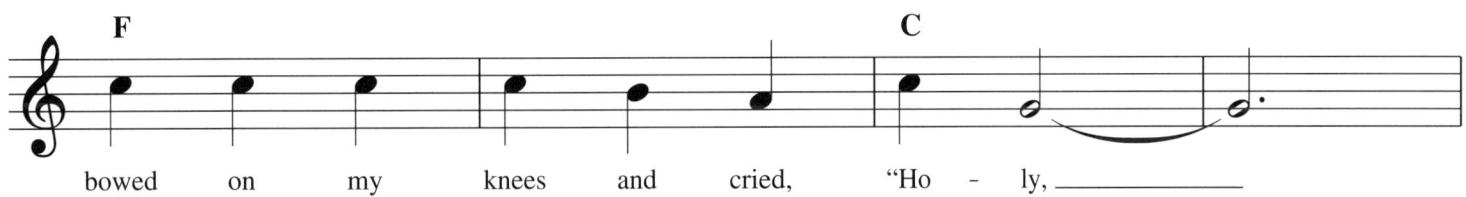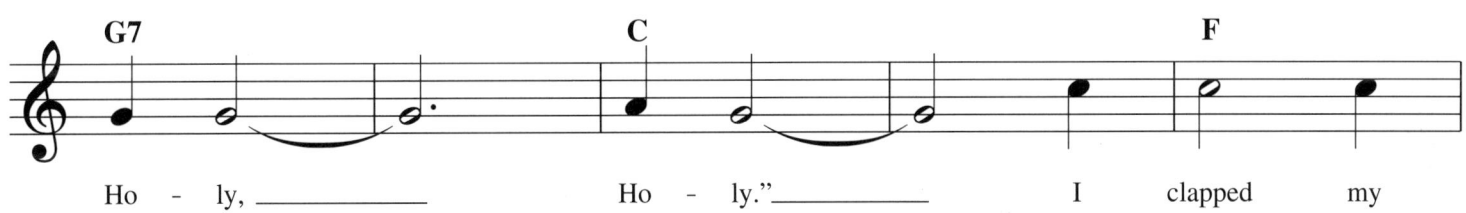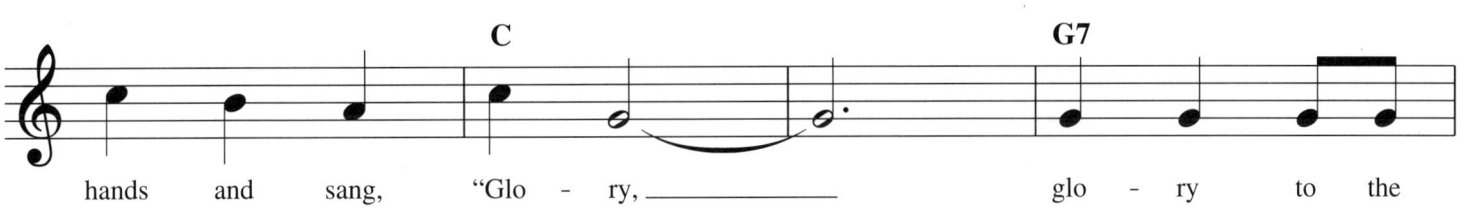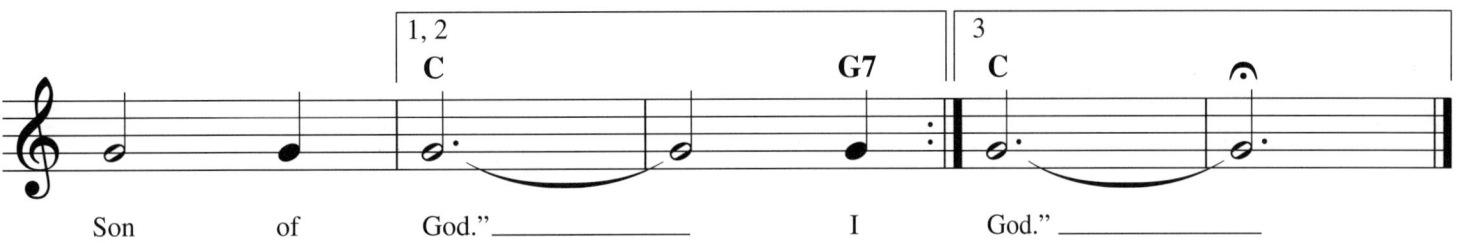

I FEEL LIKE TRAVELING ON

Words by WILLIAM HUNTER
Traditional Melody
Music Arranged by JAMES D. VAUGHAN

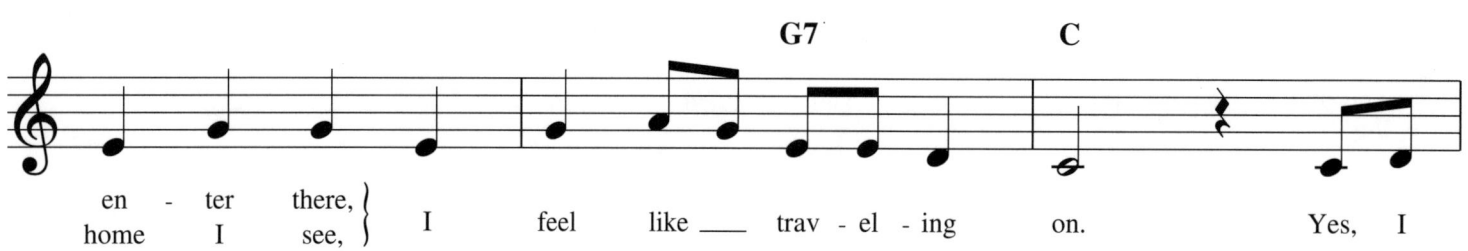
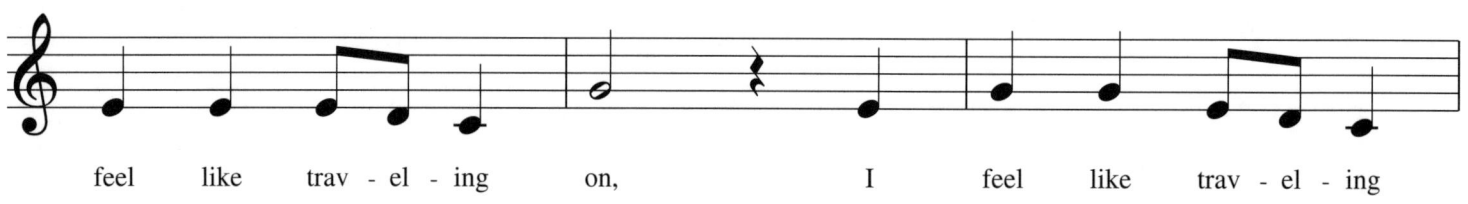
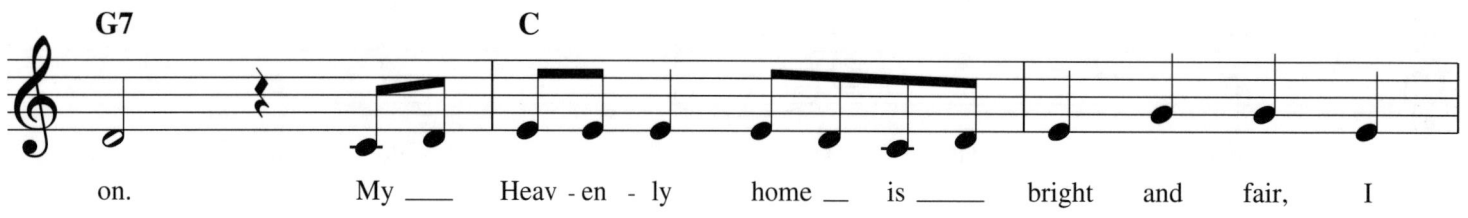
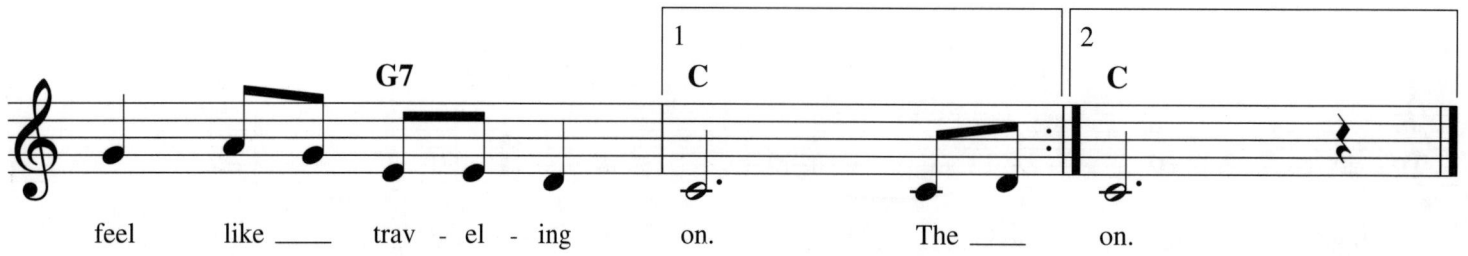

I JUST CAME TO PRAISE THE LORD

© 1975 Paragon Music Corp. (ASCAP) (a div. of Brentwood-Benson Music Publishing, Inc.)
All Rights Reserved   Used by Permission

Words and Music by
WAYNE ROMERO

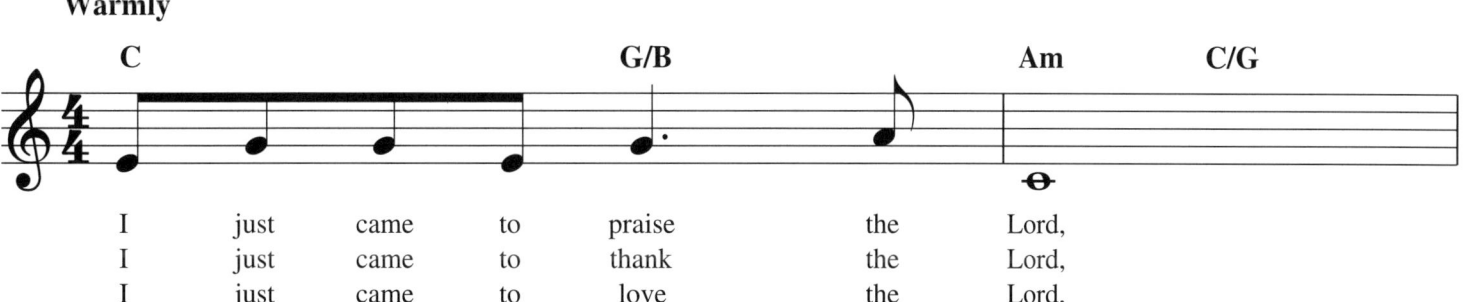

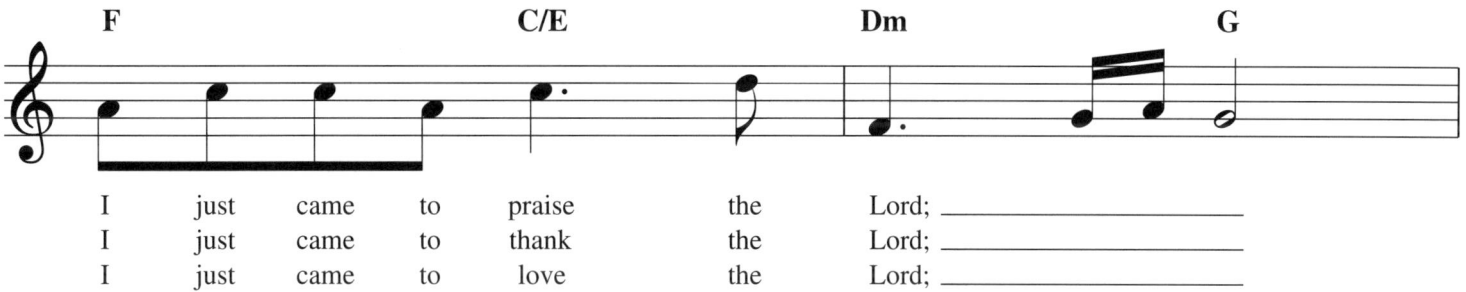

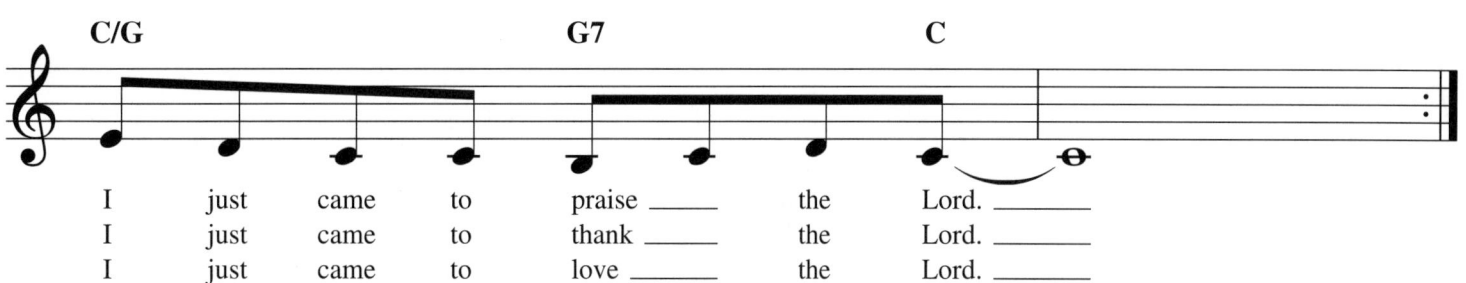

I JUST FEEL LIKE SOMETHING GOOD IS ABOUT TO HAPPEN

Copyright © 1974 William J. Gaither, Inc. (ASCAP)
All Rights Controlled by Gaither Copyright Management
All Rights Reserved   Used by Permission

Words and Music by
WILLIAM J. GAITHER

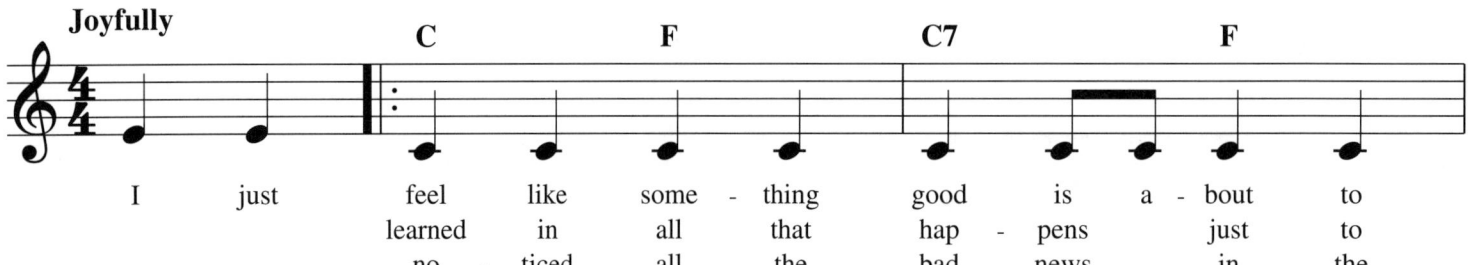

I just feel like some-thing good is a-bout to
learned in all that hap-pens just to
no-ticed all the bad news in the

hap-pen, I just feel like some-thing
praise Him, For I know He's work-ing
pa-per, And it seems like things are

good is on its way. He has
all things for my good. Ev-'ry
bleak-er ev-'ry day. But

prom-ised that He'd o-pen all of Heav-en,
fear I shed is worth all the in-vest-ment,
for this child of God it makes no dif-f'rence,

And broth-er, it could hap-pen an-y
For I know He'll see me through; He said He
Be-cause it's bound to get bet-ter ei-ther

day. When God's peo-ple hum-ble them-
would. He has prom-ised eye nor
way. I've nev-er been more

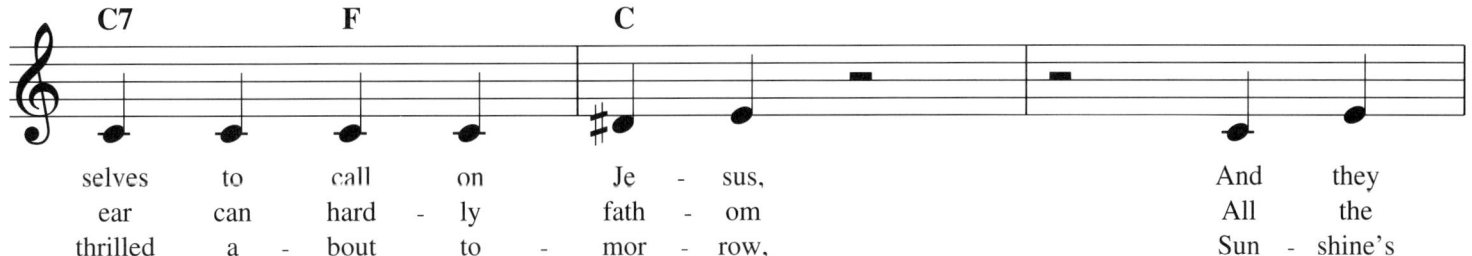
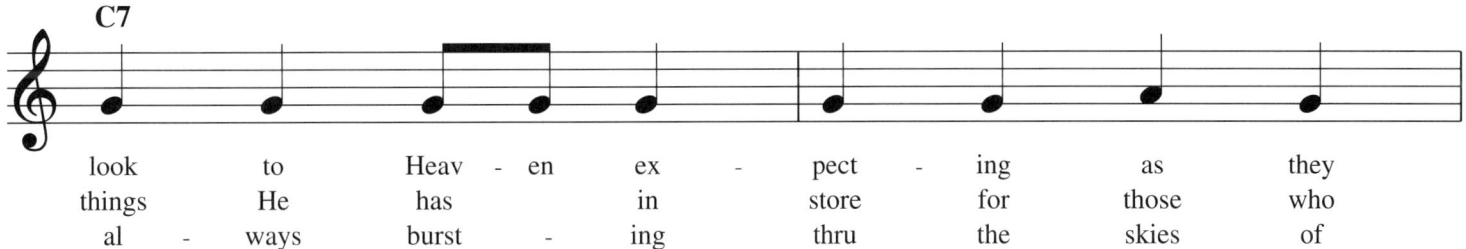
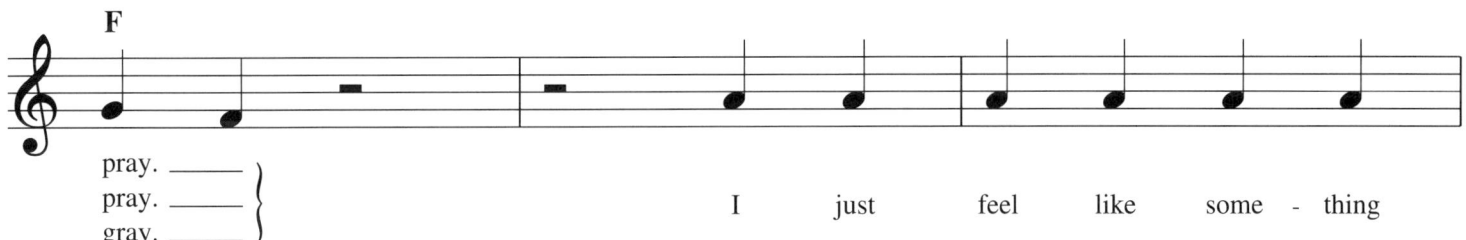
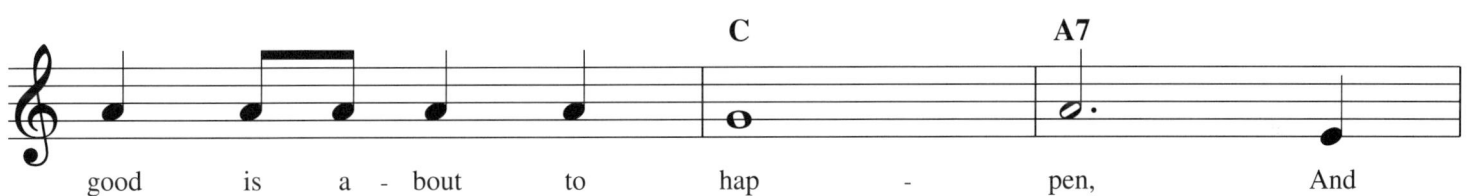
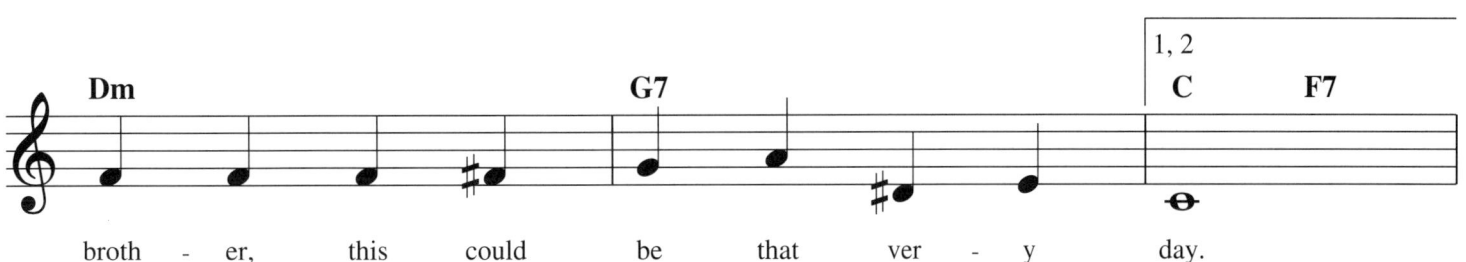
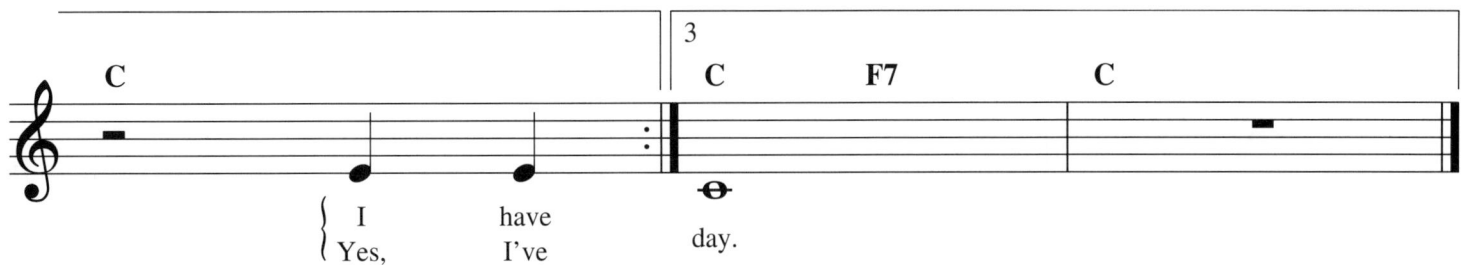

I LOVE TO TELL THE STORY

Words by A. CATHERINE HANKEY
Music by WILLIAM G. FISCHER

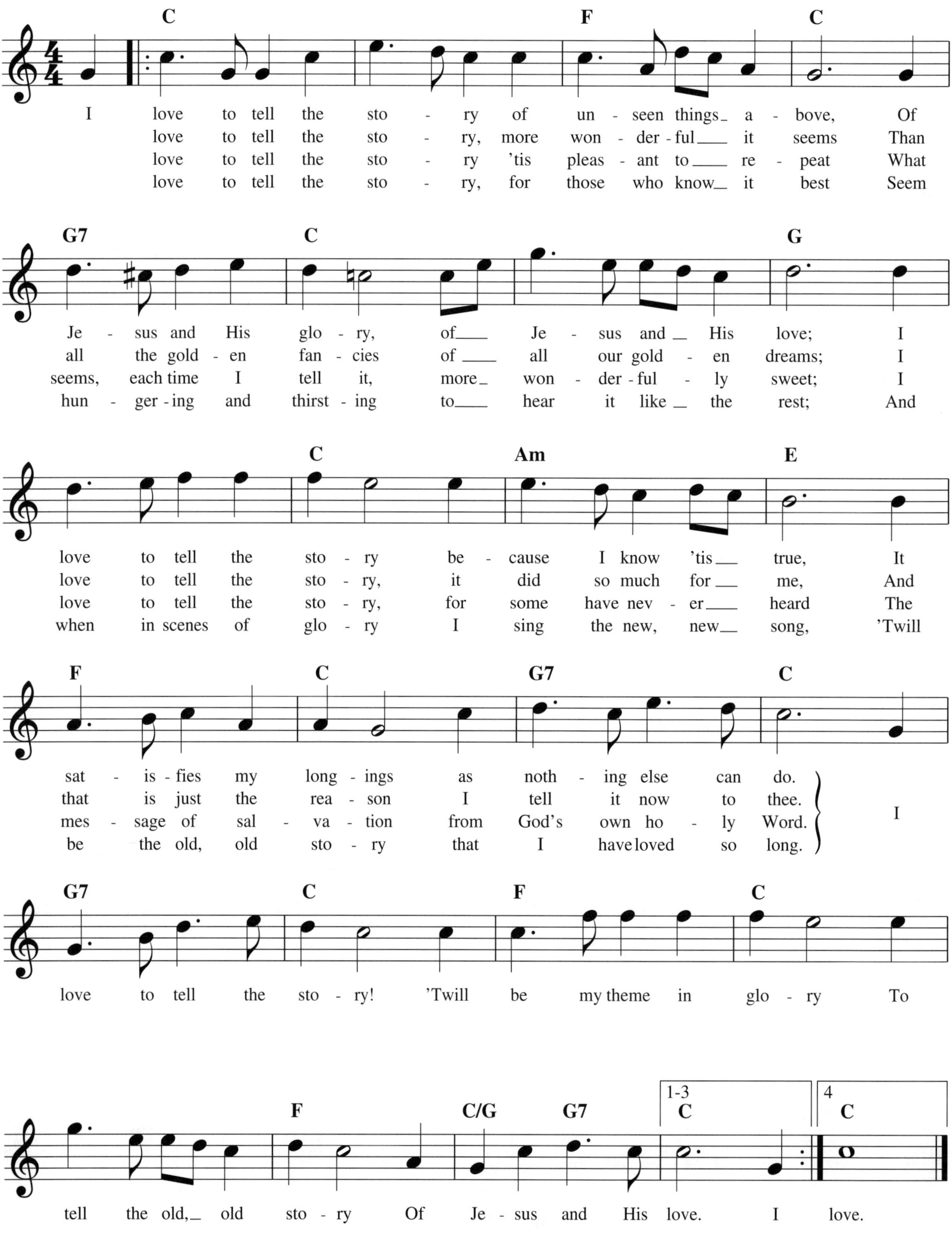
C F C
I love to tell the sto - ry of un - seen things_ a - bove, Of
love to tell the sto - ry, more won - der - ful__ it seems Than
love to tell the sto - ry 'tis pleas - ant to__ re - peat What
love to tell the sto - ry, for those who know_ it best Seem
G7 C G
Je - sus and His glo - ry, of__ Je - sus and _ His love; I
all the gold - en fan - cies of __ all our gold - en dreams; I
seems, each time I tell it, more_ won - der - ful - ly sweet; I
hun - ger - ing and thirst - ing to__ hear it like _ the rest; And
C Am E
love to tell the sto - ry be - cause I know 'tis__ true, It
love to tell the sto - ry, it did so much for __ me, And
love to tell the sto - ry, for some have nev - er__ heard The
when in scenes of glo - ry I sing the new, new_ song, 'Twill
F C G7 C
sat - is - fies my long - ings as noth - ing else can do.
that is just the rea - son I tell it now to thee.
mes - sage of sal - va - tion from God's own ho - ly Word.
be the old, old sto - ry that I have loved so long.
I
G7 C F C
love to tell the sto - ry! 'Twill be my theme in glo - ry To
F C/G G7 1-3 C 4 C
tell the old,_ old sto - ry Of Je - sus and His love. I love.

I STAND AMAZED IN THE PRESENCE
(My Savior's Love)

Words and Music by
CHARLES H. GABRIEL

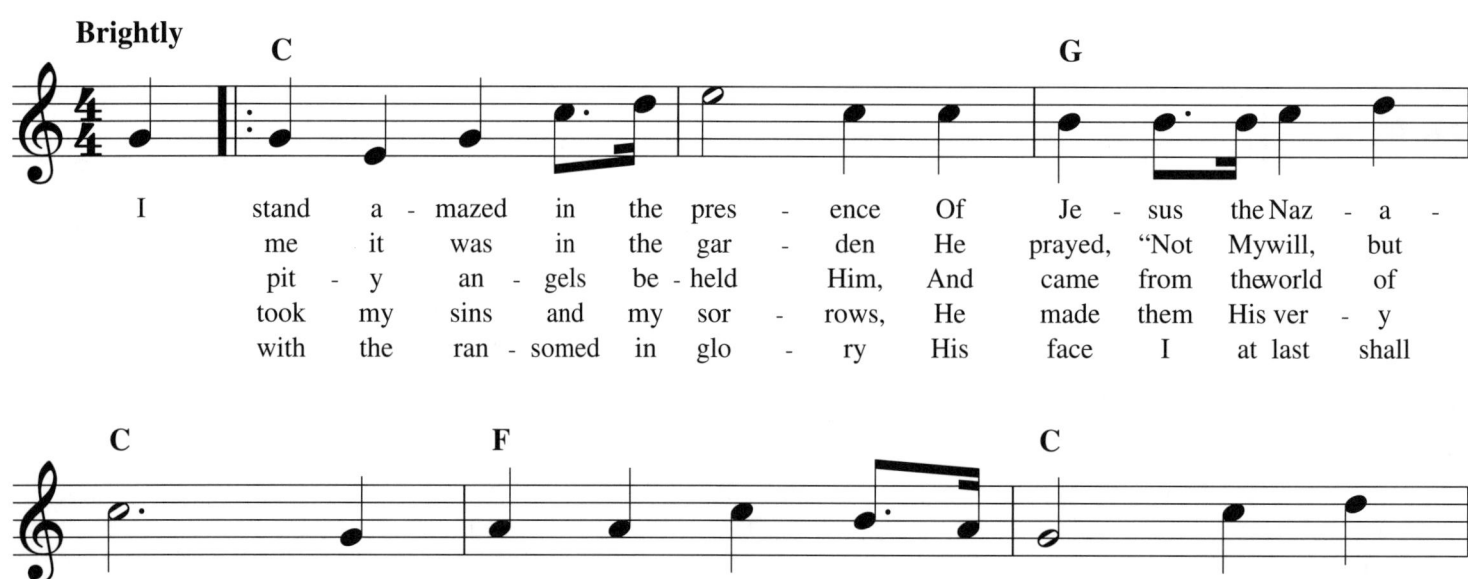

1. I stand a-mazed in the pres-ence Of Je-sus the Naz-a-rene, And won-der how He could love me, A sin-ner, con-demned, un-clean.
2. For me it was in the gar-den He prayed, "Not My will, but Thine." He had no tears for His own griefs, But sweat drops of blood for mine.
3. In pit-y an-gels be-held Him, And came from the world of light To com-fort Him in the sor-rows He bore for my soul that night.
4. He took my sins and my sor-rows, He made them His ver-y own; He bore the bur-den to Cal-v'ry, And suf-fered and died a-lone.
5. When with the ran-somed in glo-ry His face I at last shall see, 'Twill be my joy through the ag-es To sing of His love for me.

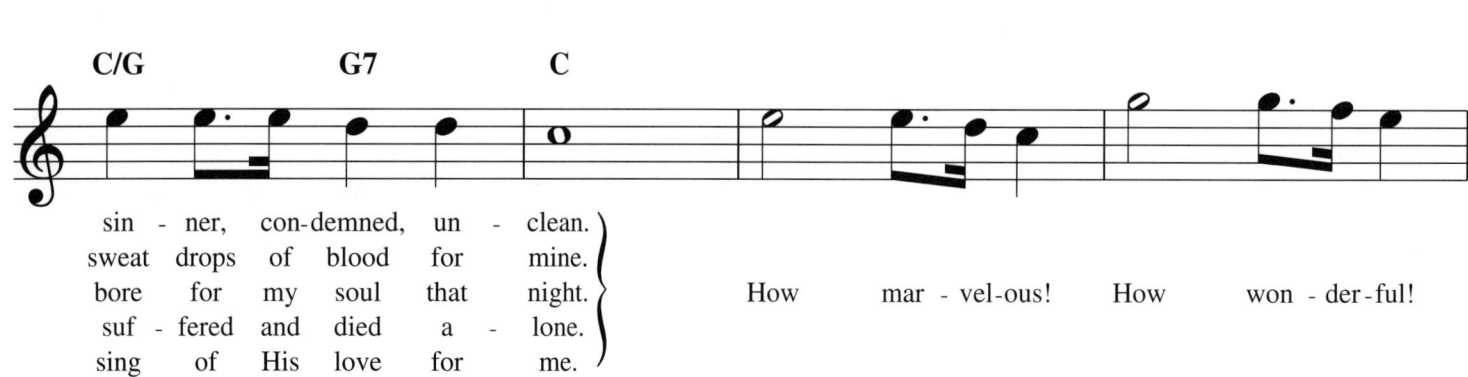

How mar-vel-ous! How won-der-ful!

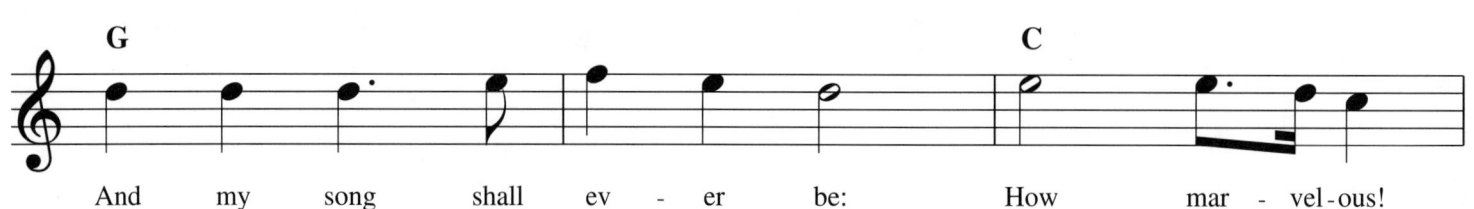

And my song shall ev-er be: How mar-vel-ous!

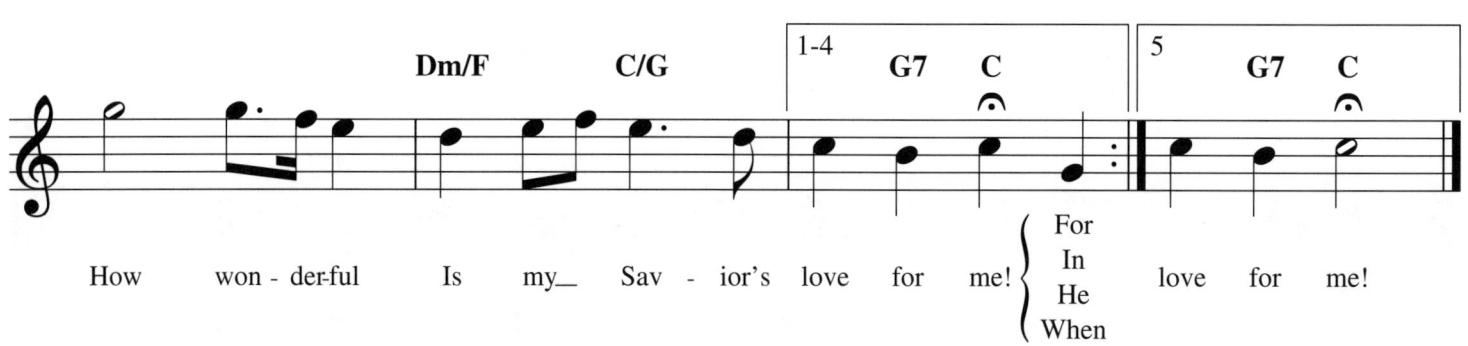

How won-der-ful Is my Sav-ior's love for me!

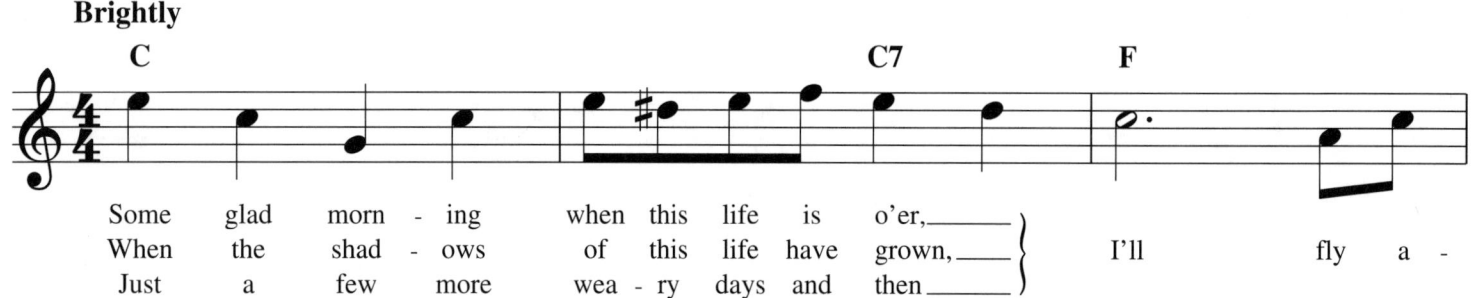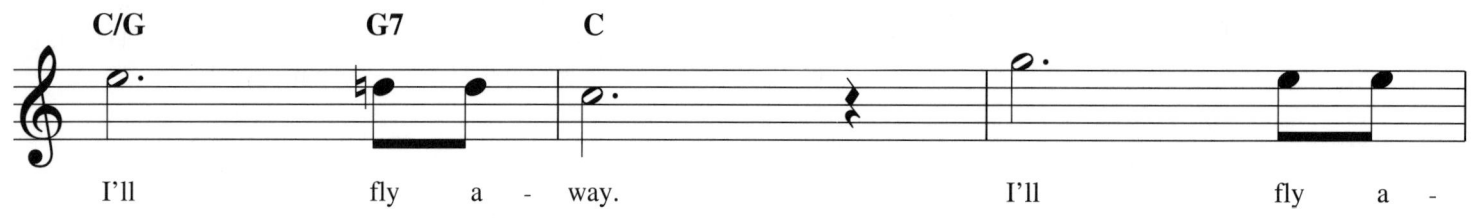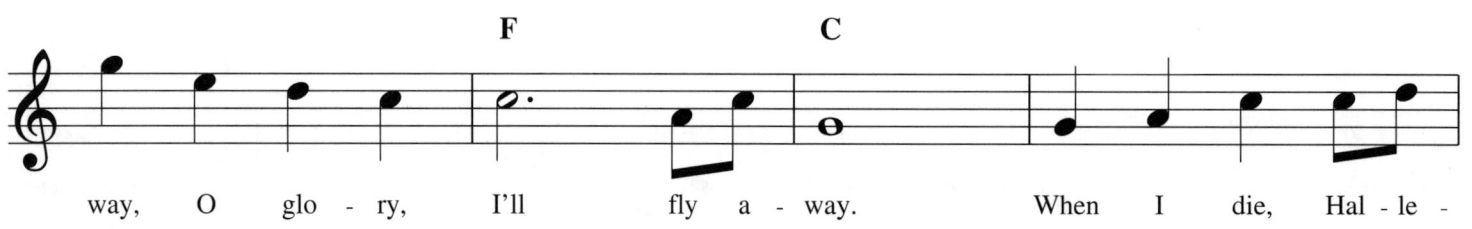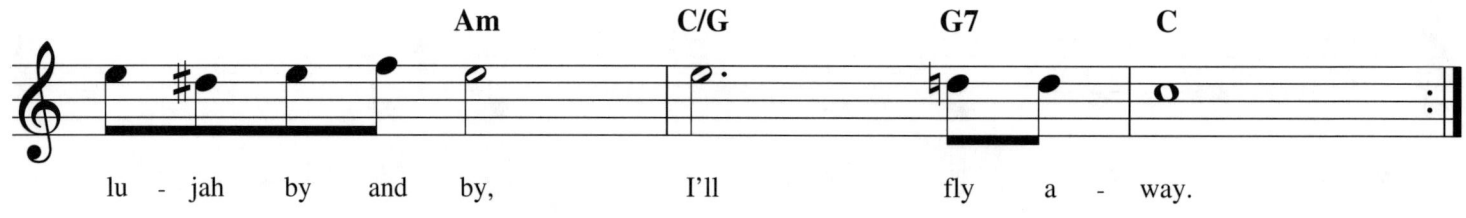

IN THE GARDEN

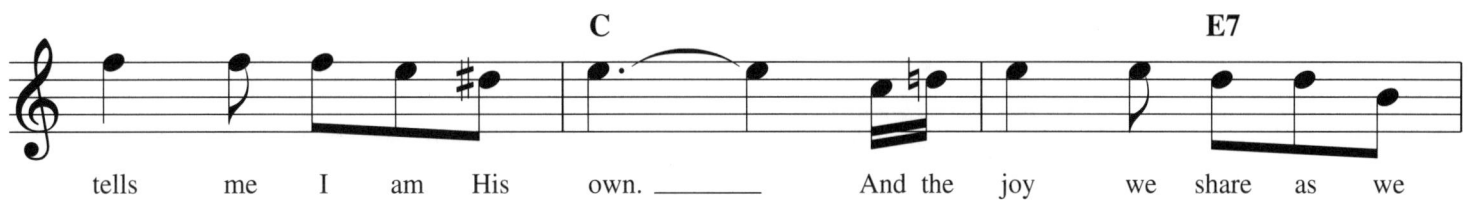
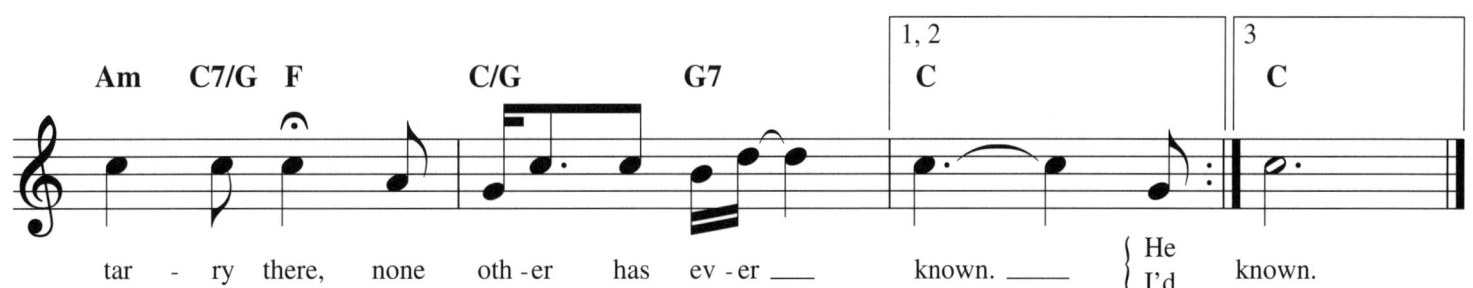

IN TIMES LIKE THESE

Copyright © 1944 by Zondervan Music Publishing Co.
Copyright Renewed
All Rights Administered by Unichappell Music Inc.
International Copyright Secured   All Rights Reserved

Words and Music by
RUTH CAYE JONES

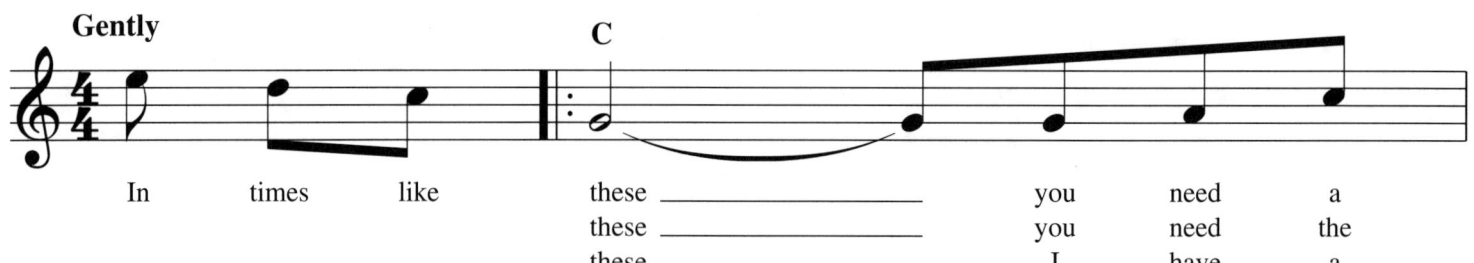

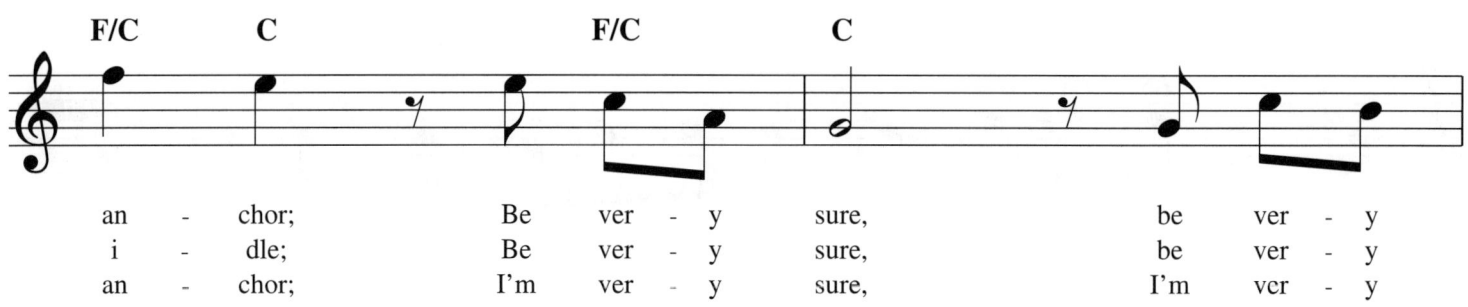

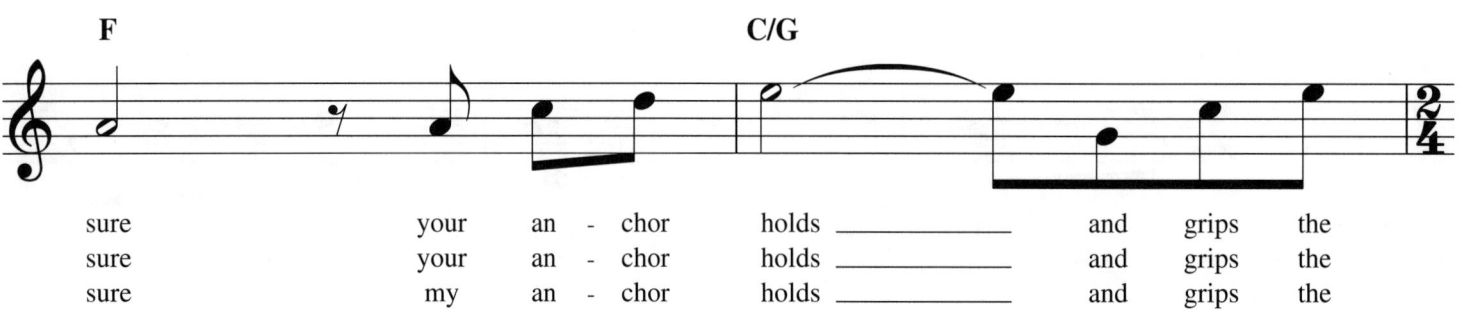

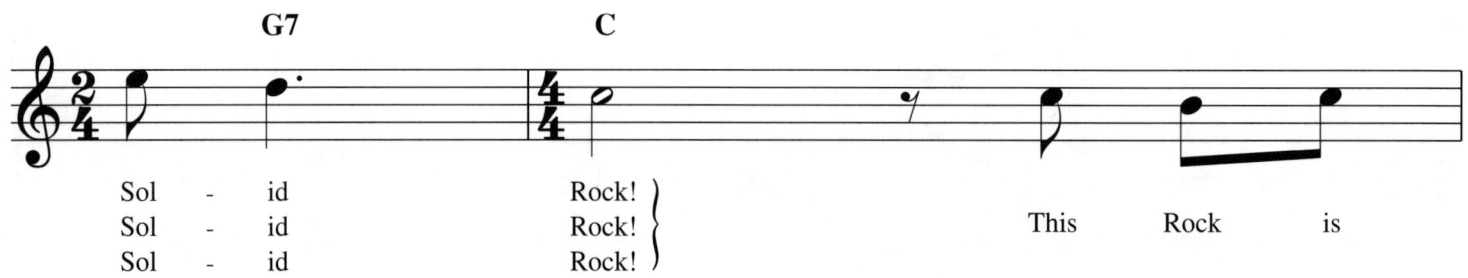

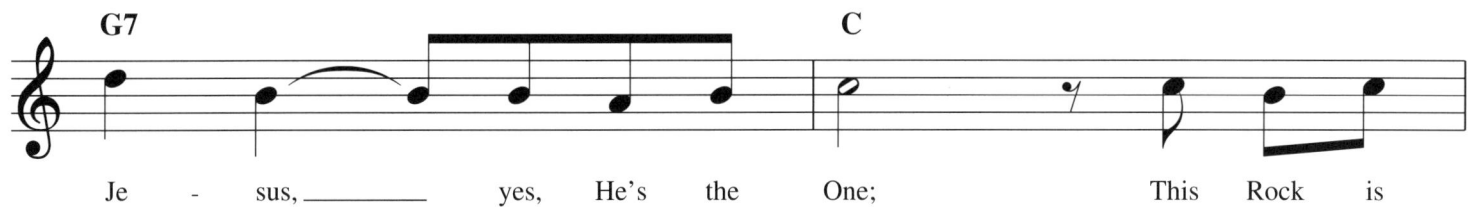
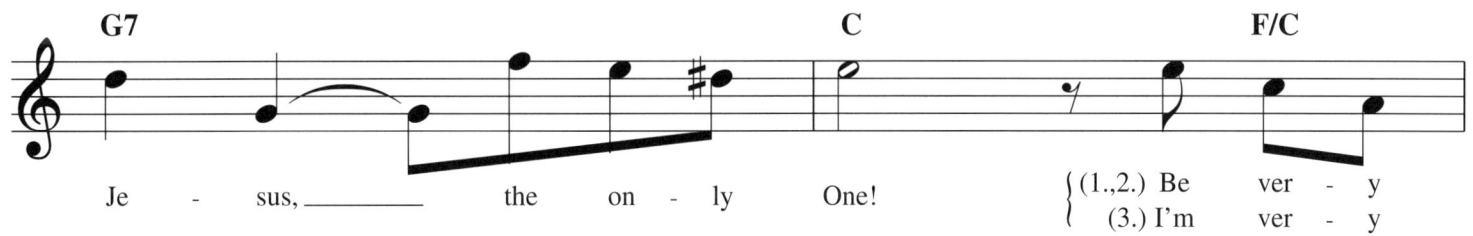
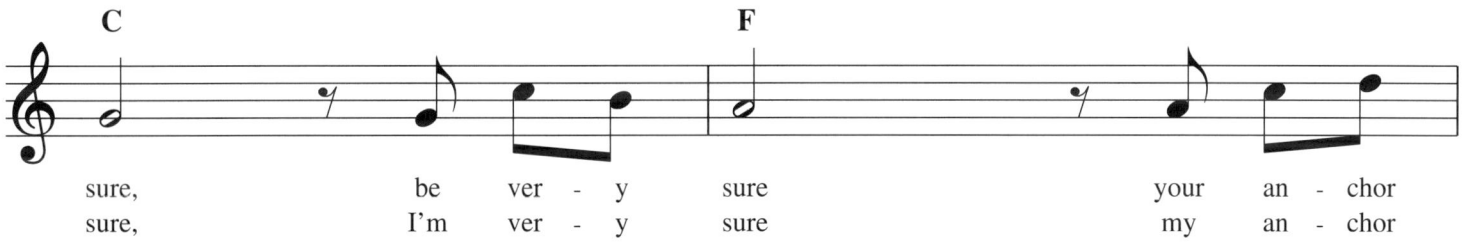
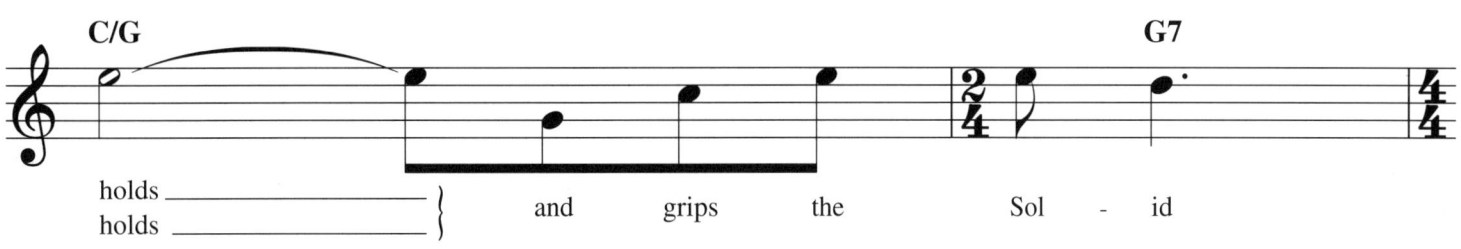
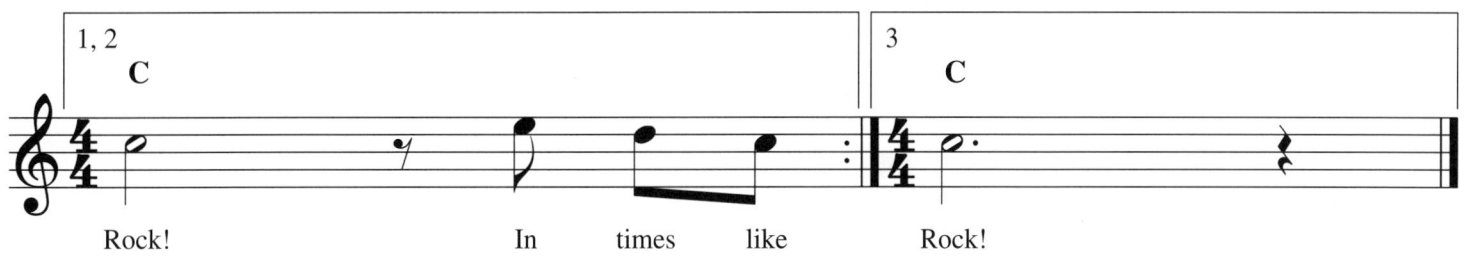

IT TOOK A MIRACLE

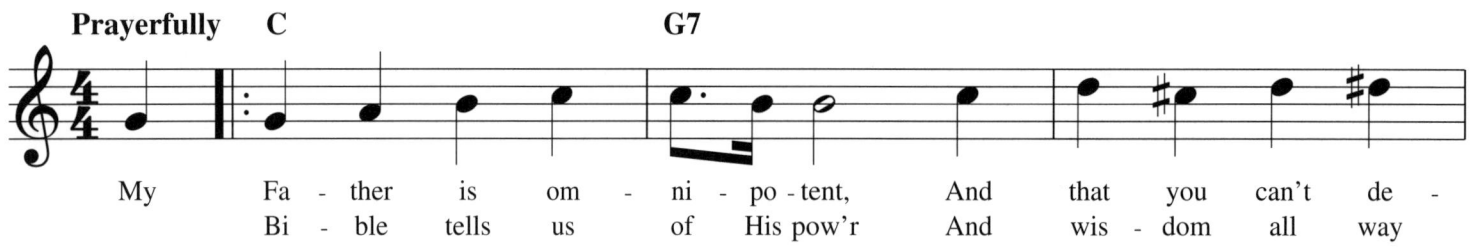
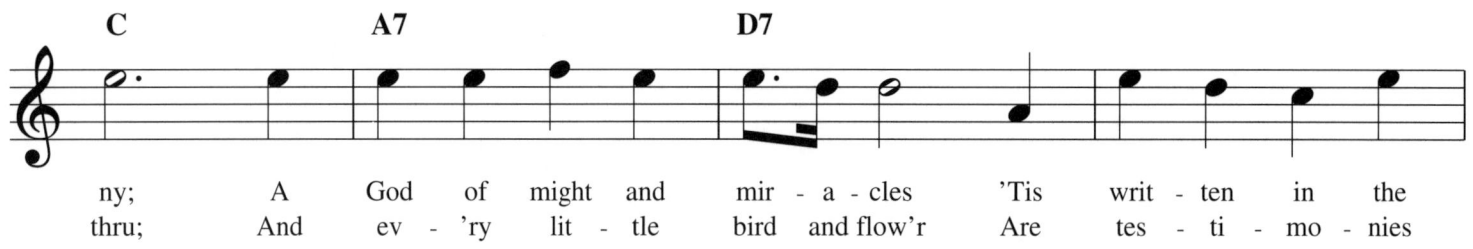

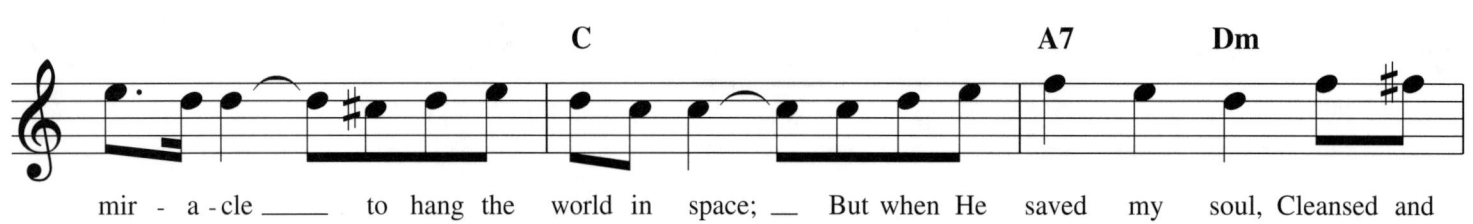
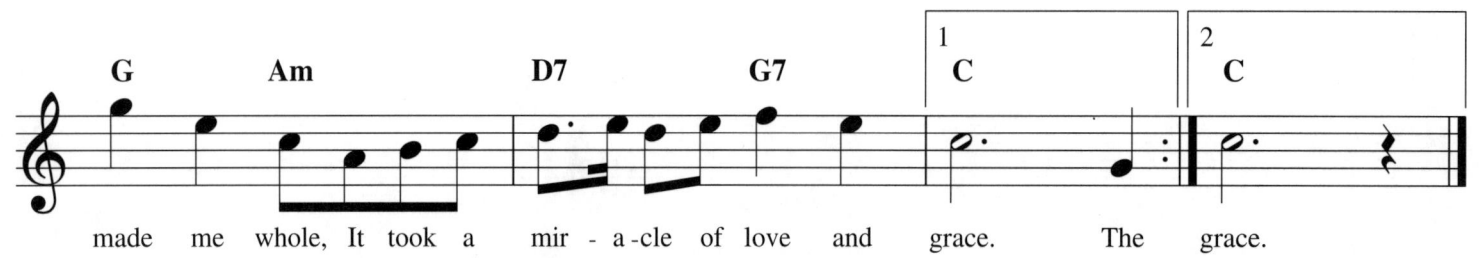

IT'S BEGINNING TO RAIN

Copyright © 1979 Gaither Music Company and Word Music, Inc.
All Rights Reserved   Used by Permission

Words by GLORIA GAITHER and AARON WILBURN
Music by WILLIAM J. GAITHER and AARON WILBURN

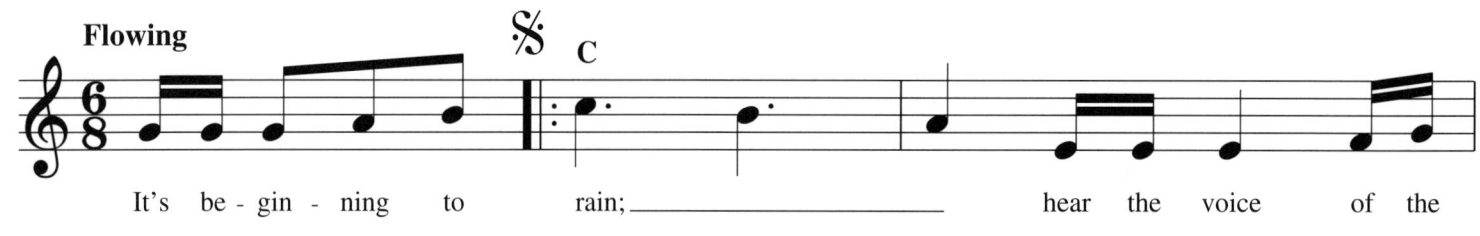
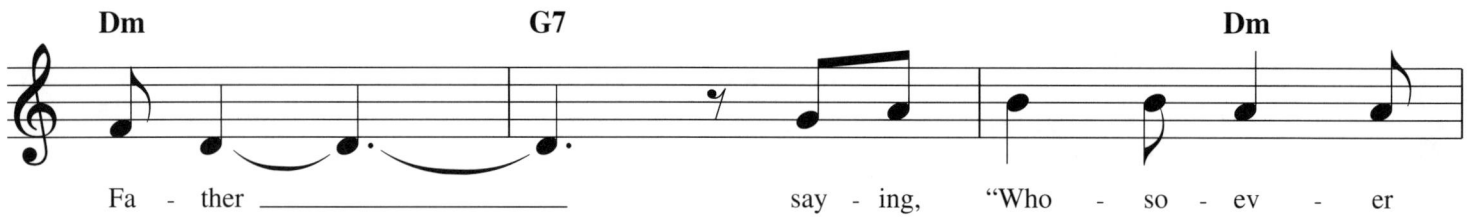
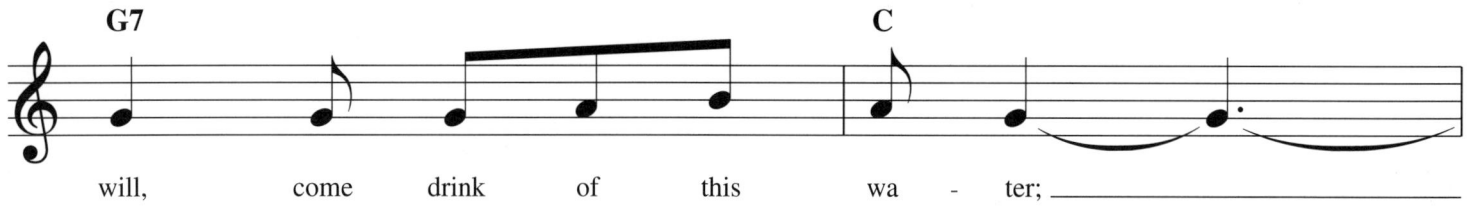
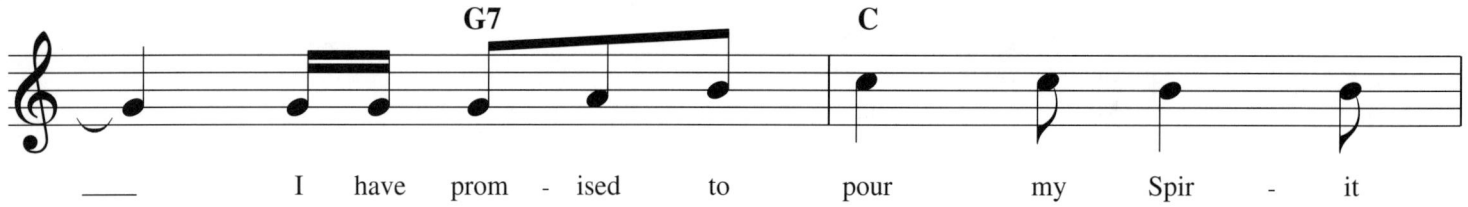

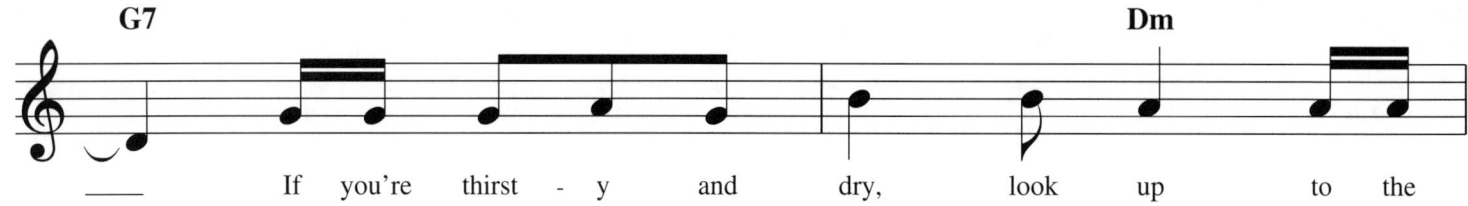
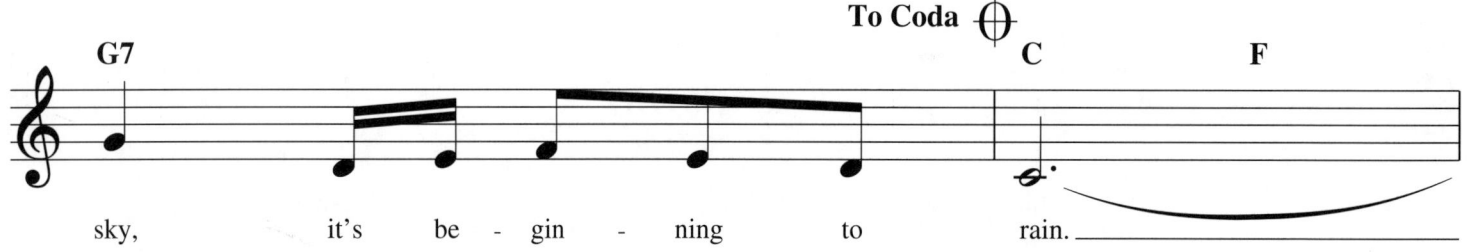

JUST A CLOSER WALK WITH THEE

Traditional
Arranged by KENNETH MORRIS

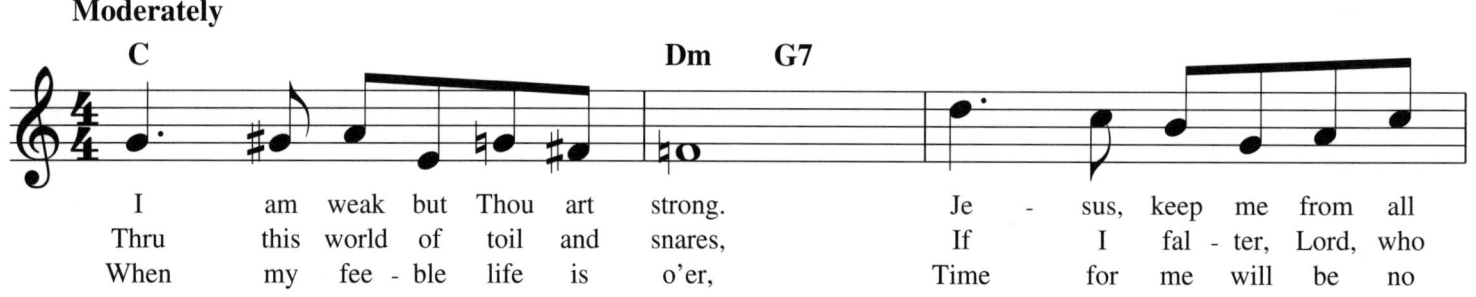
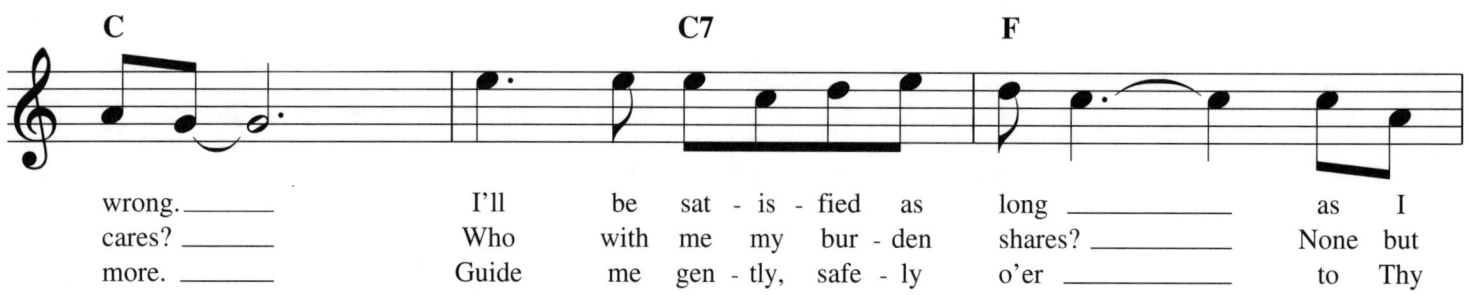
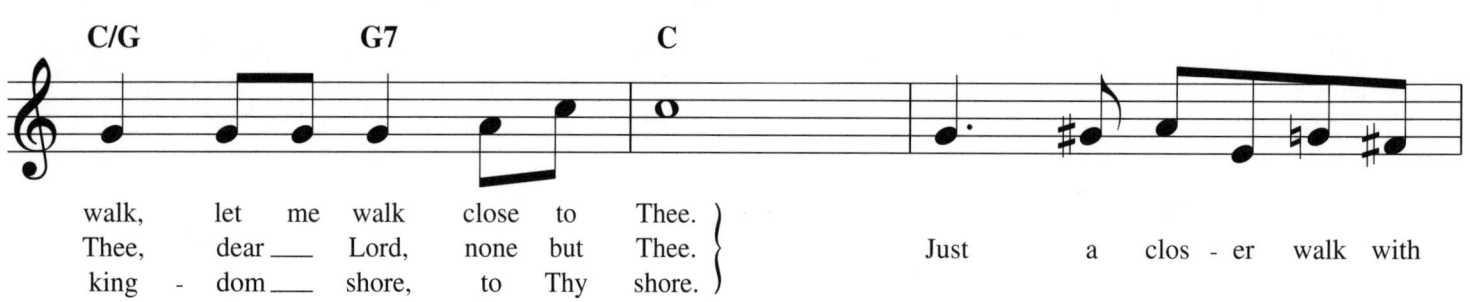

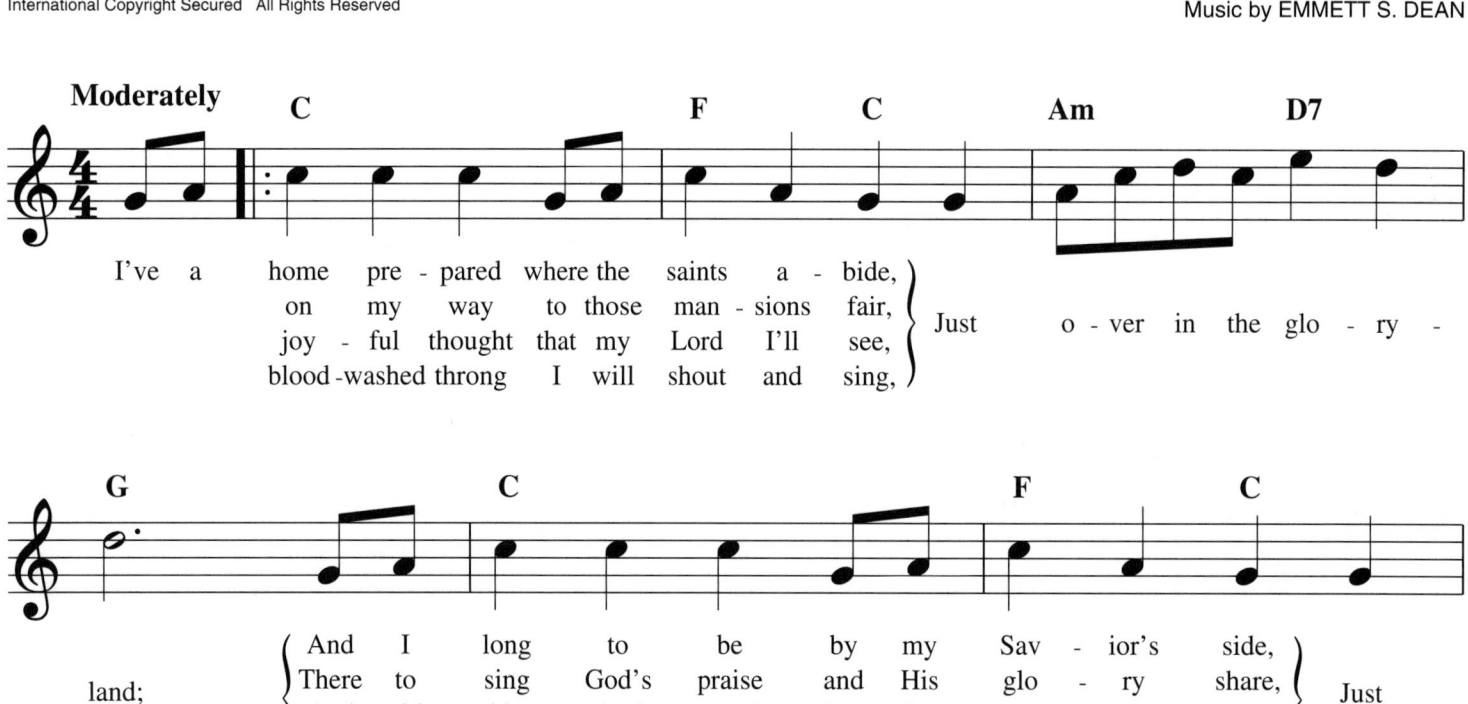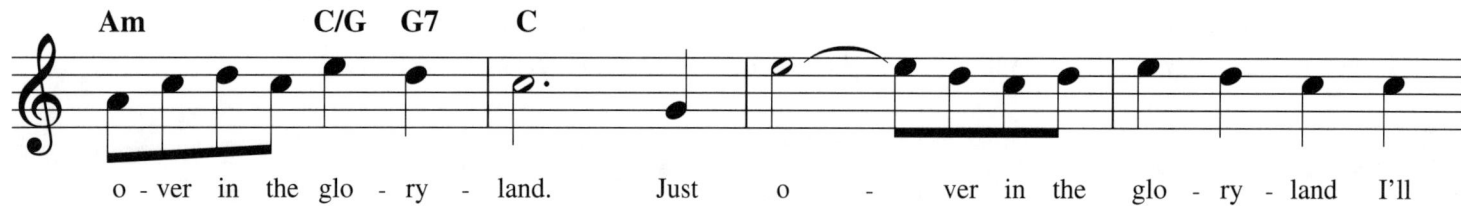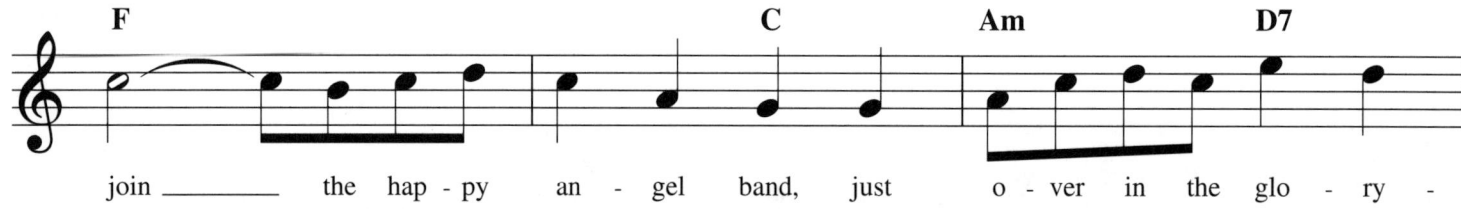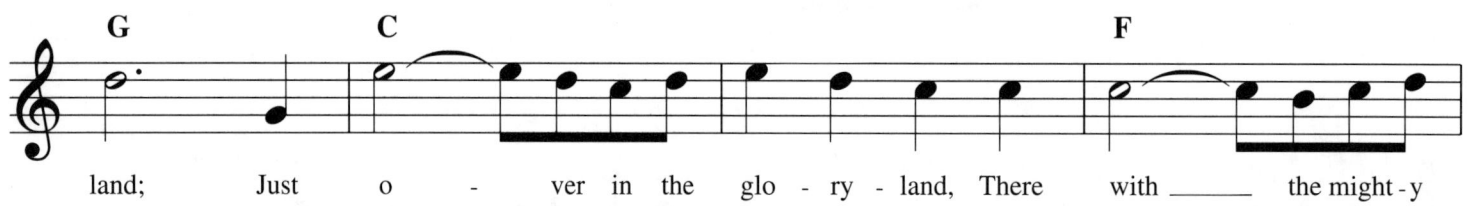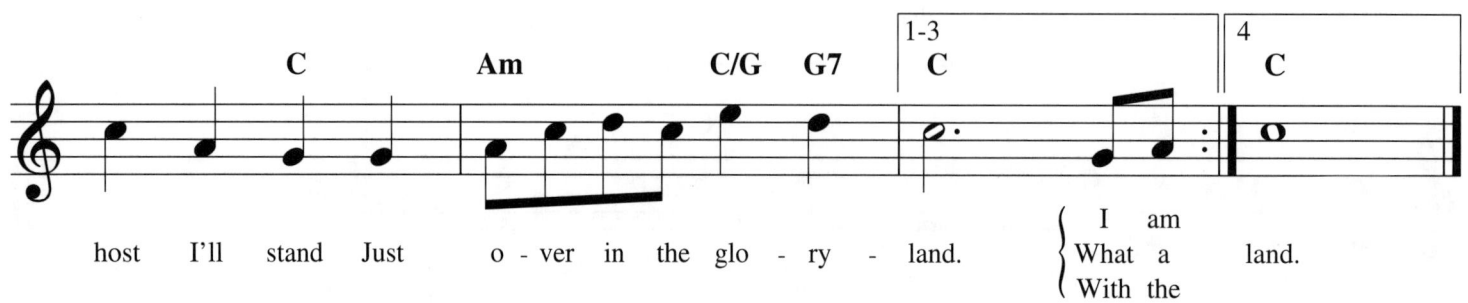

THE KING IS COMING

Copyright © 1970 (Renewed) William J. Gaither, Inc. (ASCAP)
All Rights Controlled by Gaither Copyright Management
All Rights Reserved   Used by Permission

Words by WILLIAM J. and GLORIA GAITHER
and CHARLES MILLHUFF
Music by WILLIAM J. GAITHER

The mar- ket- place is emp- ty, no more
fac- es line the hall- ways, those whose
hear the char- iots rum- ble, I can

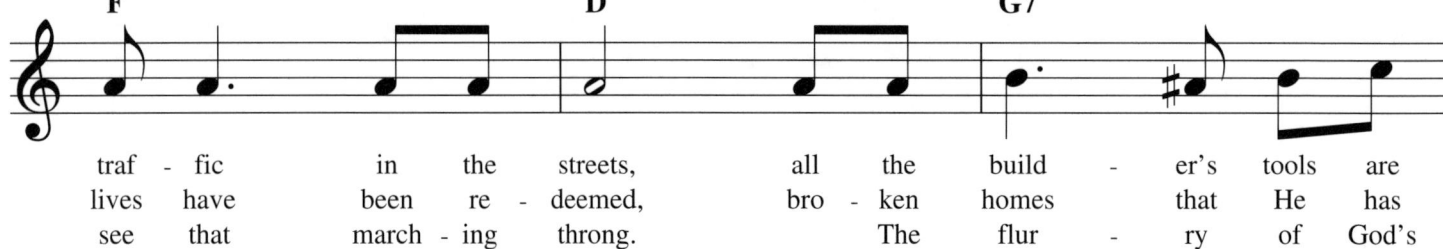

traf- fic in the streets, all the build- er's tools are
lives have been re- deemed, bro- ken homes that He has
see that march- ing throng. The flur- ry of God's

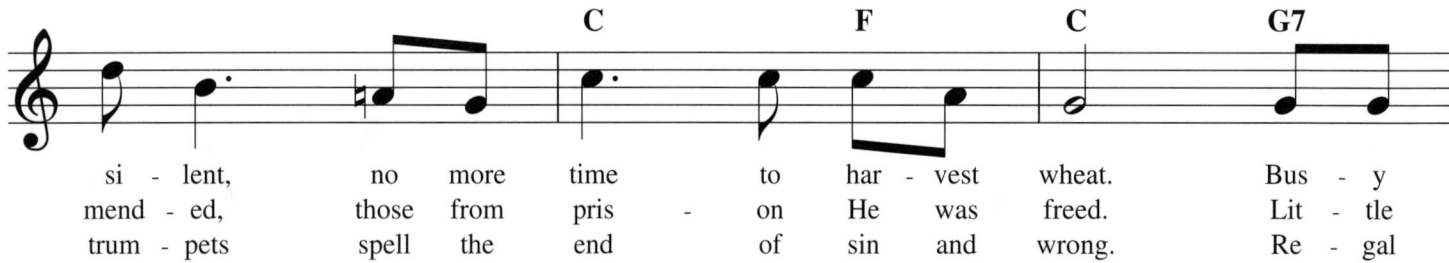

si- lent, no more time to har- vest wheat. Bus- y
mend- ed, those from pris- on He was freed. Lit- tle
trum- pets spell the end of sin and wrong. Re- gal

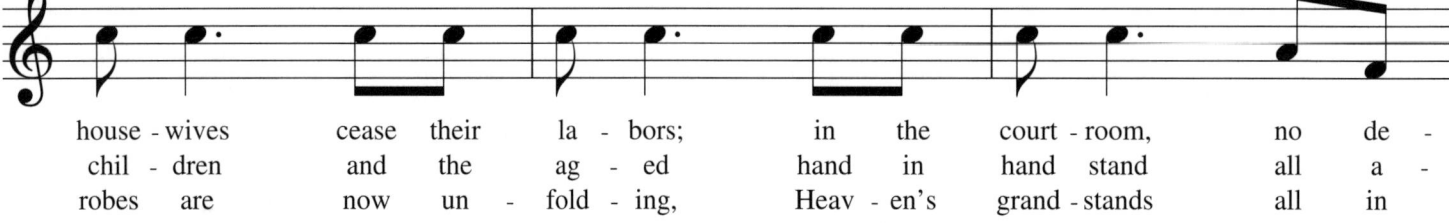

house- wives cease their la- bors; in the court- room, no de-
chil- dren and the ag- ed hand in hand stand all a-
robes are now un- fold- ing, Heav- en's grand- stands all in

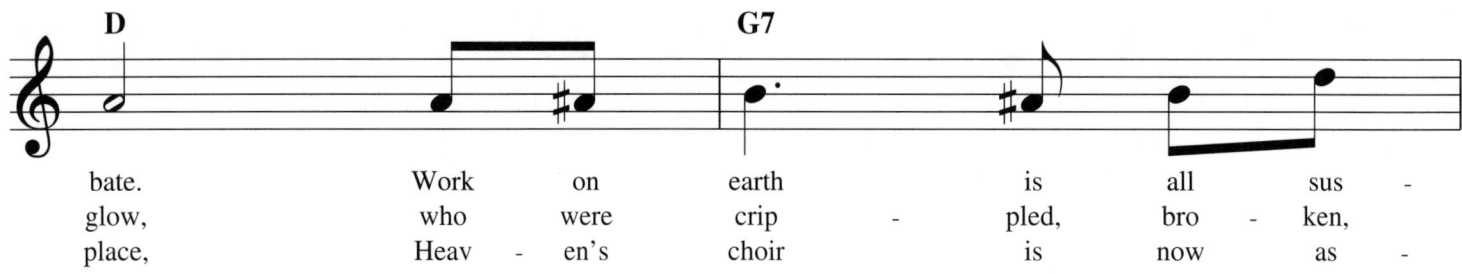

bate. Work on earth is all sus-
glow, who were crip- pled, bro- ken,
place, Heav- en's choir is now as-

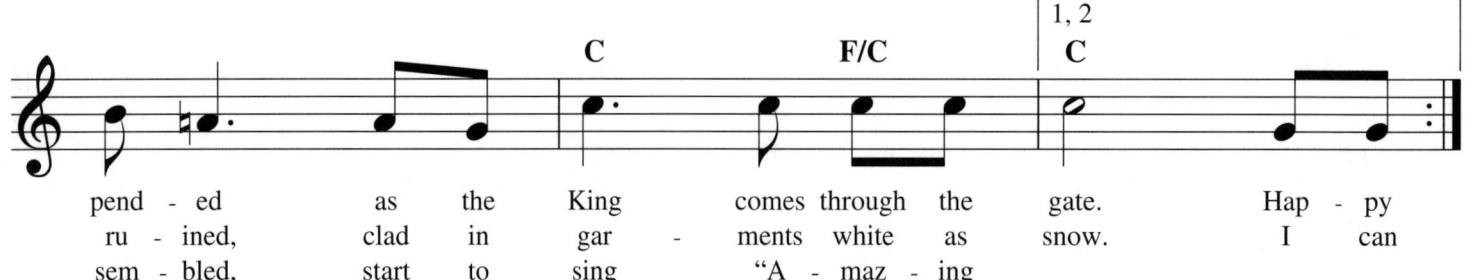

pend- ed as the King comes through the gate. Hap- py
ru- ined, clad in gar- ments white as snow. I can
sem- bled, start to sing "A- maz- ing

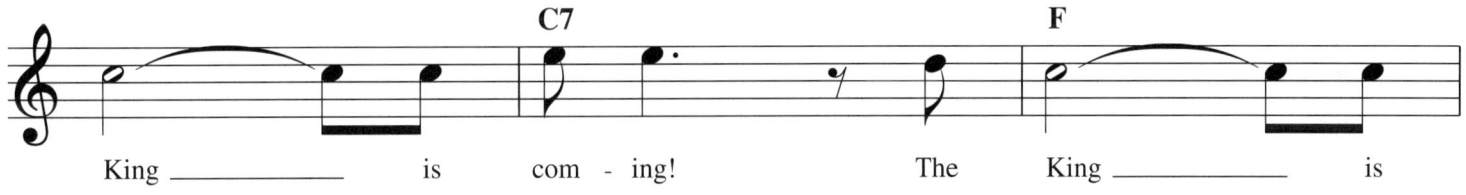
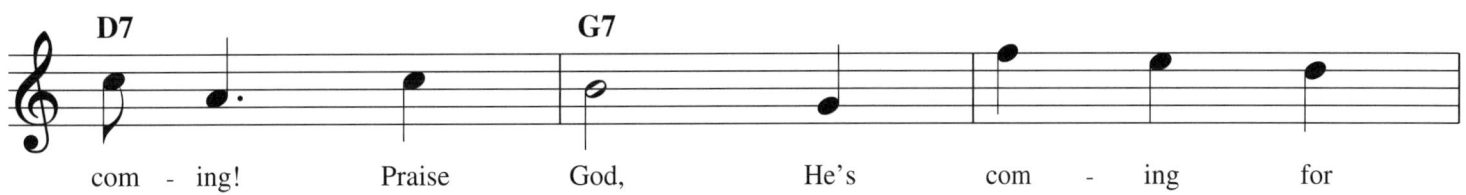
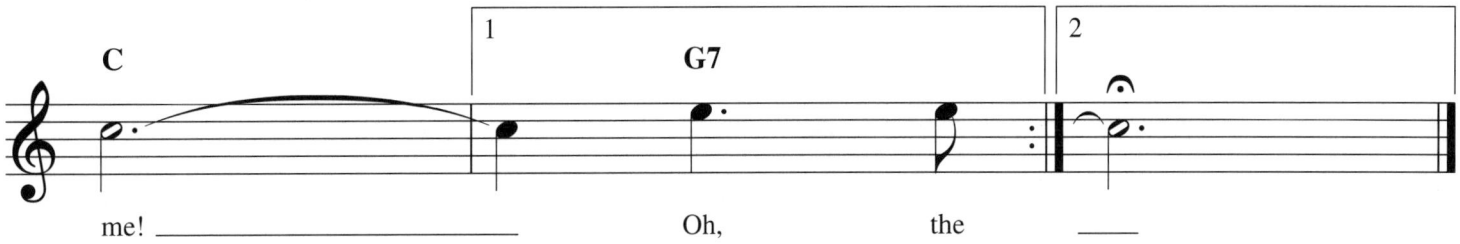

THE KING OF WHO I AM

Copyright © 1983 by BMG Songs, Inc. and Word Music, Inc.
All Rights Administered by BMG Songs, Inc.
International Copyright Secured   All Rights Reserved

Words and Music by TANYA GOODMAN
and MICHAEL SYKES

Worshipfully

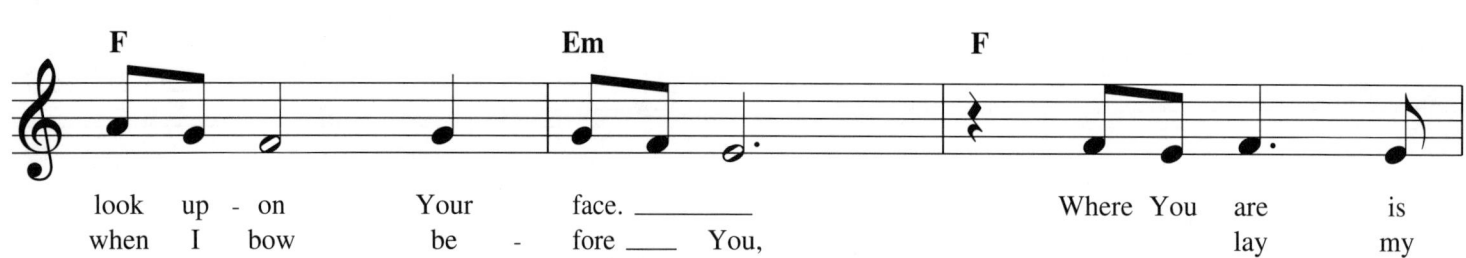

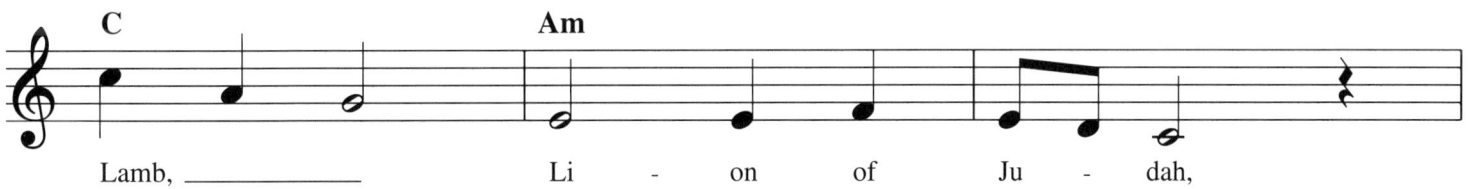

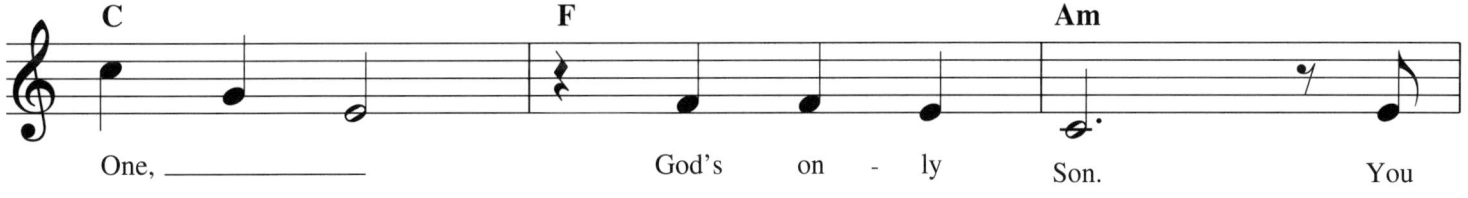
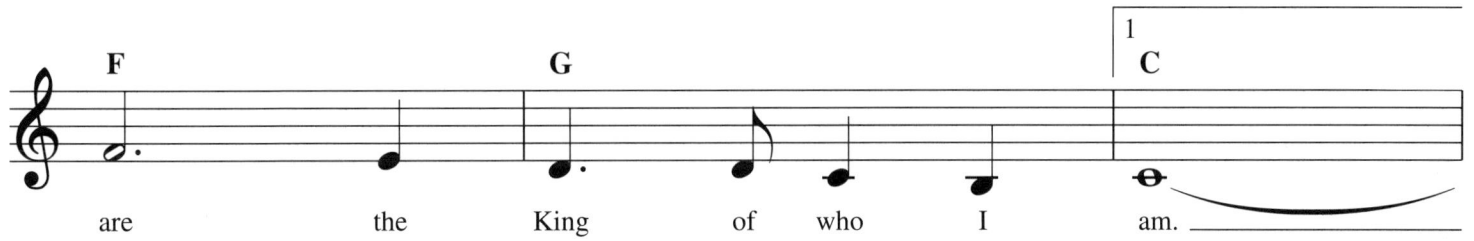
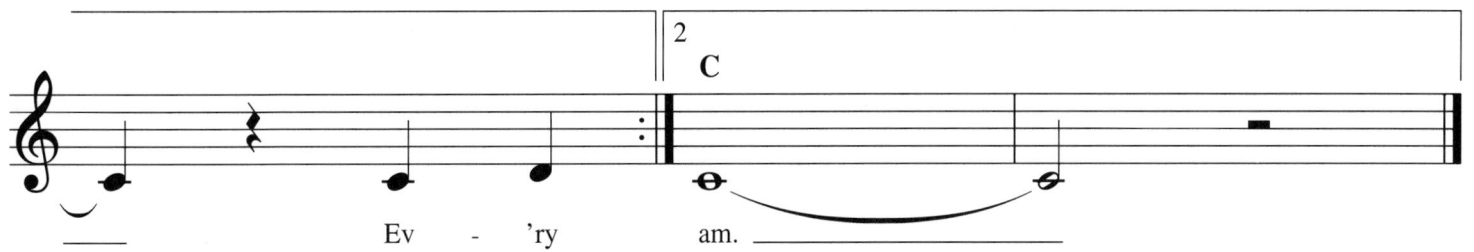

THE LILY OF THE VALLEY

Copyright © 2001 by HAL LEONARD CORPORATION
International Copyright Secured   All Rights Reserved

Words by CHARLES W. FRY
Music by WILLIAM S. HAYS

I have found a friend in Je - sus, He's ev - 'ry - thing to me, He's the
all my griefs has tak - en and all my sor - rows borne, In temp -
nev - er, nev - er leave me nor yet for - sake me here, While I

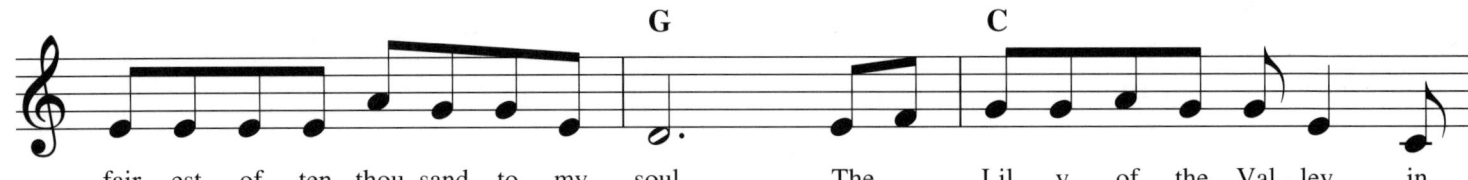

fair - est of ten thou - sand to my soul. The ___ Lil - y of the Val - ley, in
ta - tion He's my strong and might - y tow'r. I have all for Him for - sak - en and
live by faith and do His bless - ed will. A ___ wall of fire a - bout me, I've

Him a - lone I see All I need to cleanse and make me ful - ly whole. In
all my i - dols torn From my heart, and now He keeps me by His pow'r. Though
noth - ing now to fear; With His man - na He my hun - gry soul shall fill. Then

sor - row He's my com - fort, in trou - ble He's my stay, He ___ tells me ev - 'ry care on Him to
all the world for - sake me and Sa - tan tempt me sore, Through ___ Je - sus I shall safe - ly reach the
sweep - ing up to glo - ry I'll see His bless - ed face Where ___ riv - ers of de - light shall ev - er

roll.
goal.   He's the Lil - y of the Val - ley, the Bright and Morn - ing Star, He's the
roll.

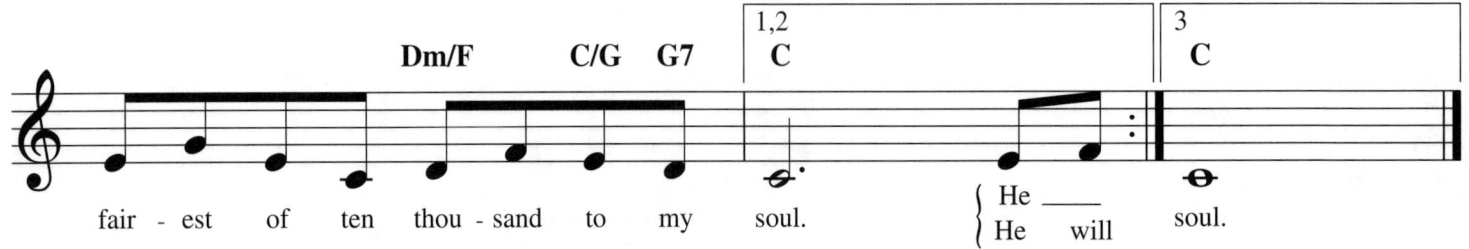

fair - est of ten thou - sand to my soul.   He ___
                                              He will soul.

THE LONGER I SERVE HIM

Copyright © 1965 (Renewed) William J. Gaither, Inc. (ASCAP)
All Rights Controlled by Gaither Copyright Management
All Rights Reserved   Used by Permission

Words and Music by
WILLIAM J. GAITHER

Reflectively

Since I started for the Kingdom, Since my life He controls, _____ Since I gave my heart to Jesus, } The longer I serve Him, the sweeter He grows. _____ The longer I serve Him, the sweeter He grows; _____ The more that I love Him, more love He bestows. Each day is like heaven, my heart over-flows; The longer I serve Him, the sweeter He grows.

Ev-'ry need He is sup-ply-ing, Plen-teous grace He be-stows, _____ Ev-'ry day my way gets brighter;

LOVE LIFTED ME

Words by JAMES ROWE
Music by HOWARD E. SMITH

Joyfully, in 2

I was sink - ing deep in sin,
All my heart to Him I give,
Souls in dan - ger, look a - bove;

far from the peace - ful shore, Ver - y deep - ly
ev - er to Him I'll cling, In His bless - ed
Je - sus com - plete - ly saves. He will lift you

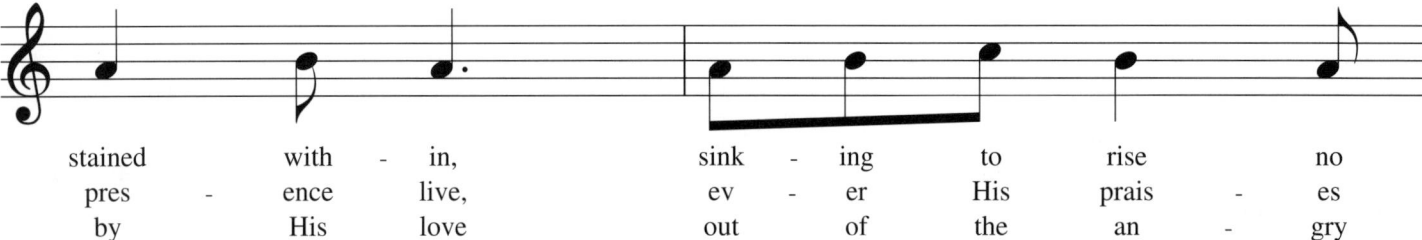
stained with - in, sink - ing to rise no
pres - ence live, ev - er His prais - es
by His love out of the an - gry

more. But the Mas - ter of the sea
sing. Love so might - y and so true
waves; He's the Mas - ter of the sea,

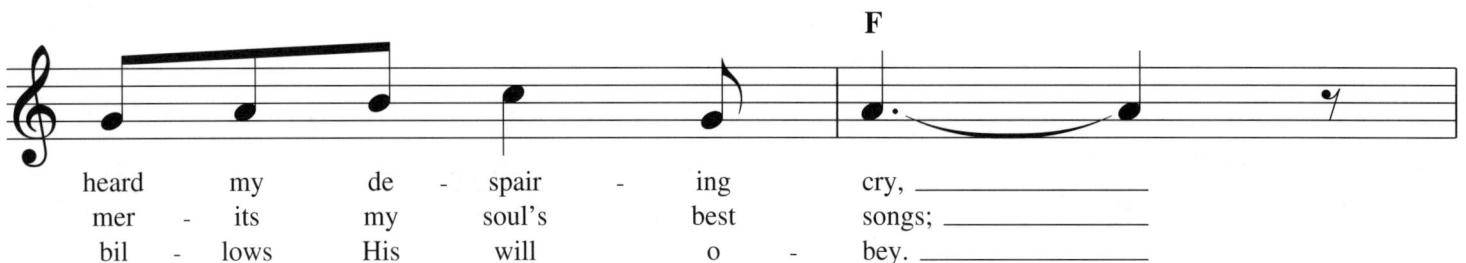
heard my de - spair - ing cry,
mer - its my soul's best songs;
bil - lows His will o - bey.

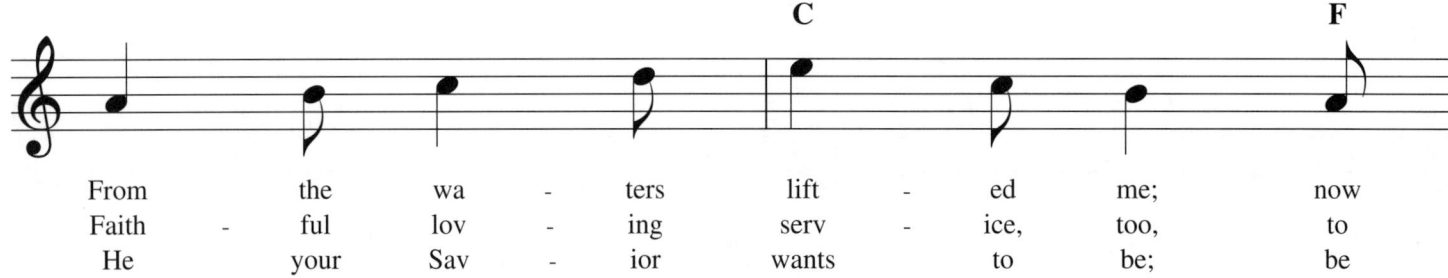
From the wa - ters lift - ed me; now
Faith - ful lov - ing serv - ice, too, to
He your Sav - ior wants to be; be

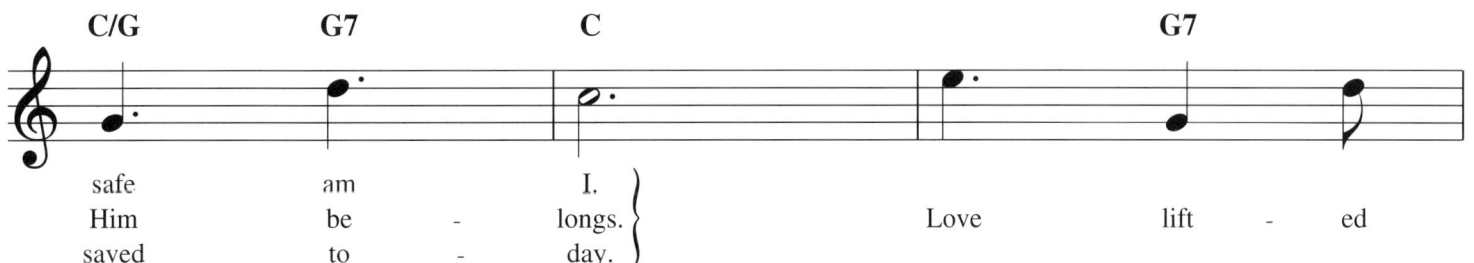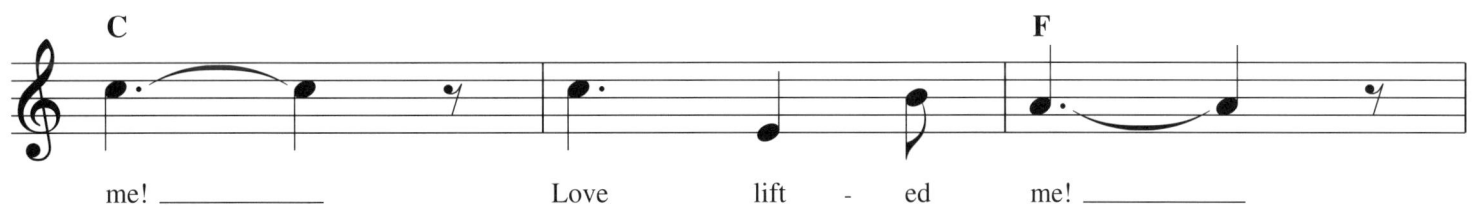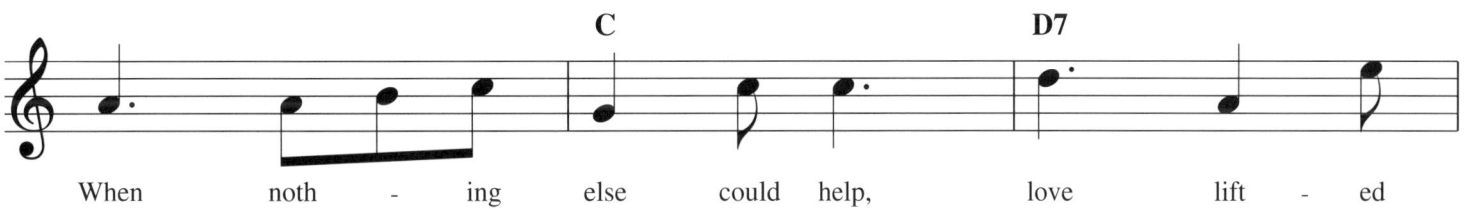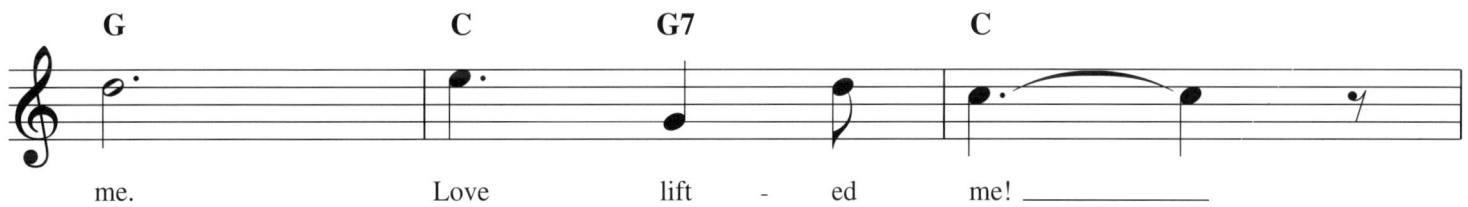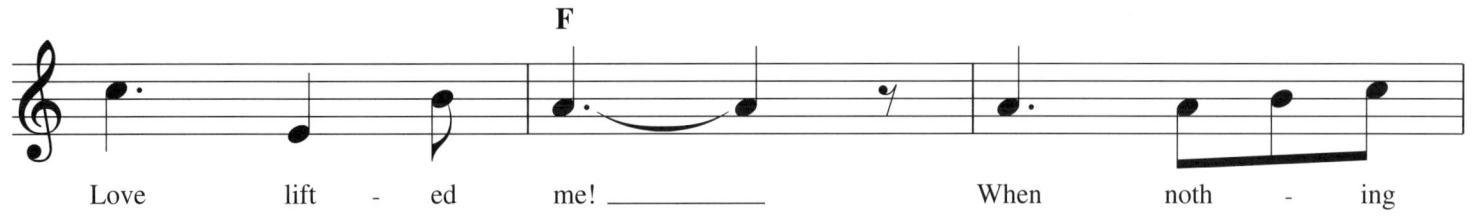

MANSION OVER THE HILLTOP

Words and Music by
IRA F. STANPHILL

With an easy flow

I'm sat-is-fied with just a cot-tage be-low, A lit-tle sil-ver and a lit-tle gold. But in that cit-y where the ran-somed will shine, I want a gold one that's sil-ver-lined.

tempt-ed, tor-ment-ed and test-ed, And like the proph-et, my pil-low a stone, And tho' I find here no per-ma-nent dwell-ing, I know He'll give me a man-sion my own.

poor or de-sert-ed or lone-ly; I'm not dis-cour-aged, I'm heav-en-bound. I'm just a pil-grim in search of a cit-y; I want a man-sion, a harp and a crown.

I've got a man-sion just o-ver the hill-top in that bright land where we'll nev-er grow old. And some-day yon-der we will nev-er-more wan-der, But walk the streets that are pur-est gold.

Though of-ten
Don't think me gold.

MIDNIGHT CRY

Words and Music by GREG DAY
and CHUCK DAY

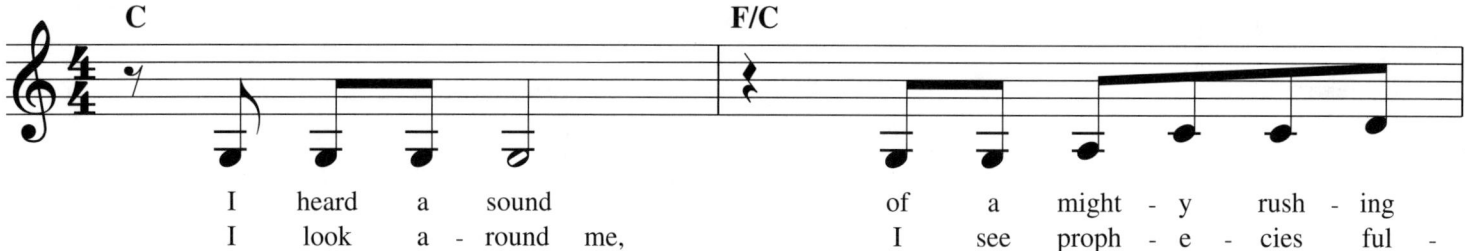
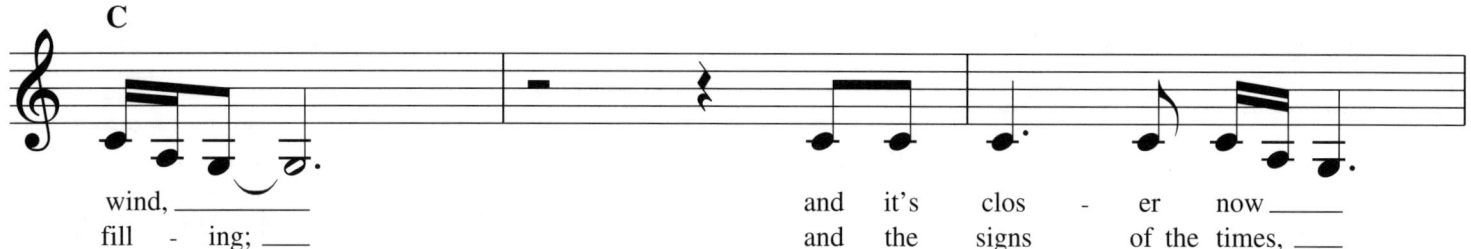

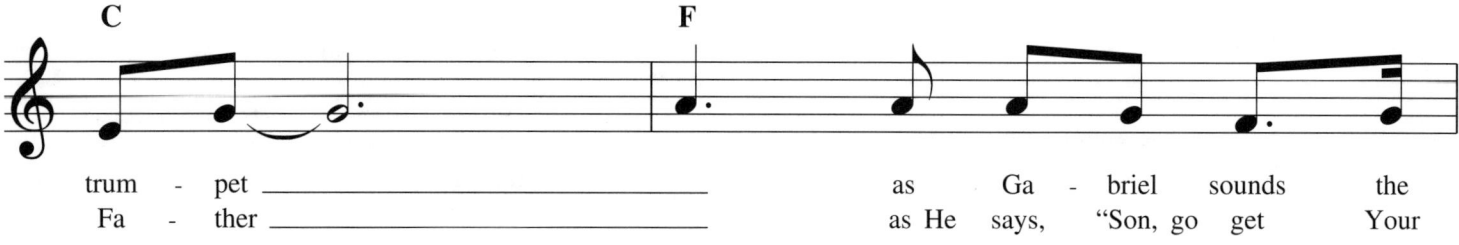
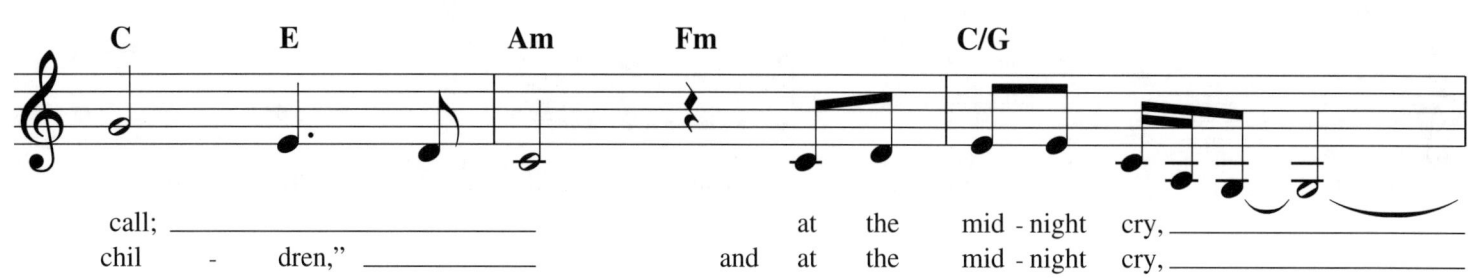
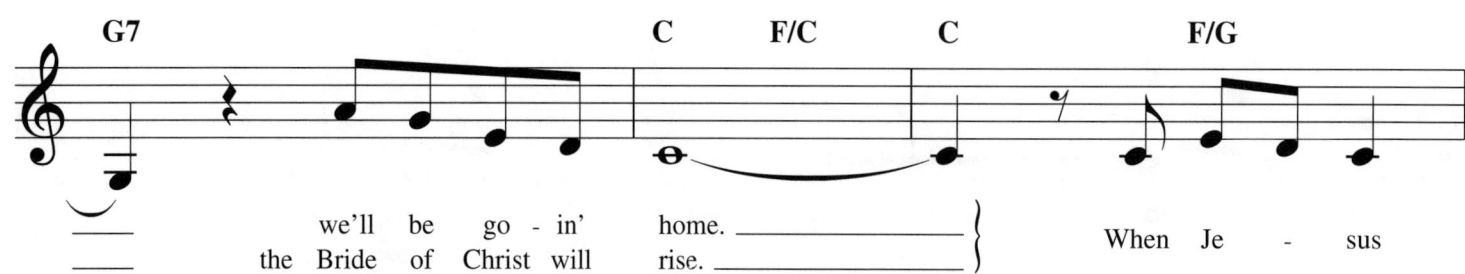

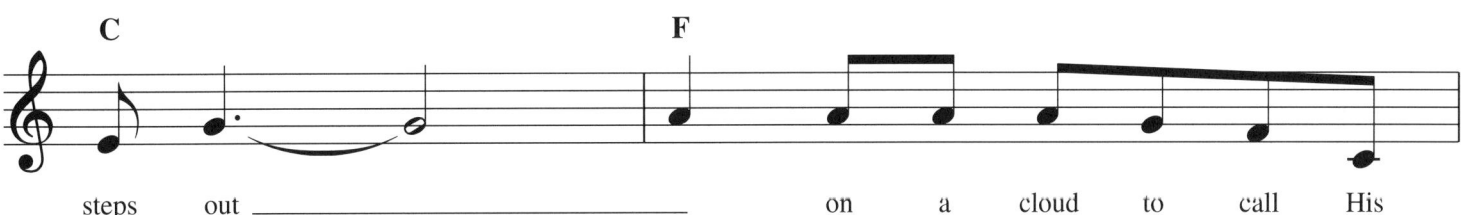
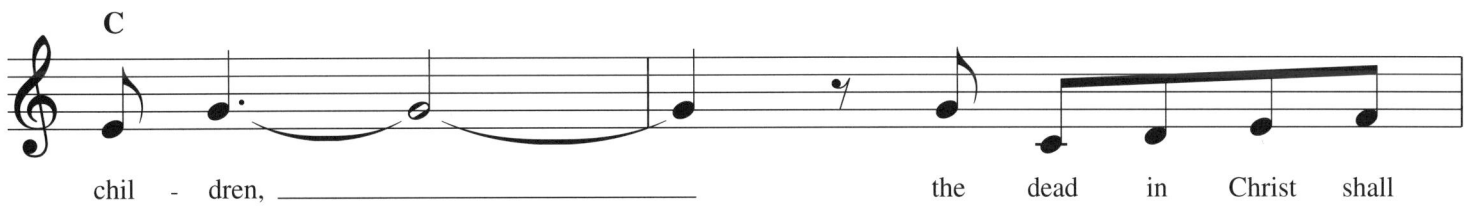
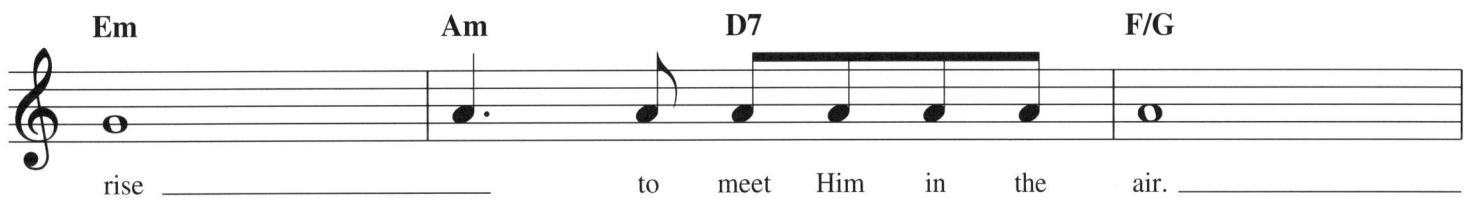
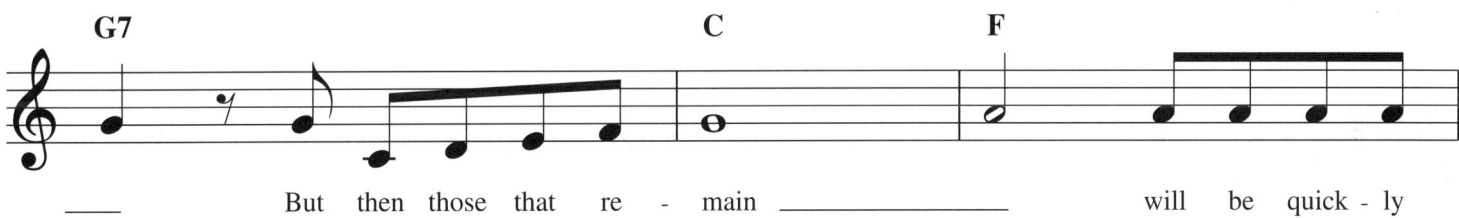
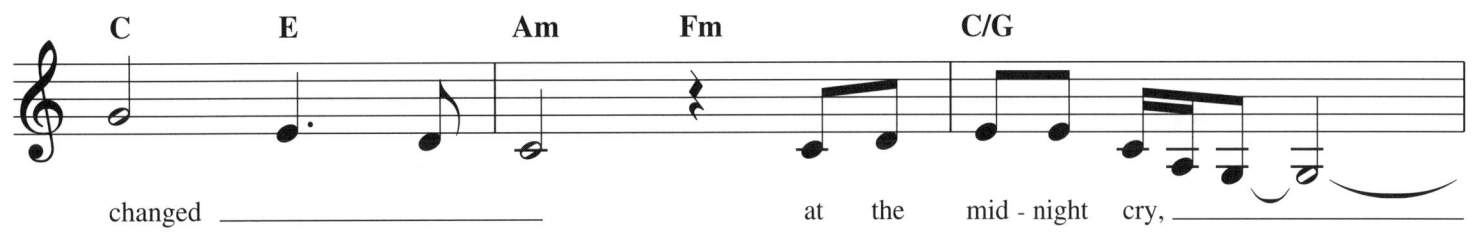
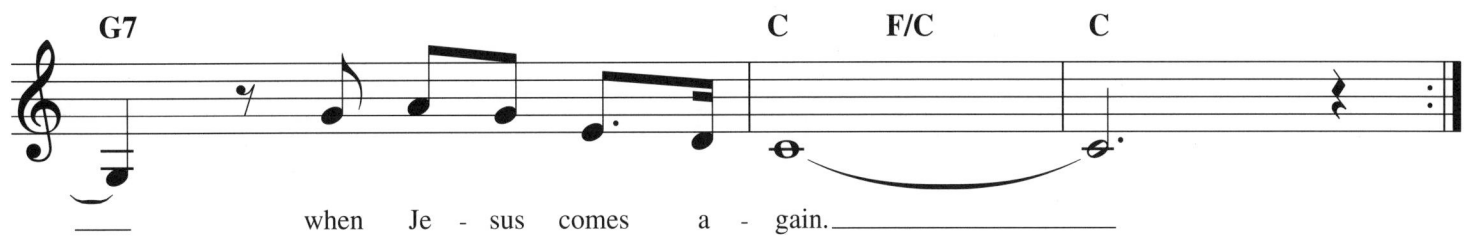

MORE THAN WONDERFUL

Copyright © 1983 Lanny Wolfe Music Company
All Rights Controlled by Gaither Copyright Management
All Rights Reserved   Used by Permission

Words and Music by
LANNY WOLFE

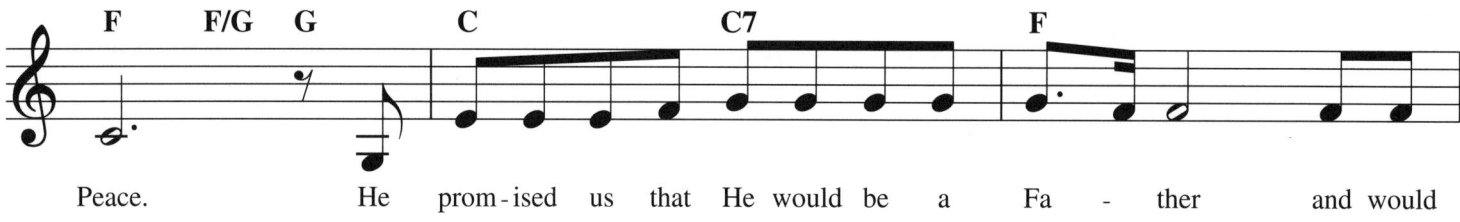

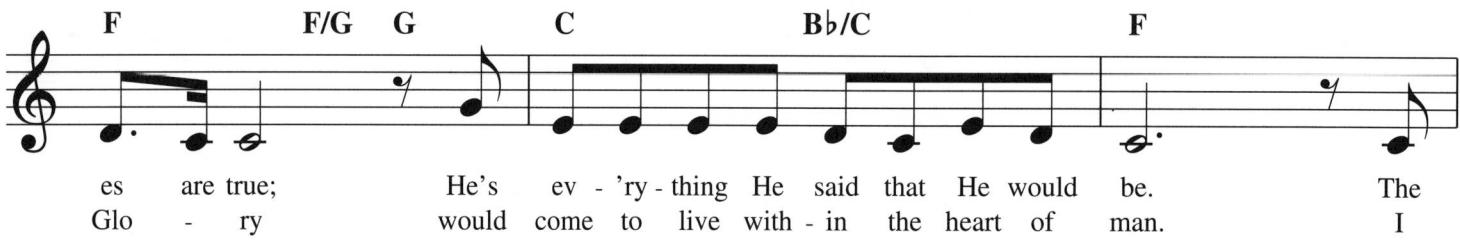

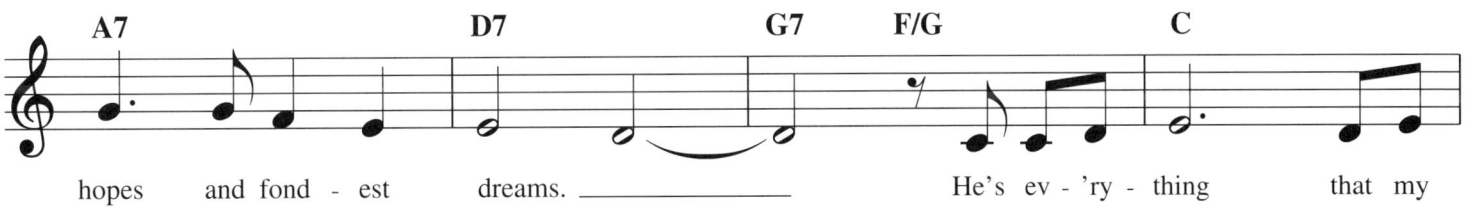

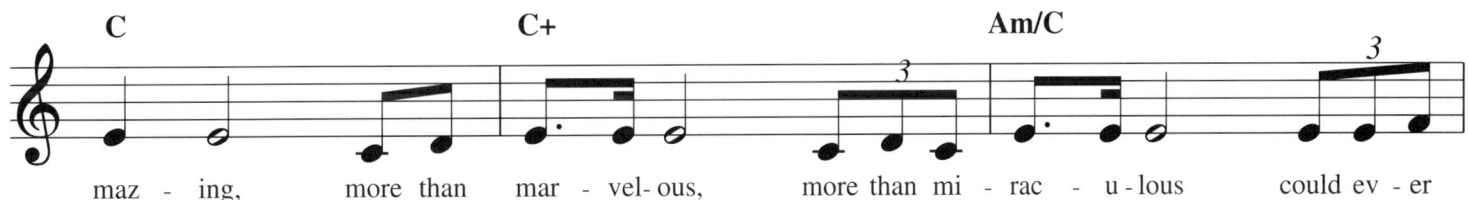

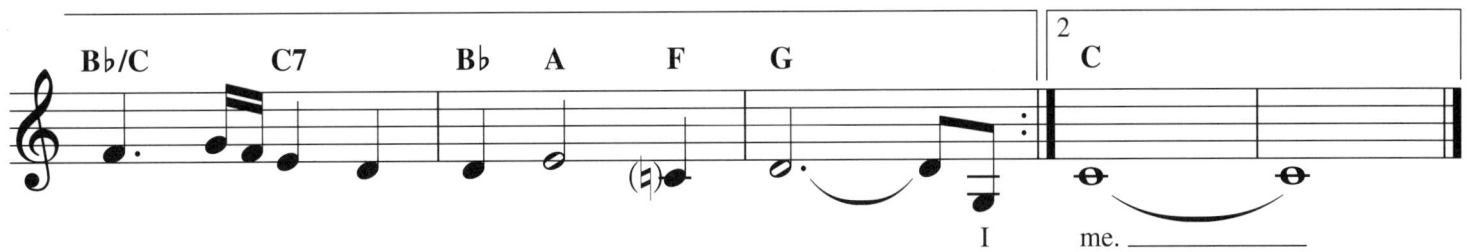

MOVIN' UP TO GLORYLAND

© Copyright 1983 Abernathy Publishing Co. (ASCAP)/(admin. by ICG)
All Rights Reserved   Used by Permission

Words and Music by
LEE ROY ABERNATHY

I love to think a - bout a par - a - dise
I made my res - er - va - tion long a - go

some - where be - yond the blue,
the day I gave up sin,

A man - sion wait - ing in the dis - tant skies
And when my man - sion's read - y, this I know:

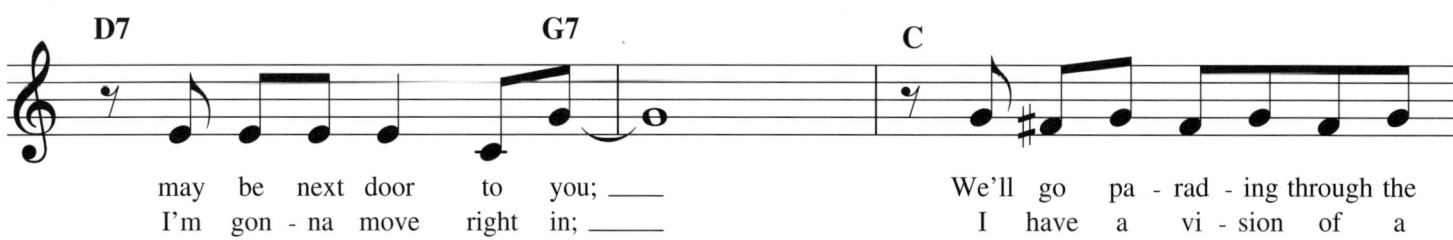

may be next door to you;   We'll go pa - rad - ing through the
I'm gon - na move right in;   I have a vi - sion of a

dis - tant stars,   right down the Milk - y Way,
hap - py place   where friends and loved ones meet,

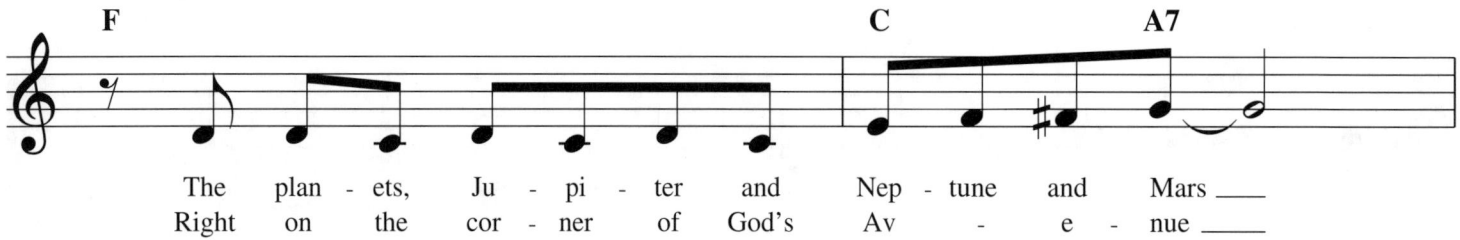

The plan - ets, Ju - pi - ter and Nep - tune and Mars
Right on the cor - ner of God's Av - e - nue

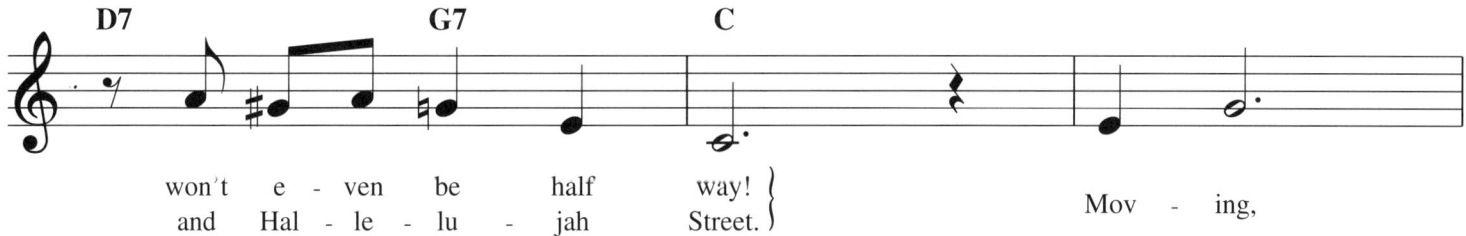
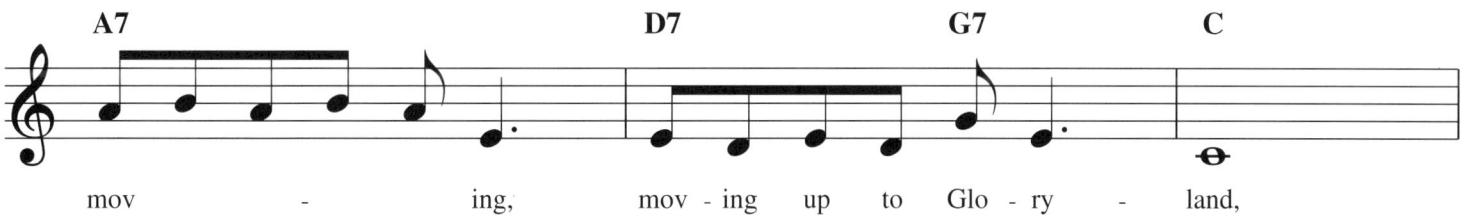

MY TRIBUTE

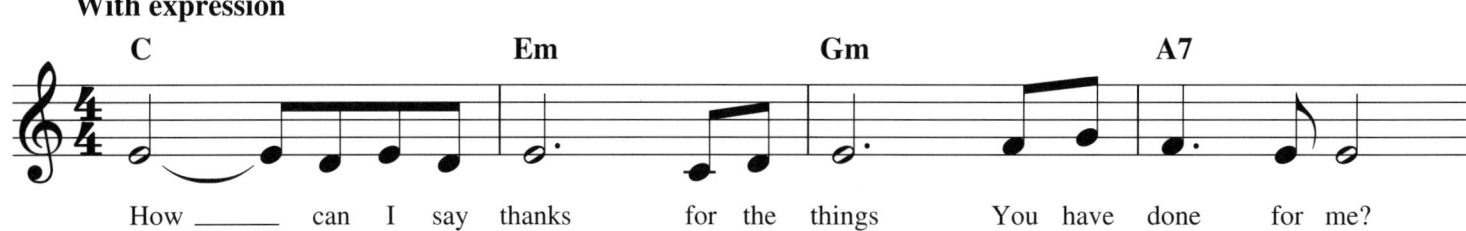
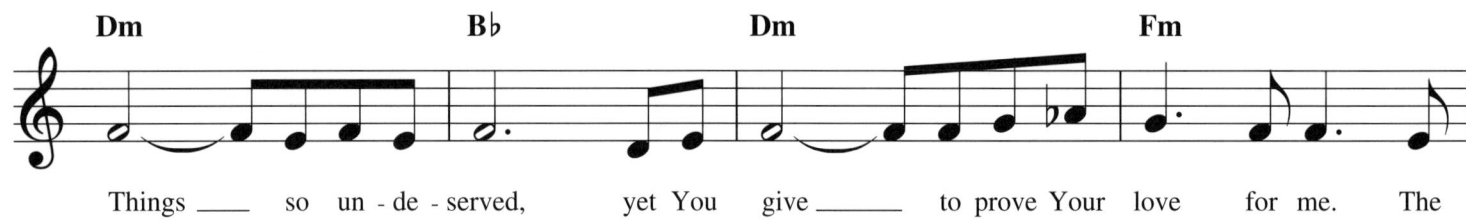
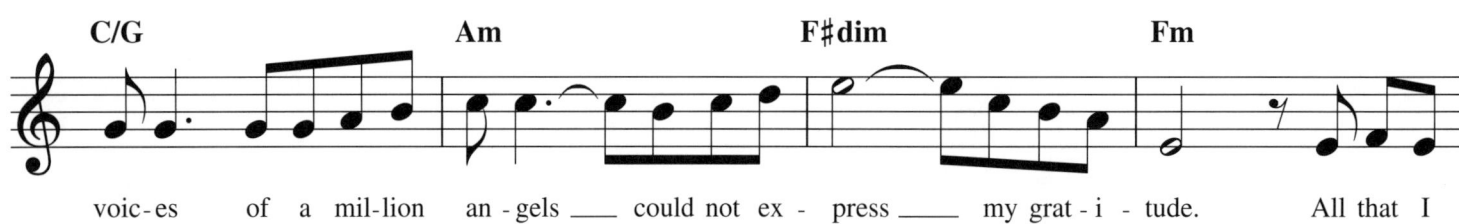
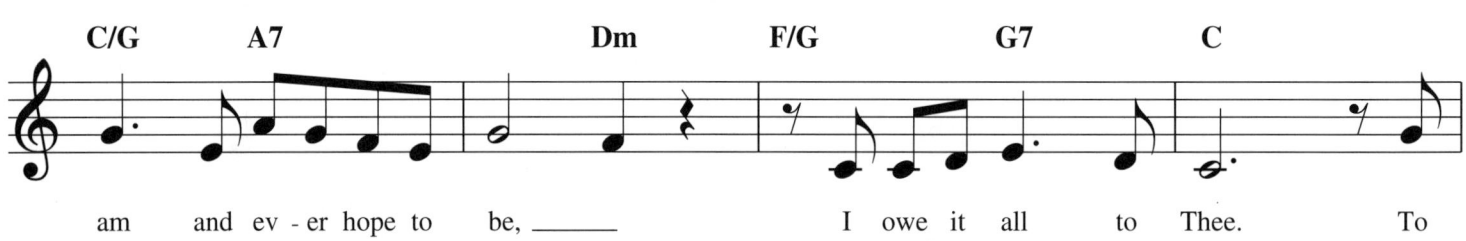
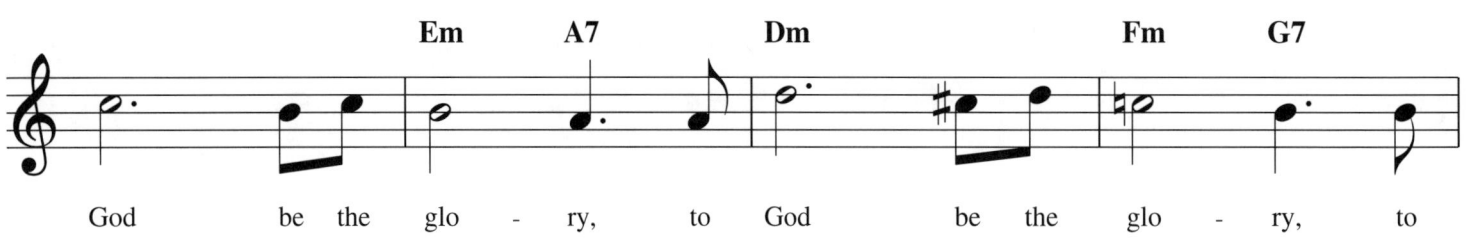

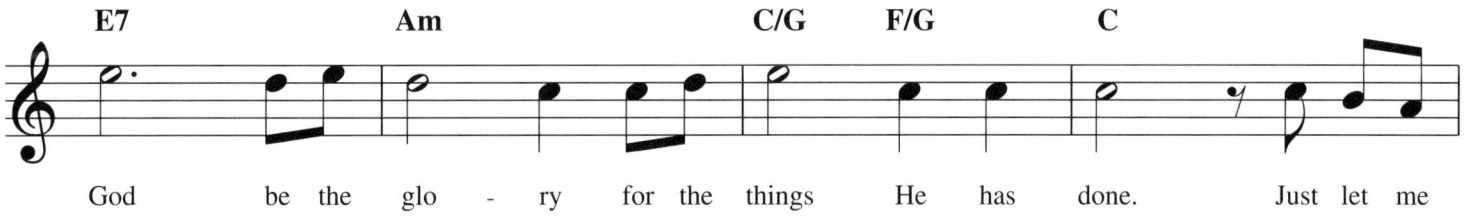

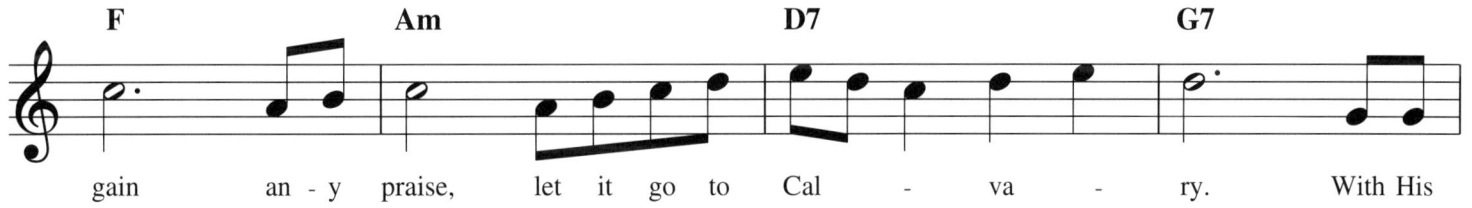

NOW I BELONG TO JESUS

© 1938 (Renewed 1967) Wordspring Music, Inc.
All Rights Reserved   Used by Permission

Words and Music by
NORMAN J. CLAYTON

Je - sus, my Lord, will love me for - ev - er. From Him no pow'r of
Once I was lost in sin's deg - ra - da - tion; Je - sus came down to
Joy floods my soul, for Je - sus has saved me, Freed me from sin that

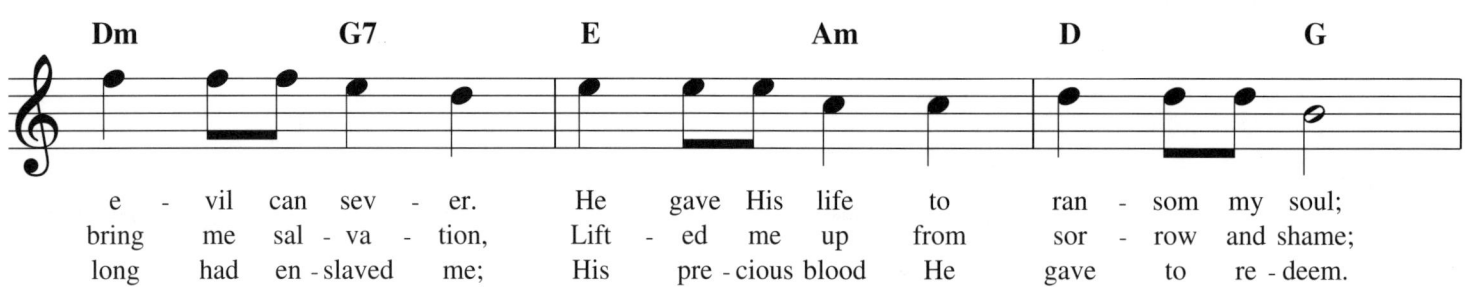

e - vil can sev - er. He gave His life to ran - som my soul;
bring me sal - va - tion, Lift - ed me up from sor - row and shame;
long had en - slaved me; His pre - cious blood He gave to re - deem.

Now I be - long to Him.
Now I be - long to Him.   Now I be - long to
Now I be - long to Him.

Je - sus, Je - sus be - longs to me;

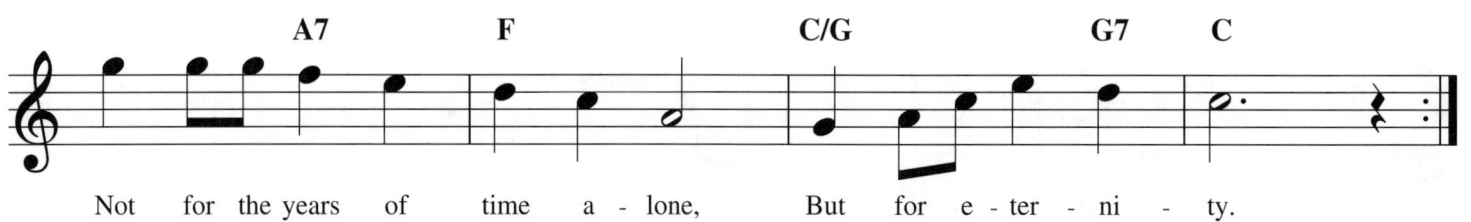

Not for the years of time a - lone, But for e - ter - ni - ty.

THE OLD RUGGED CROSS

Words and Music by
REV. GEORGE BENNARD

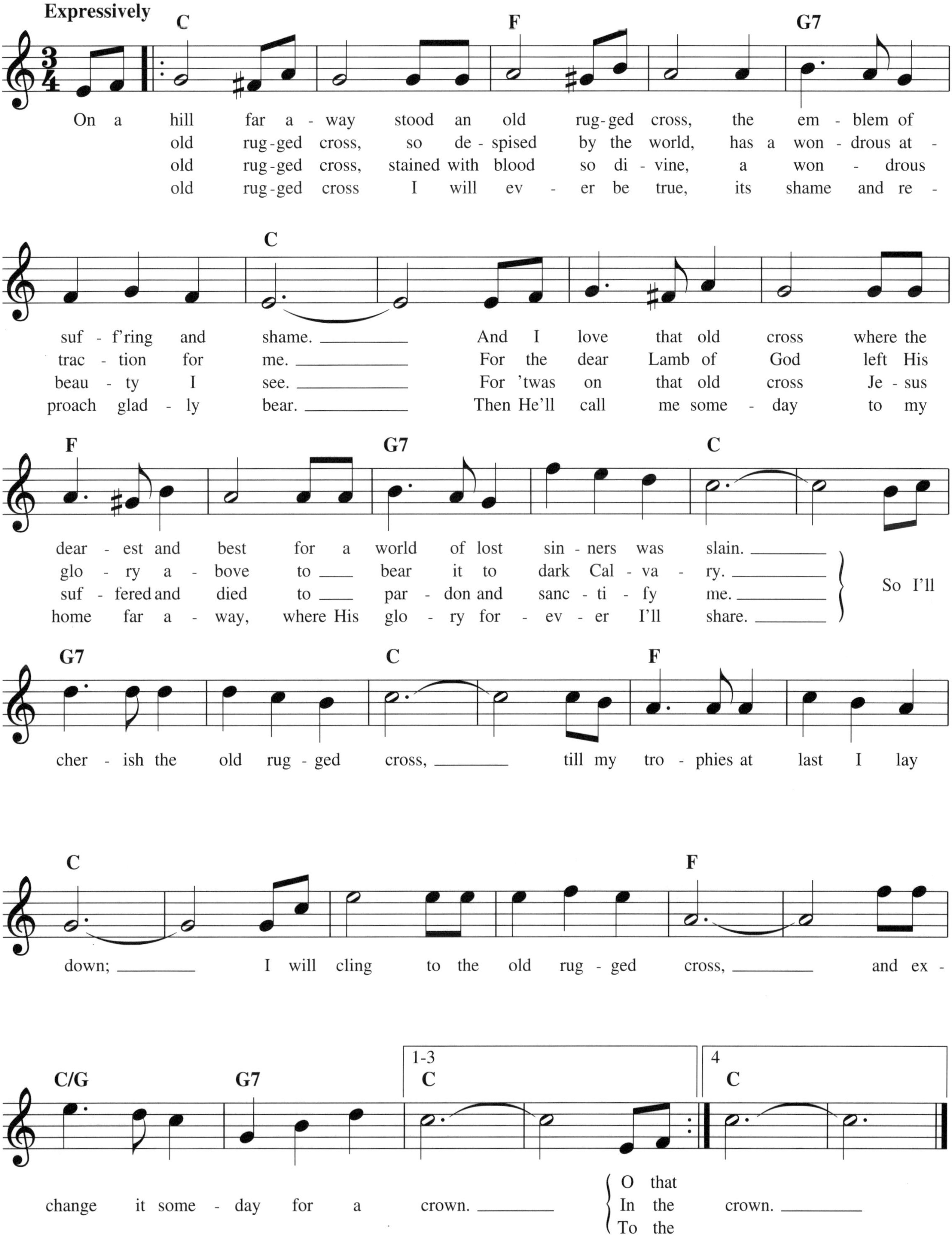
Expressively
C F G7
On a hill far a - way stood an old rug-ged cross, the em - blem of
old rug-ged cross, so de - spised by the world, has a won - drous at -
old rug-ged cross, stained with blood so di - vine, a won - drous
old rug-ged cross I will ev - er be true, its shame and re -
C
suf - f'ring and shame. And I love that old cross where the
trac - tion for me. For the dear Lamb of God left His
beau - ty I see. For 'twas on that old cross Je - sus
proach glad - ly bear. Then He'll call me some - day to my
F G7 C
dear - est and best for a world of lost sin - ners was slain.
glo - ry a - bove to bear it to dark Cal - va - ry.
suf - fered and died to par - don and sanc - ti - fy me.
home far a - way, where His glo - ry for - ev - er I'll share.
So I'll
G7 C F
cher - ish the old rug - ged cross, till my tro - phies at last I lay
C F
down; I will cling to the old rug - ged cross, and ex -
C/G G7 1-3 C 4 C
change it some - day for a crown. O that In the To the crown.

PART THE WATERS

© 1975 Word Music, Inc.
All Rights Reserved   Used by Permission

Words and Music by
CHARLES F. BROWN

Moderate Gospel feel

When I think I'm go-in' un-der, part the wa-ters, Lord. When I

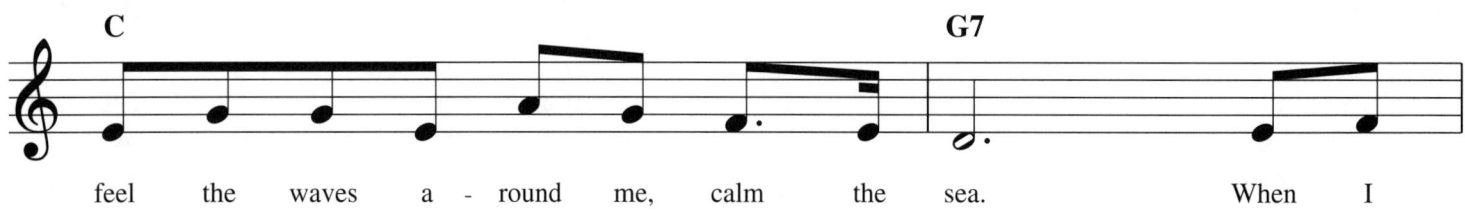

feel the waves a-round me, calm the sea. When I

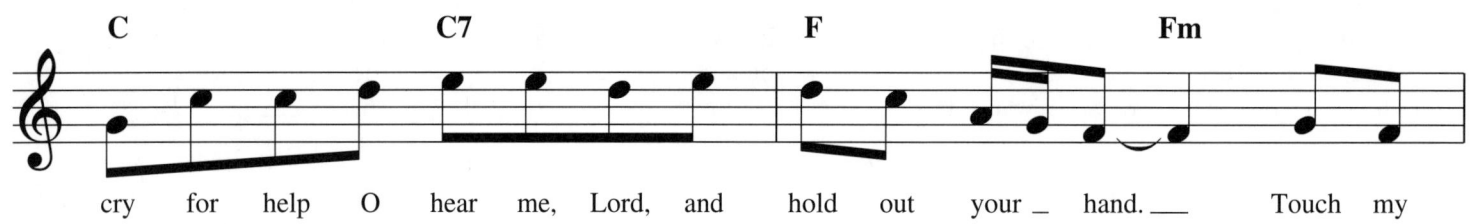

cry for help O hear me, Lord, and hold out your hand. Touch my

To Coda

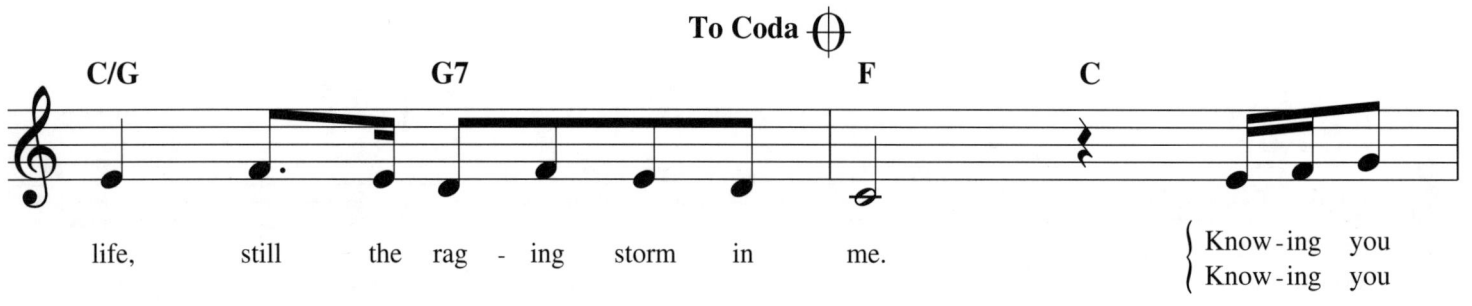

life, still the rag-ing storm in me. Know-ing you / Know-ing you

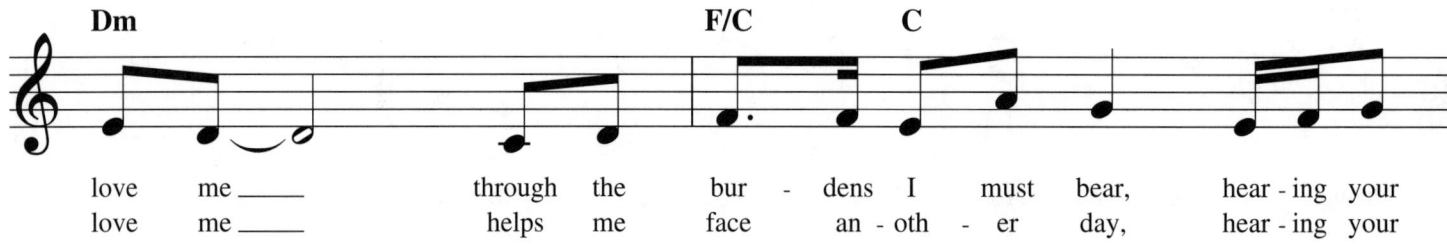

love me through the bur-dens I must bear, hear-ing your
love me helps me face an-oth-er day, hear-ing your

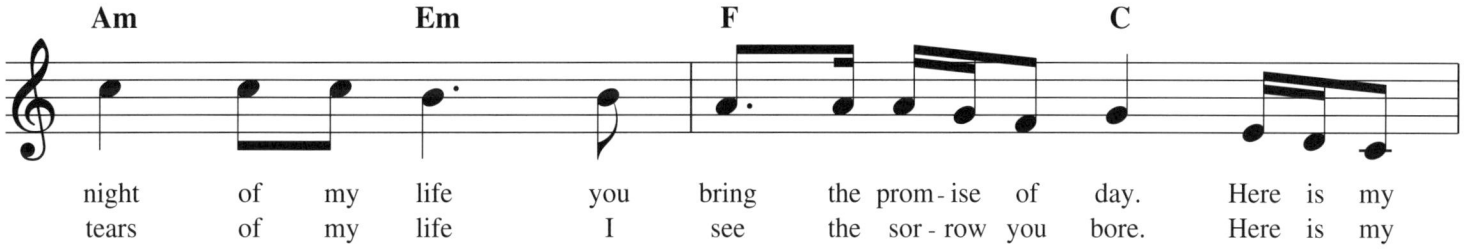
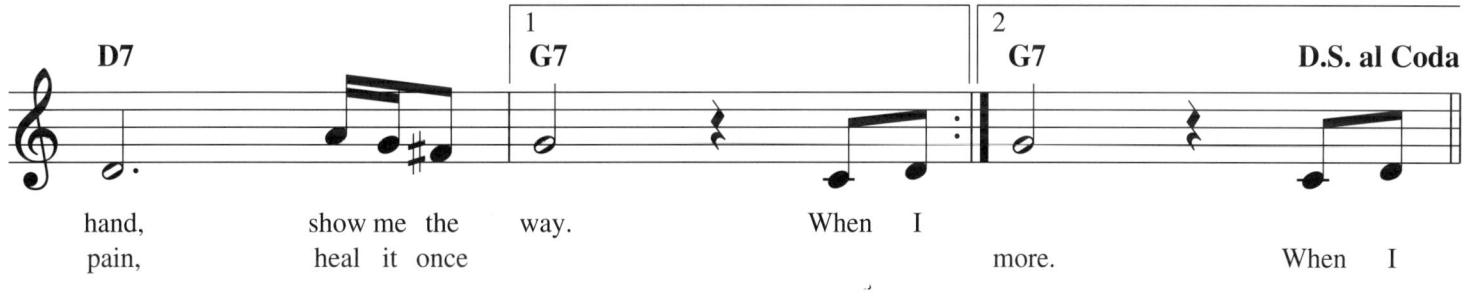
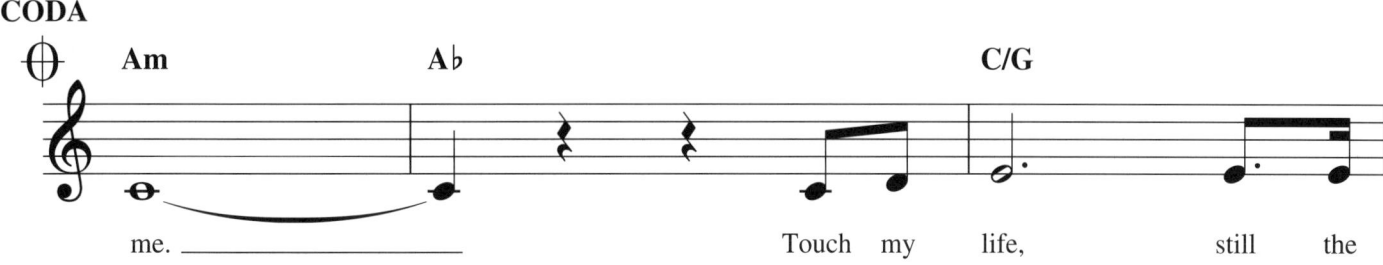
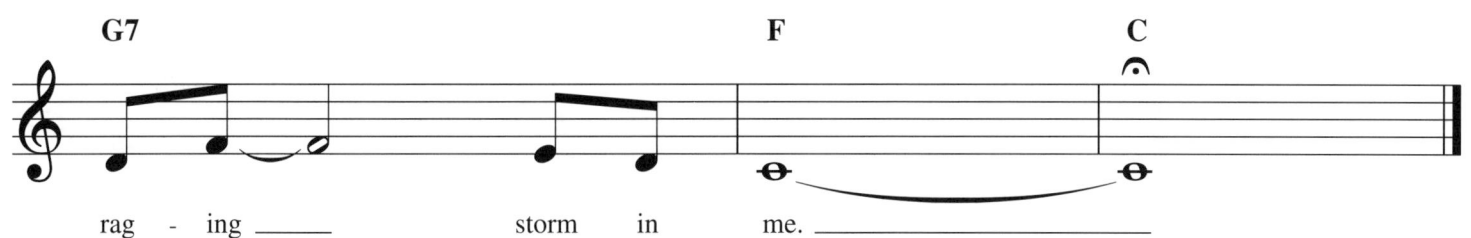

(There'll Be) PEACE IN THE VALLEY (For Me)

Copyright © 1939 by Thomas A. Dorsey
Copyright Renewed, Assigned to Unichappell Music Inc.
International Coyright Secured   All Rights Reserved

Words and Music by
THOMAS A. DORSEY

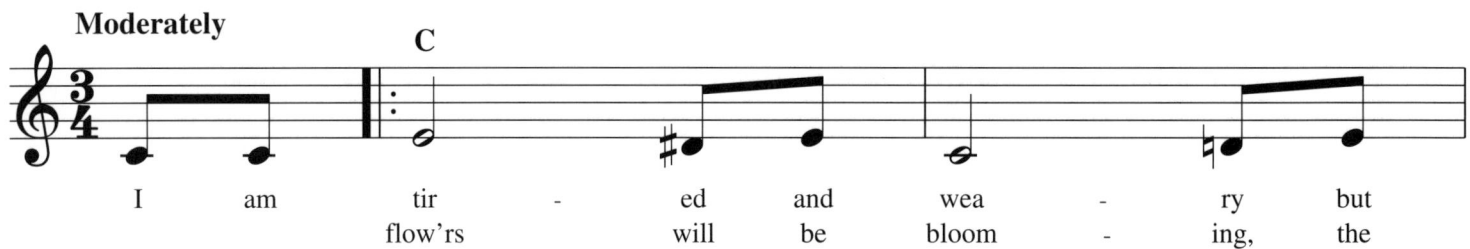
I am tir - ed and wea - ry but
flow'rs will be bloom - ing, the

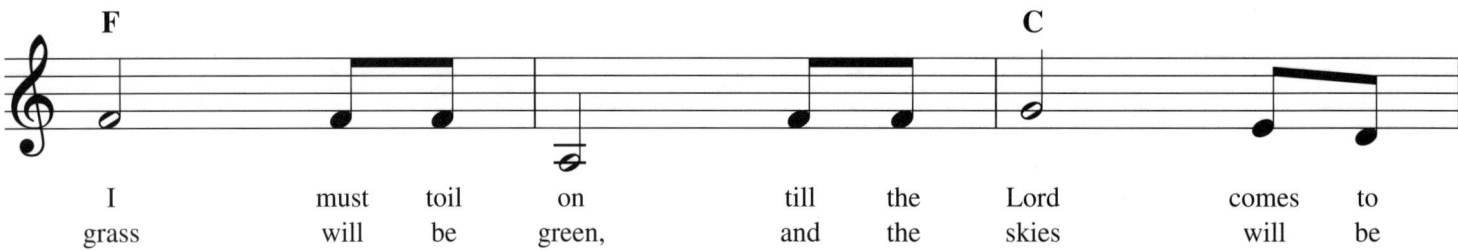
I must toil on till the Lord comes to
grass will be green, and the skies will be

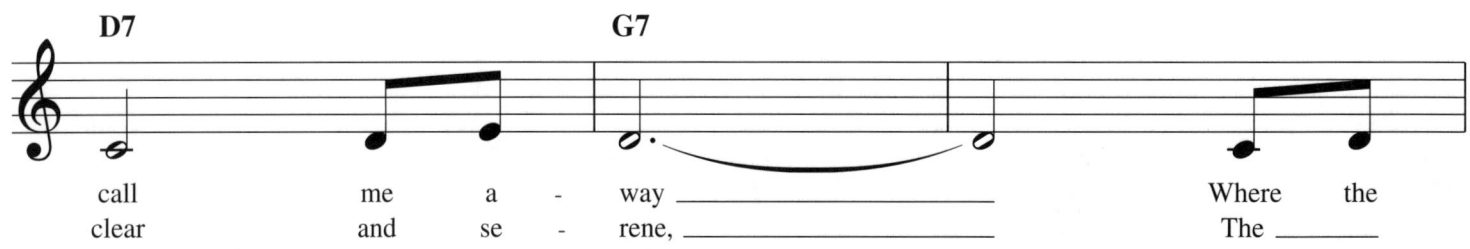
call me a - way Where the
clear and se - rene, The

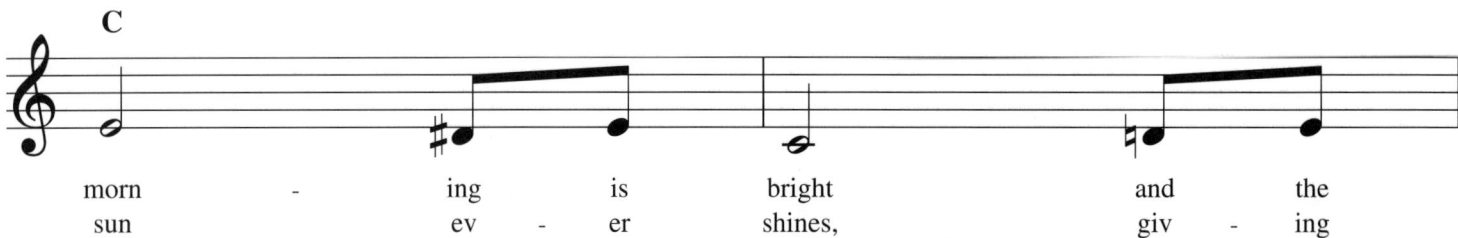
morn - ing is bright and the
sun ev - er shines, giv - ing

Lamb is the light and the night is as
one end - less beam and no clouds there will

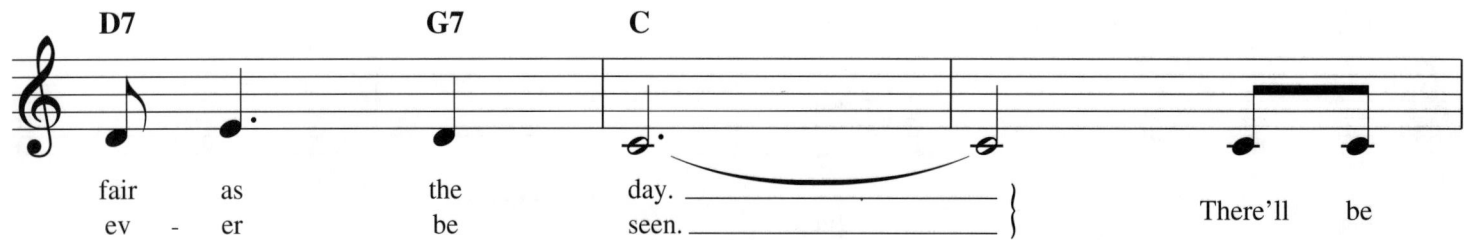
fair as the day.
ev - er be seen. There'll be

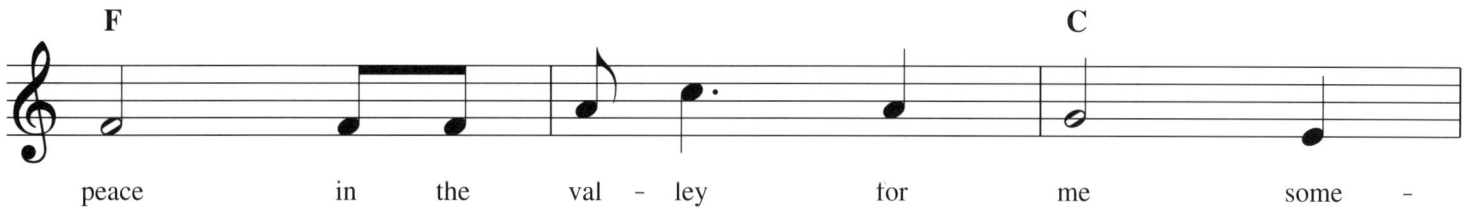
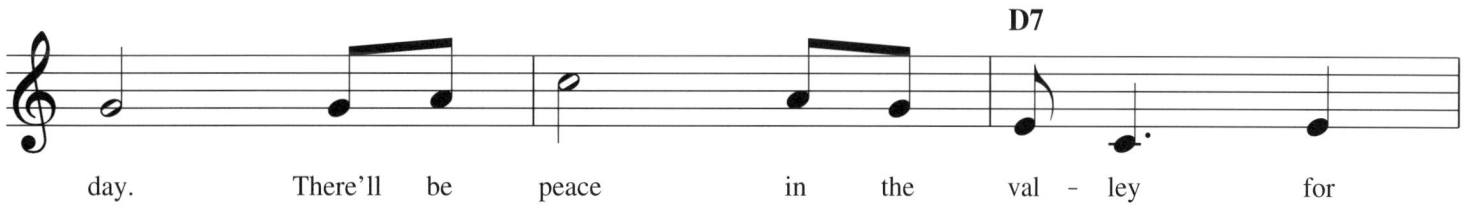
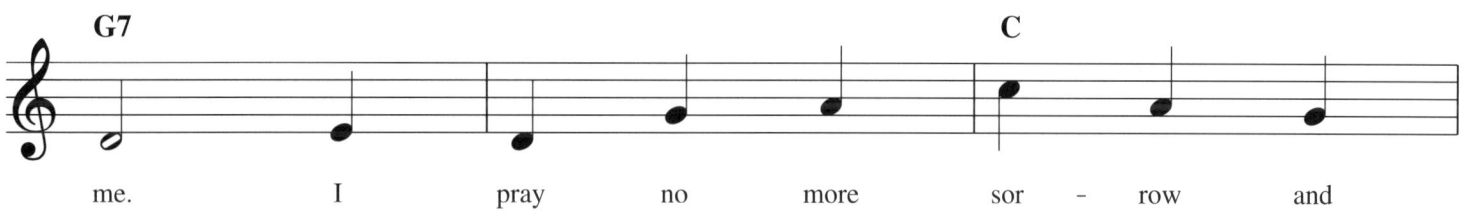
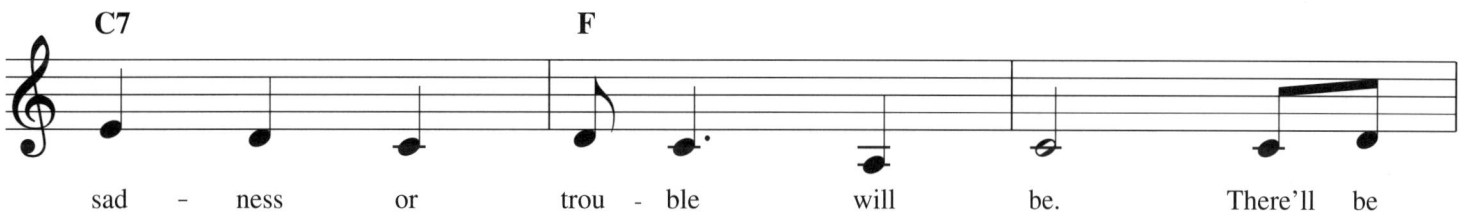
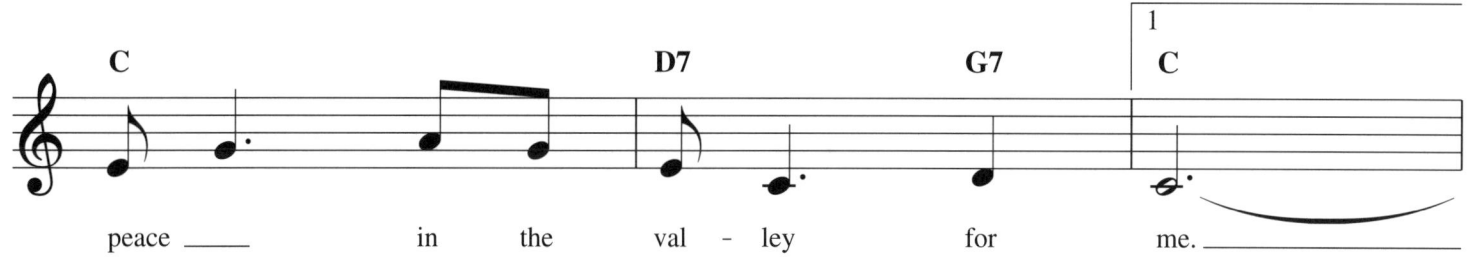
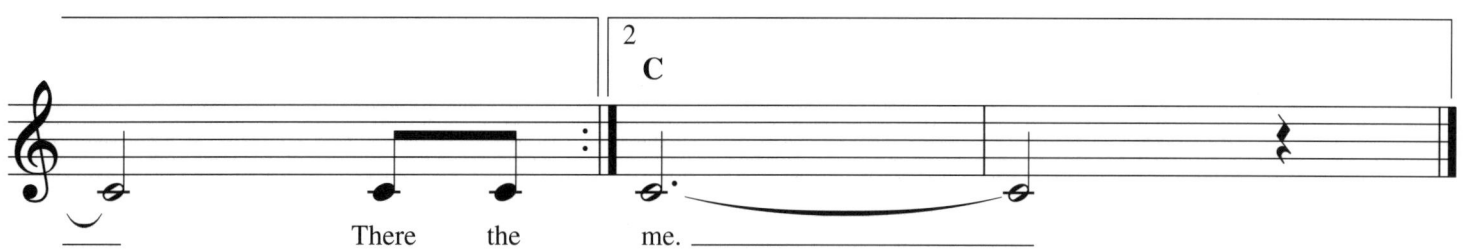

PRECIOUS LORD, TAKE MY HAND
(Take My Hand, Precious Lord)

Copyright © 1938 by Unichappell Music Inc.
Copyright Renewed
International Copyright Secured   All Rights Reserved

Words and Music by
THOMAS A. DORSEY

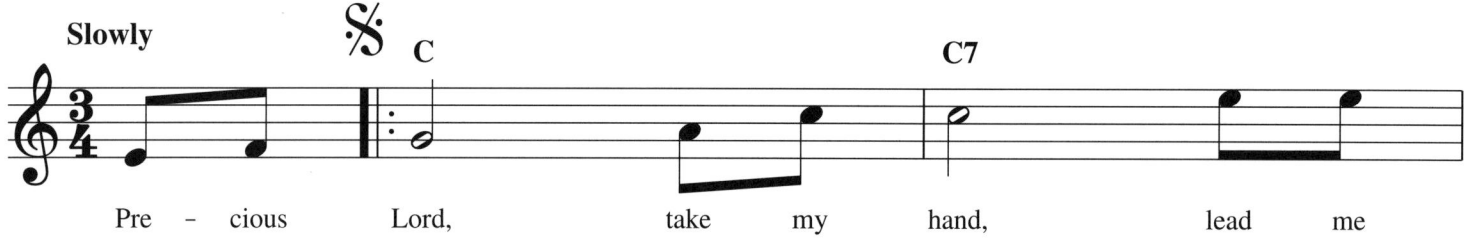

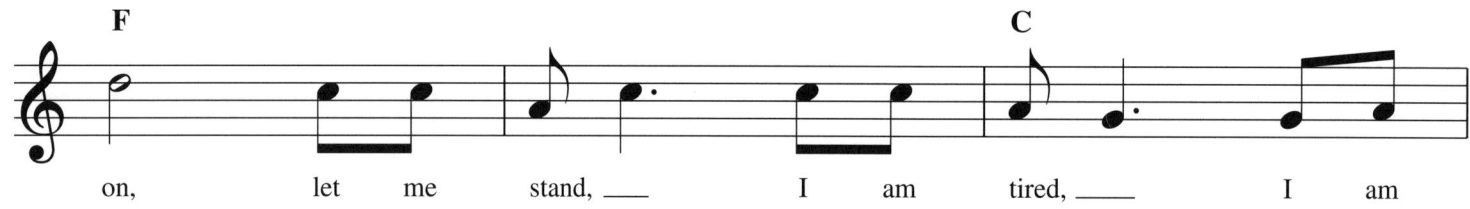

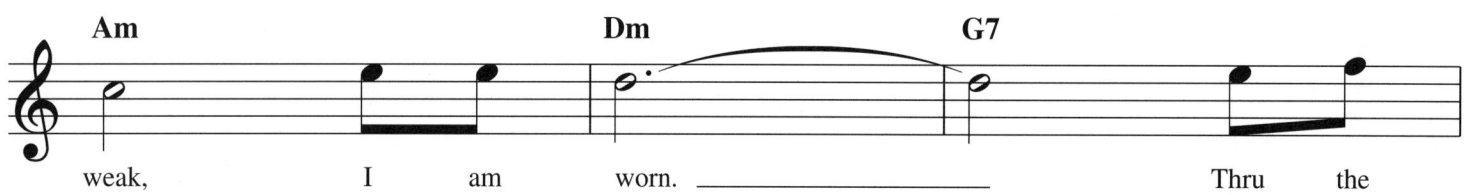

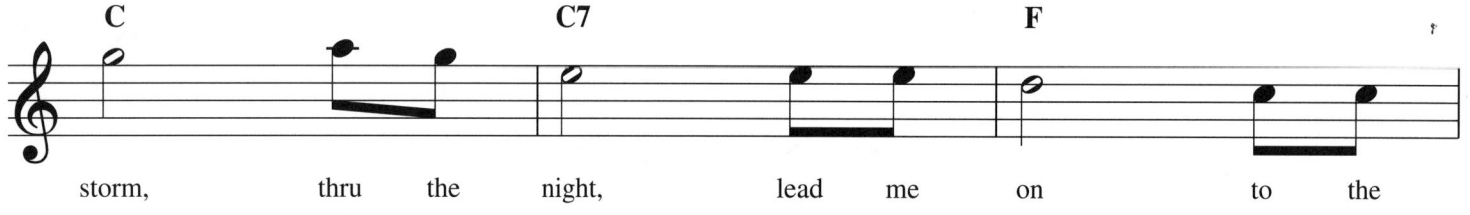

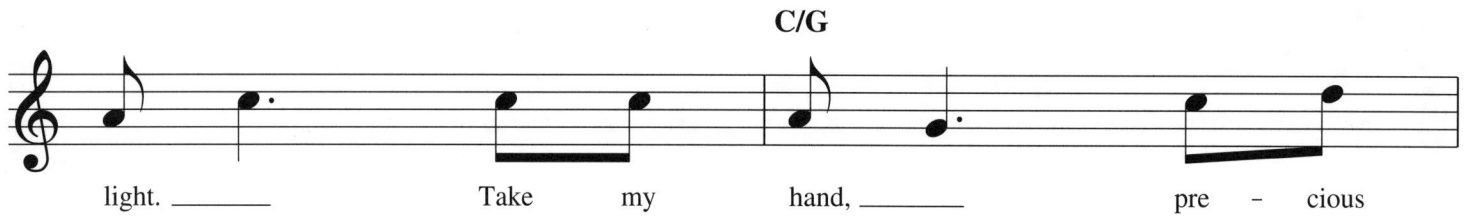

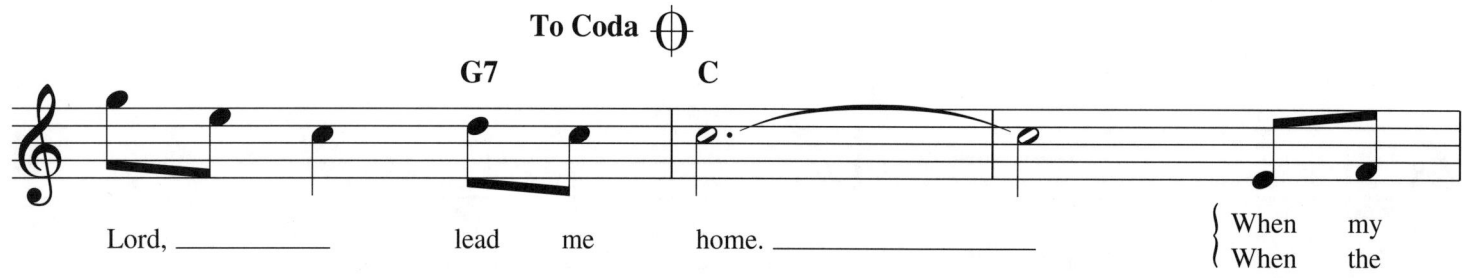

PRECIOUS MEMORIES

Copyright © 2001 by HAL LEONARD CORPORATION
International Copyright Secured   All Rights Reserved

Words and Music by
J.B.F. WRIGHT

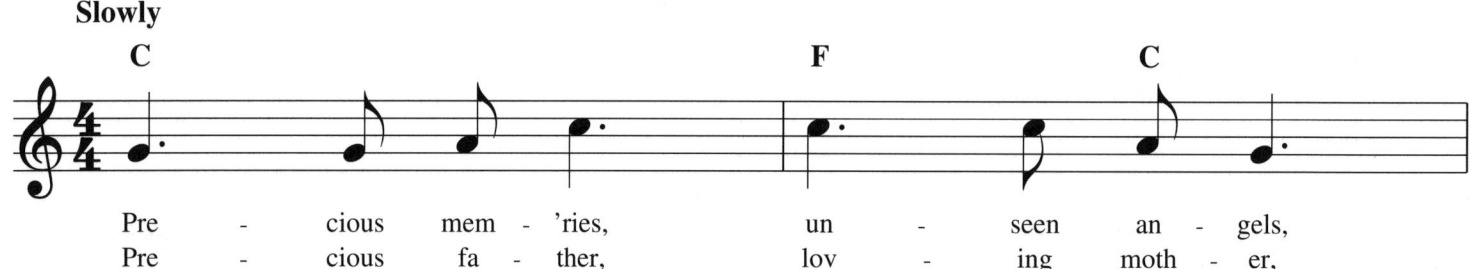
Pre - cious mem - 'ries, un - seen an - gels,
Pre - cious fa - ther, lov - ing moth - er,

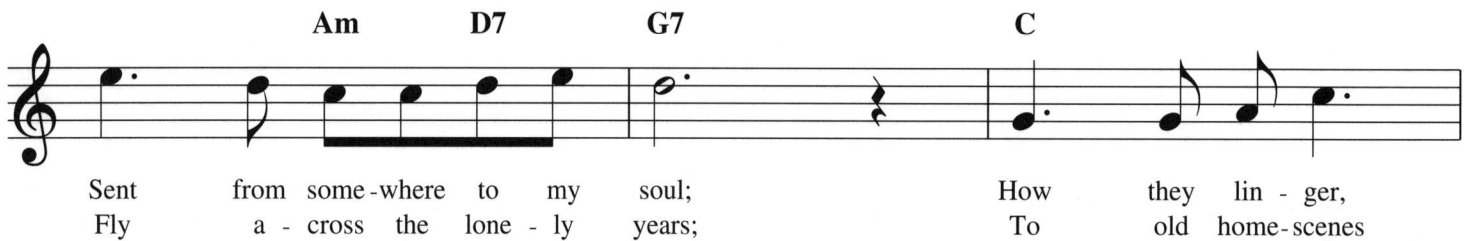
Sent from some - where to my soul; How they lin - ger,
Fly a - cross the lone - ly years; To old home - scenes

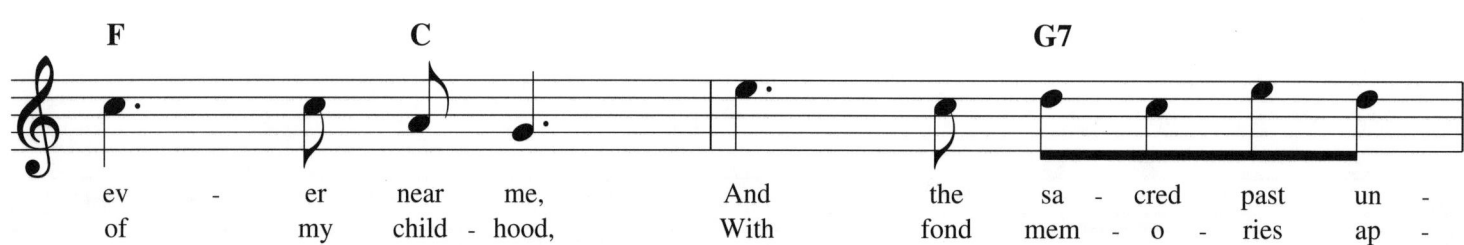
ev - er near me, And the sa - cred past un -
of my child - hood, With fond mem - o - ries ap -

fold.
pear. } Pre - cious mem - 'ries, how they lin - ger,

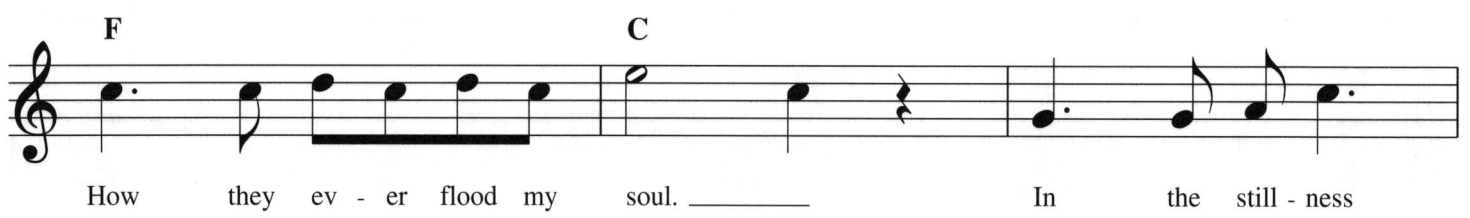
How they ev - er flood my soul. _____ In the still - ness

of the mid - night, Pre - cious sa - cred scenes un - fold.

ROCK OF AGES

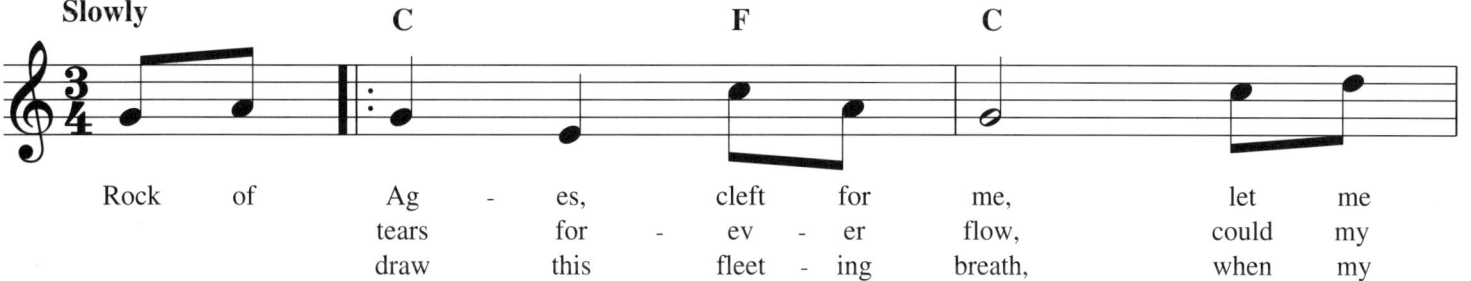
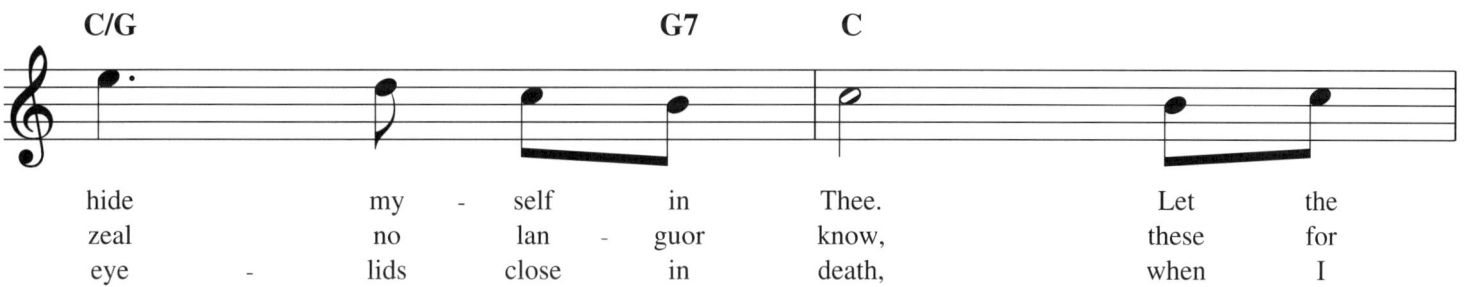
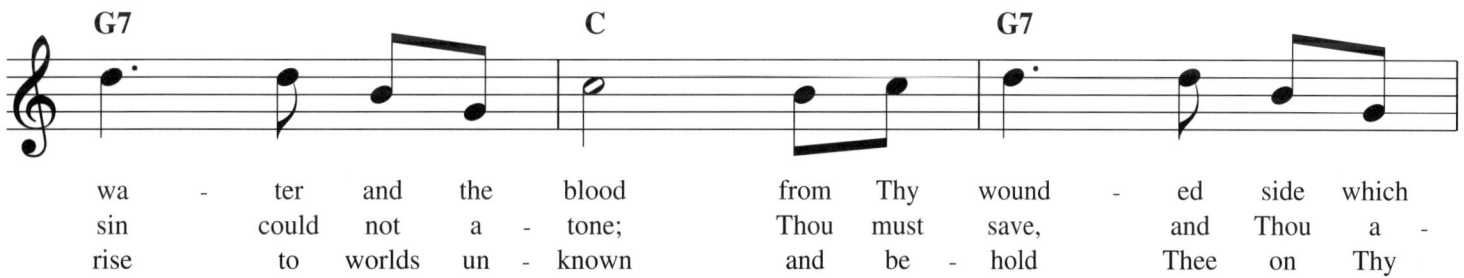
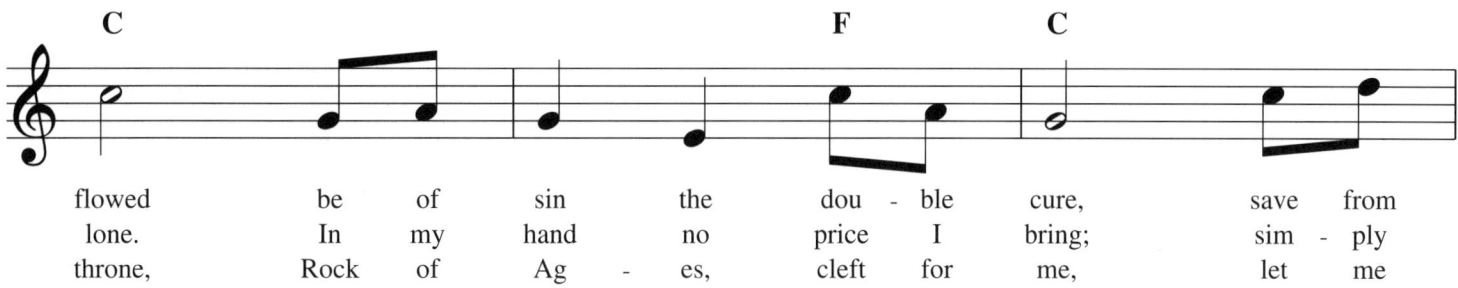
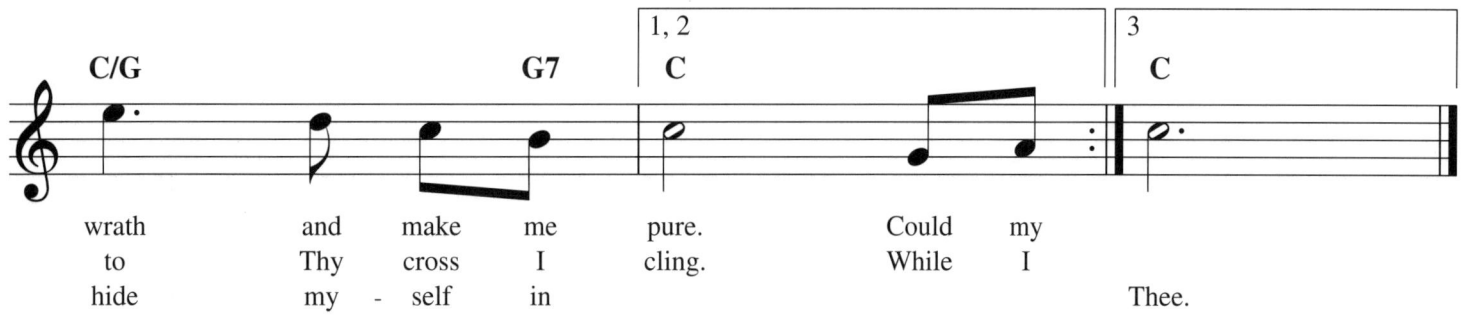

PUT YOUR HAND IN THE HAND

© 1970 (Renewed 1998) BEECHWOOD MUSIC OF CANADA
All Rights for the U.S.A. Controlled and Administered by BEECHWOOD MUSIC CORP.
All Rights Reserved   International Copyright Secured   Used by Permission

Words and Music by
GENE MacLELLAN

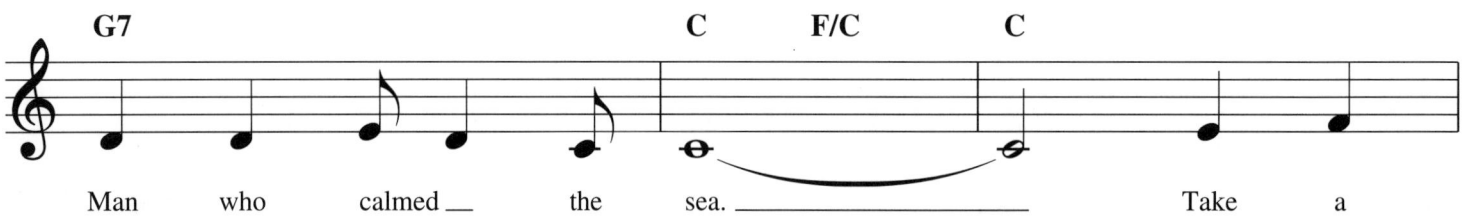

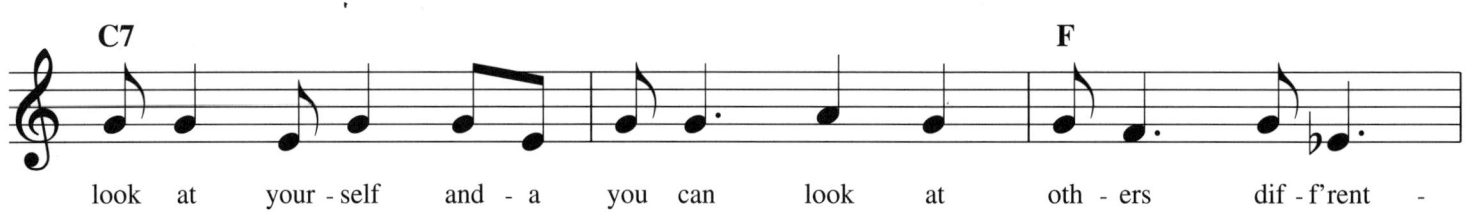

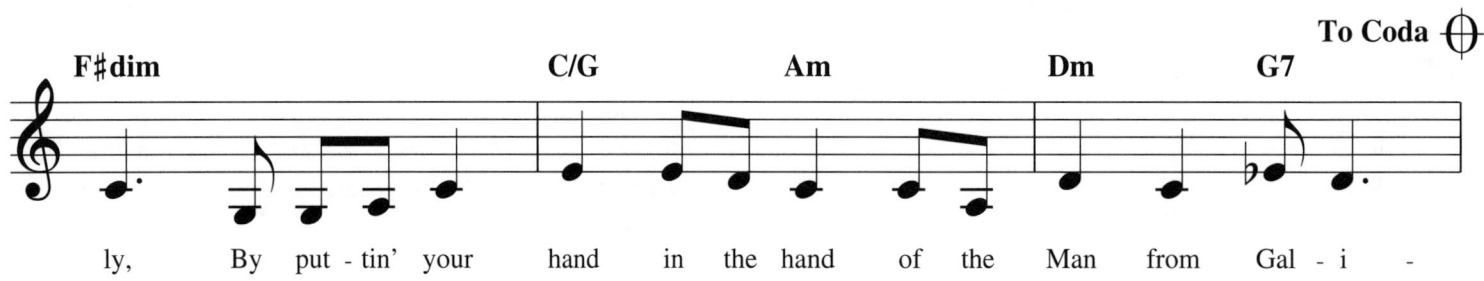

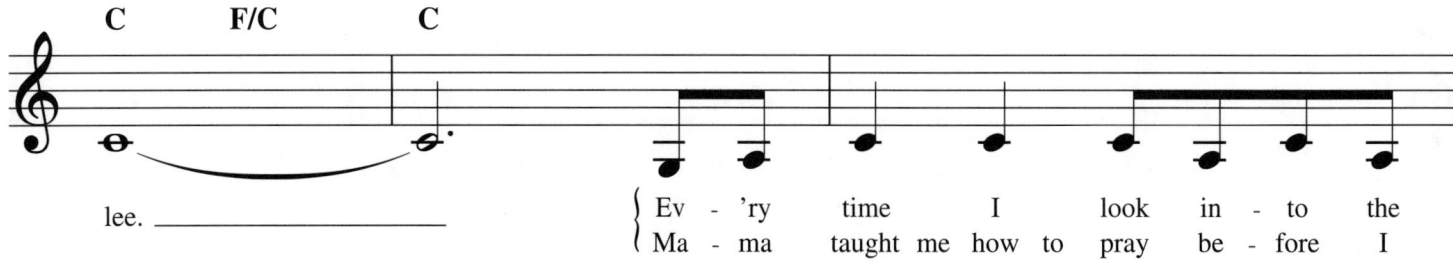

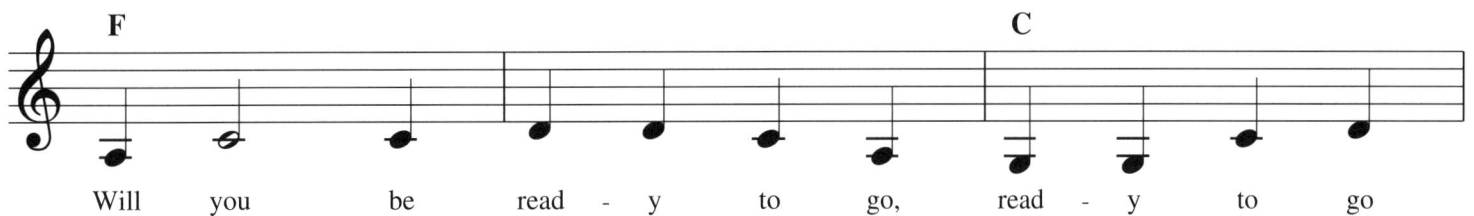
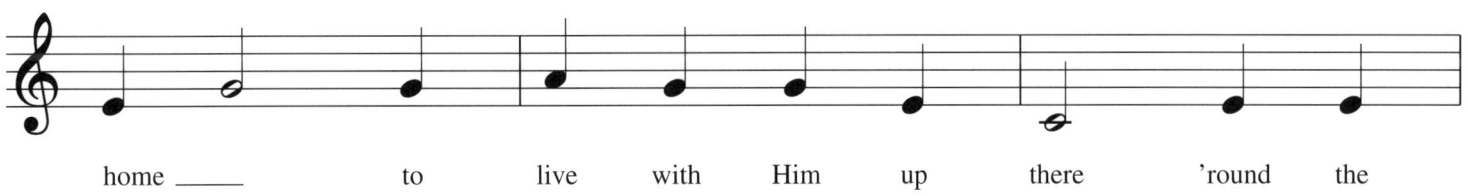

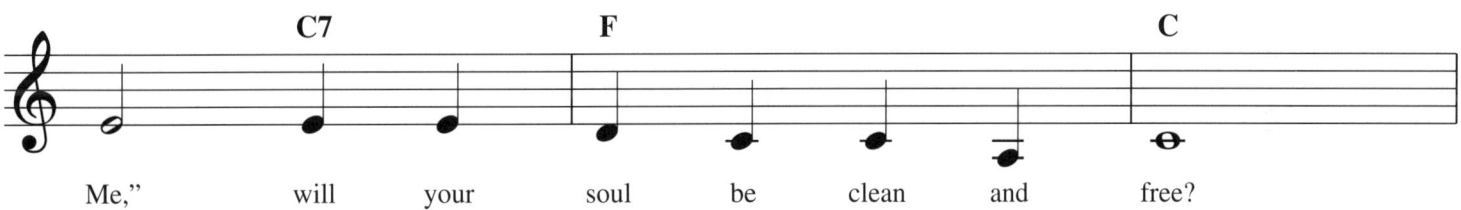

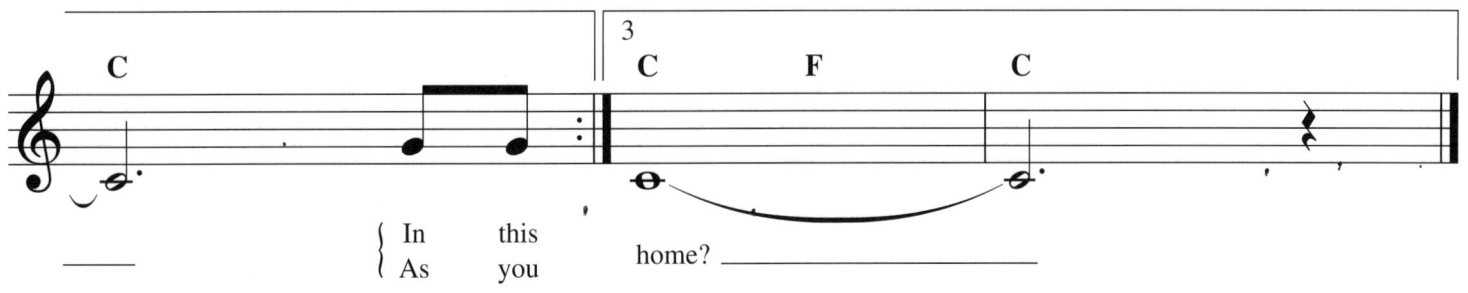

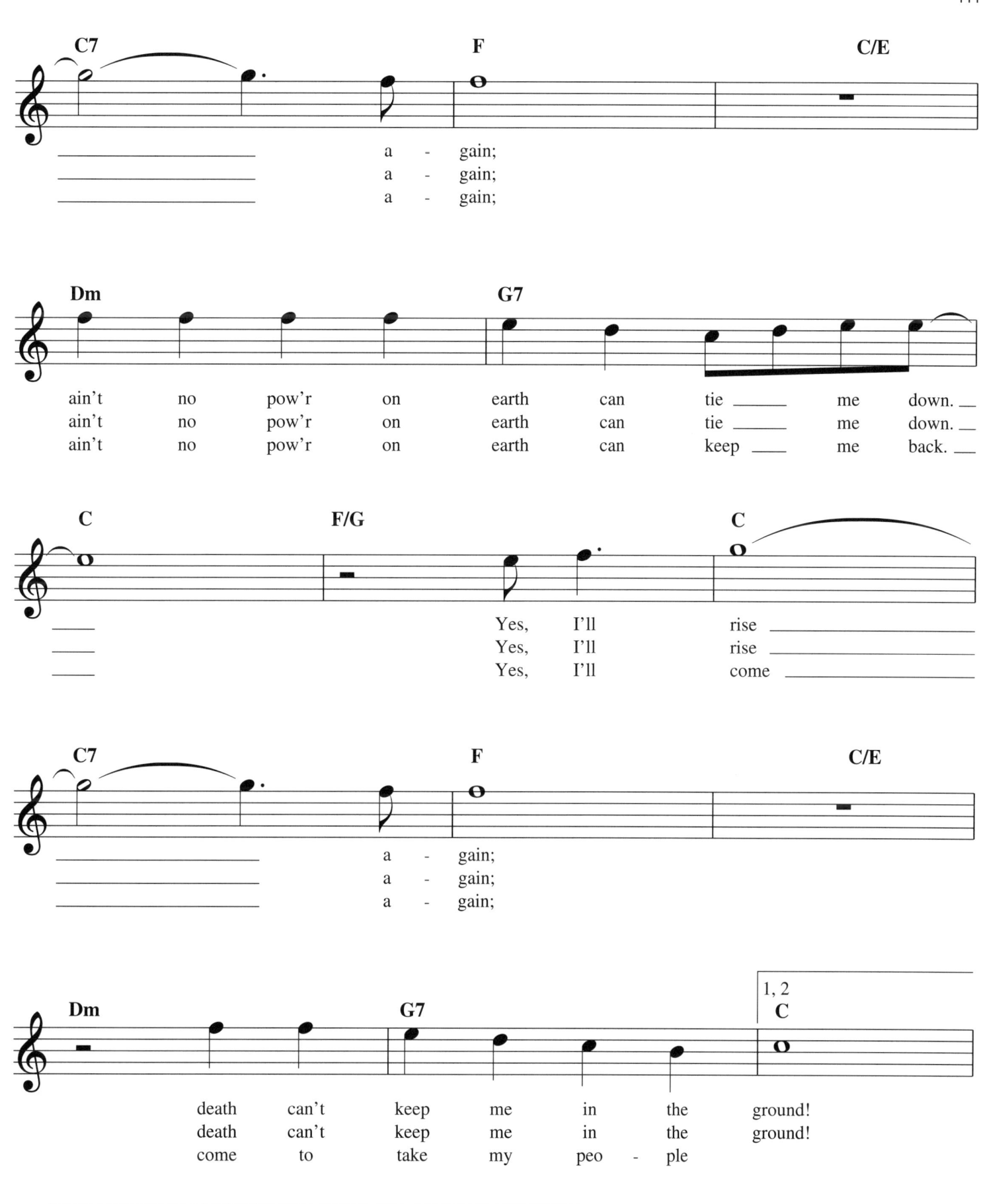

SEND THE LIGHT

Words and Music by
CHARLES H. GABRIEL

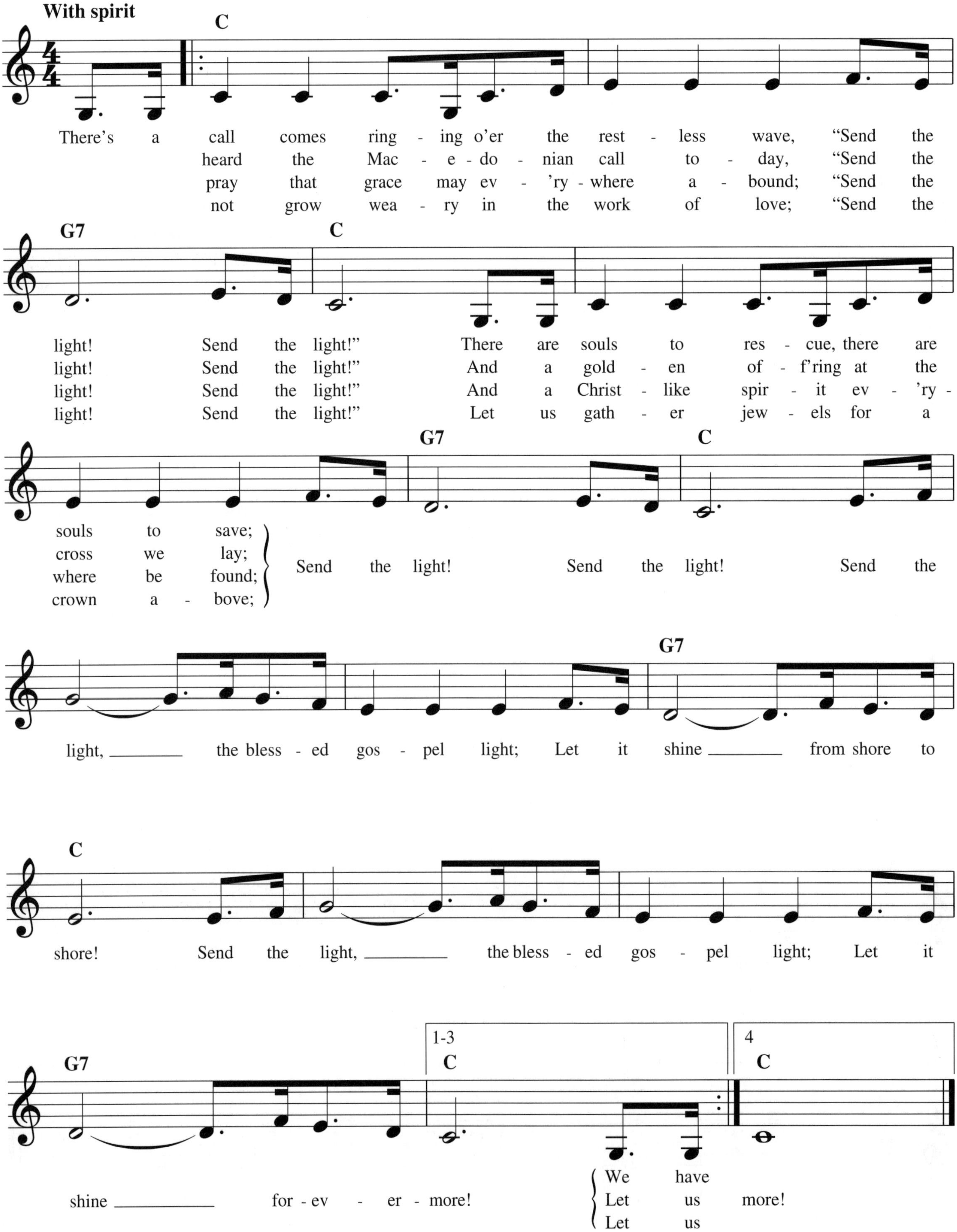
With spirit
C
There's a call comes ring - ing o'er the rest - less wave, "Send the
heard the Mac - e - do - nian call to - day, "Send the
pray that grace may ev - 'ry - where a - bound; "Send the
not grow wea - ry in the work of love; "Send the
G7 C
light! Send the light!" There are souls to res - cue, there are
light! Send the light!" And a gold - en of - f'ring at the
light! Send the light!" And a Christ - like spir - it ev - 'ry -
light! Send the light!" Let us gath - er jew - els for a
G7 C
souls to save;
cross we lay;
where be found;
crown a - bove;
Send the light! Send the light! Send the
G7
light, the bless - ed gos - pel light; Let it shine from shore to
C
shore! Send the light, the bless - ed gos - pel light; Let it
G7
shine for - ev - er - more!
1-3 C
We have
Let us
Let us
4 C
more!

SHALL WE GATHER AT THE RIVER?

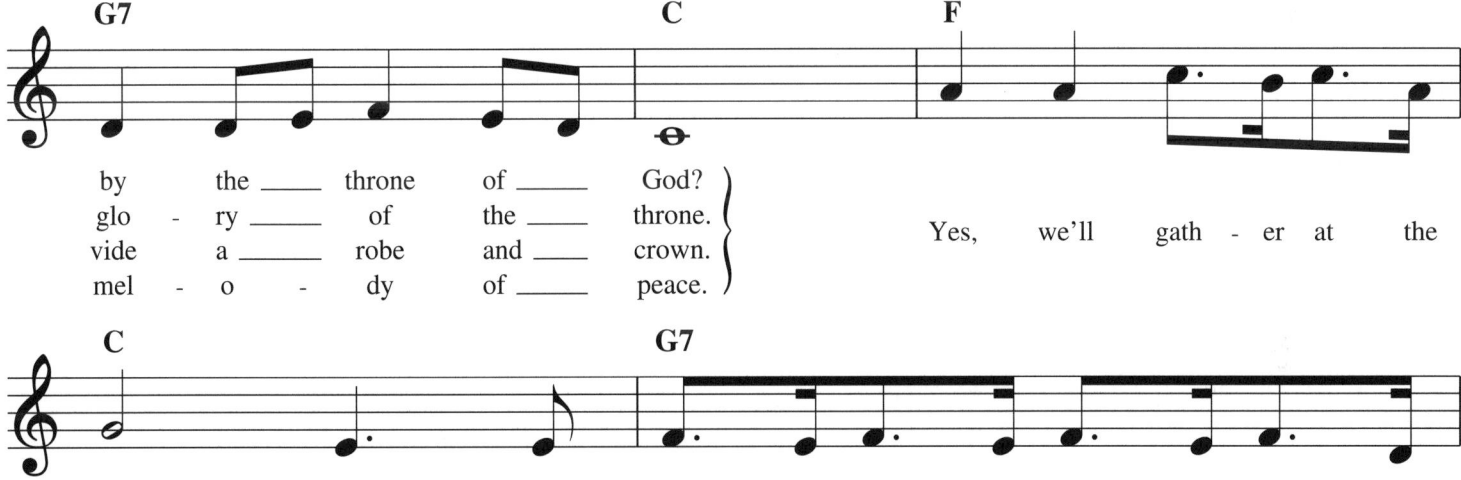

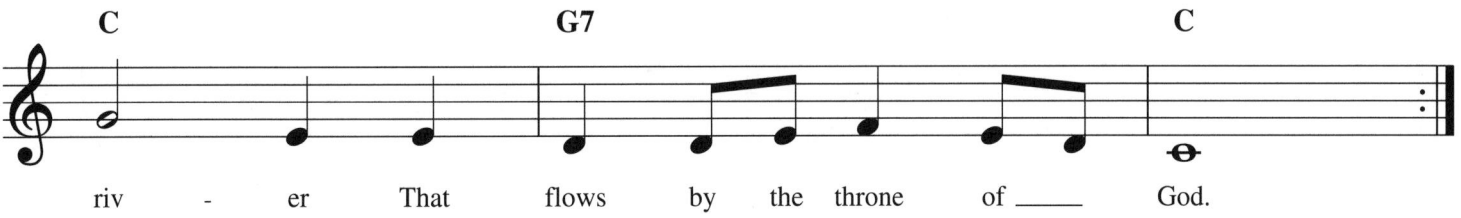

SHELTERED IN THE ARMS OF GOD

Copyright © 1969 by Peermusic Ltd.
Copyright Renewed
International Copyright Secured   All Rights Reserved

Words and Music by DOTTIE RAMBO
and JIMMIE DAVIS

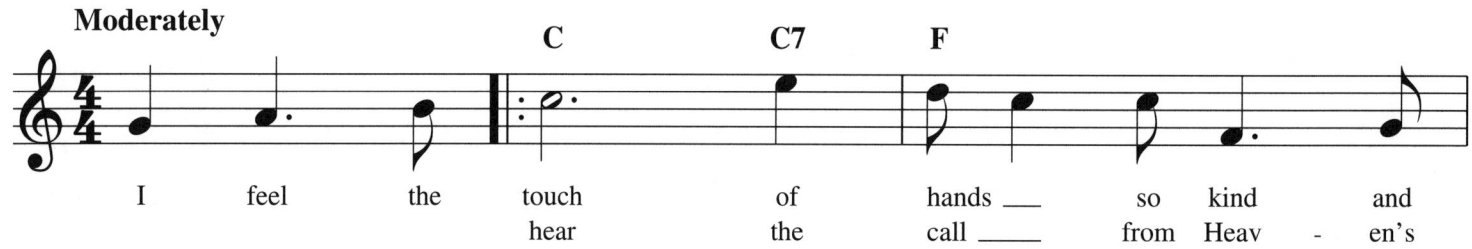
I feel the touch of hands so kind and
hear the call from Heav-en's

ten - der, They're lead-ing me in
por - tals, "Come home, my child, it's the

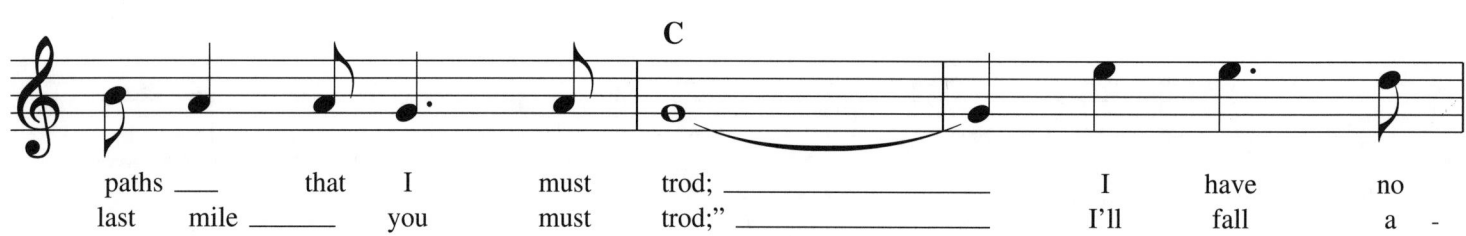
paths that I must trod; I have no
last mile you must trod;" I'll fall a-

fear when Je - sus walks be - side me,
sleep and wake in God's new Heav - en,

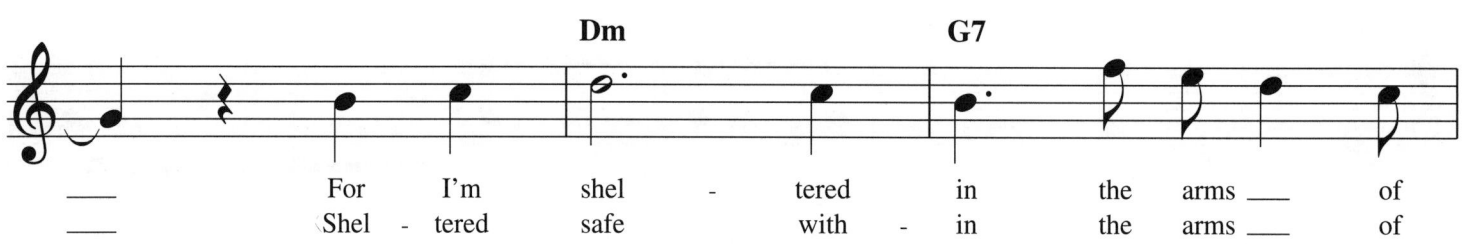
For I'm shel - tered in the arms of
Shel - tered safe with - in the arms of

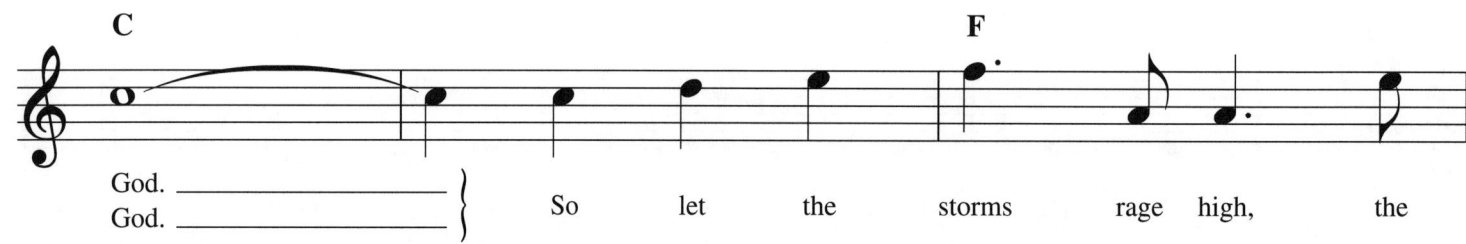
God.
God. So let the storms rage high, the

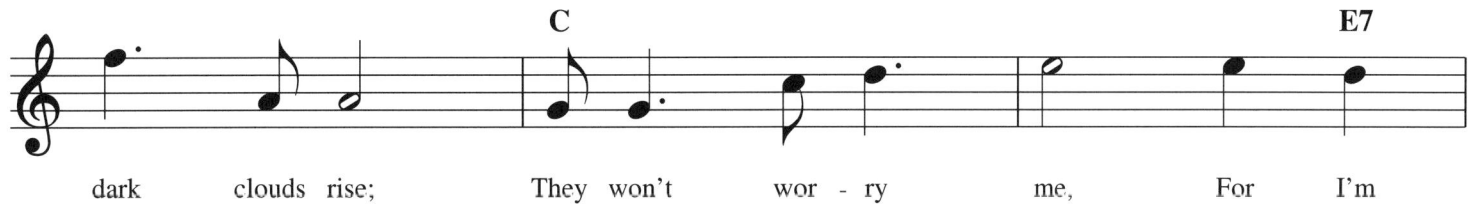
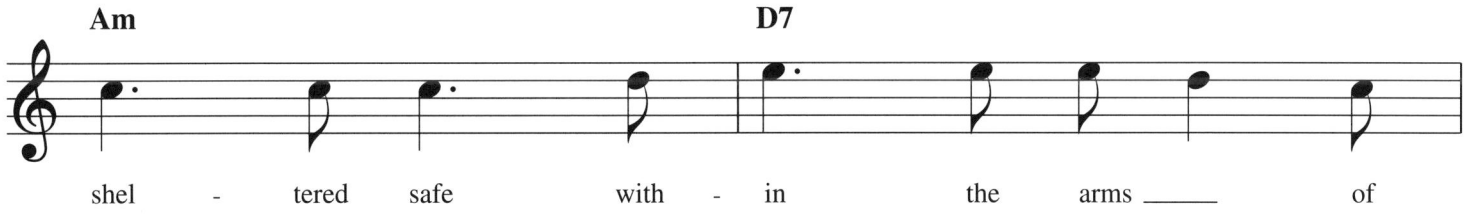
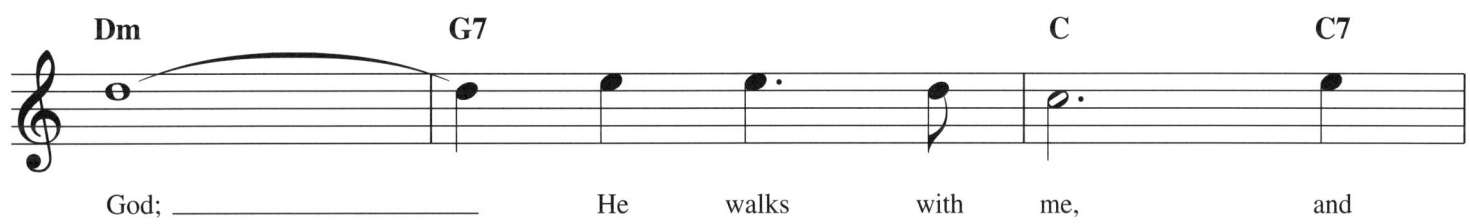
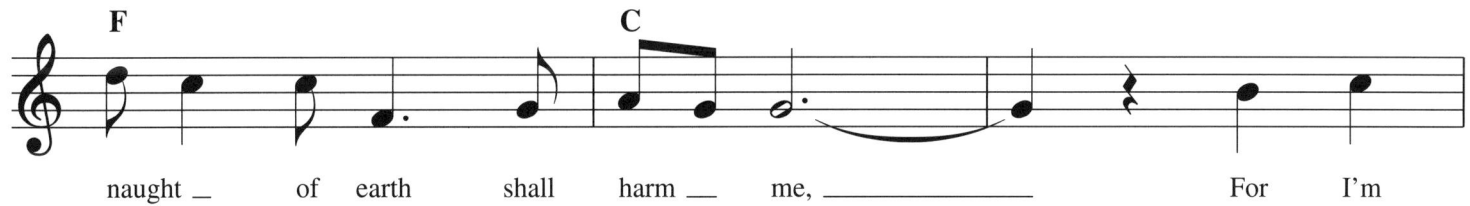
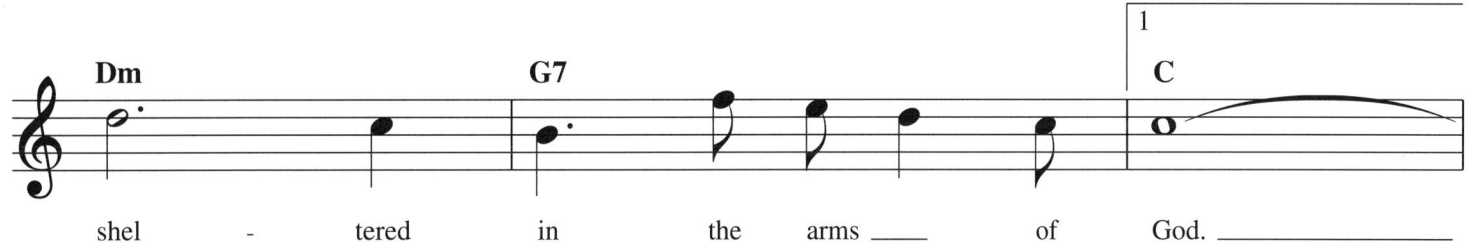
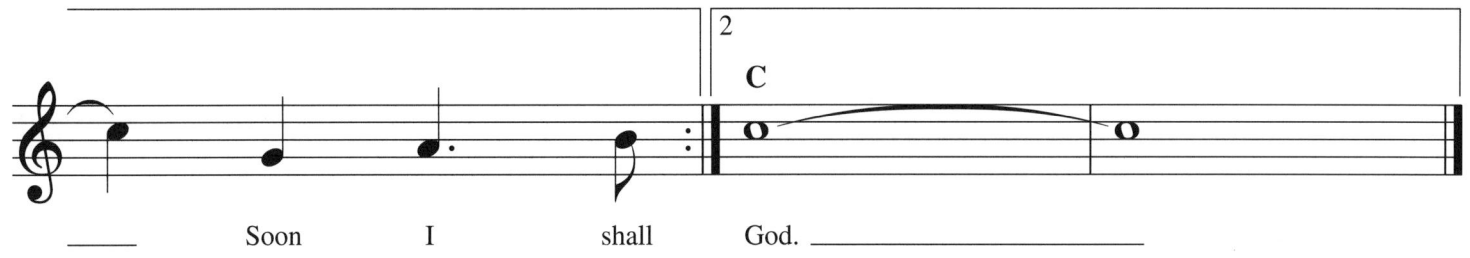

SINCE JESUS CAME INTO MY HEART

Words by RUFUS H. McDANIEL
Music by CHARLES H. GABRIEL

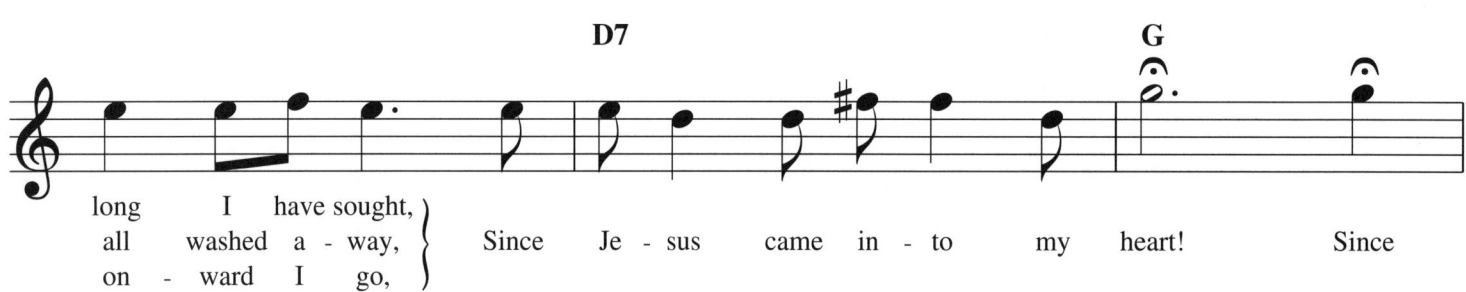

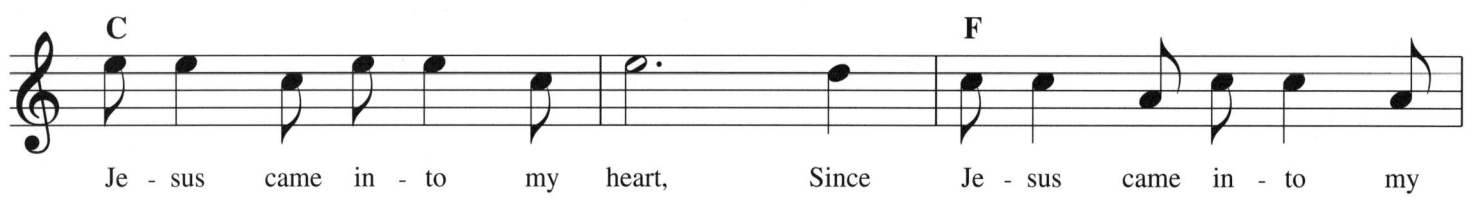

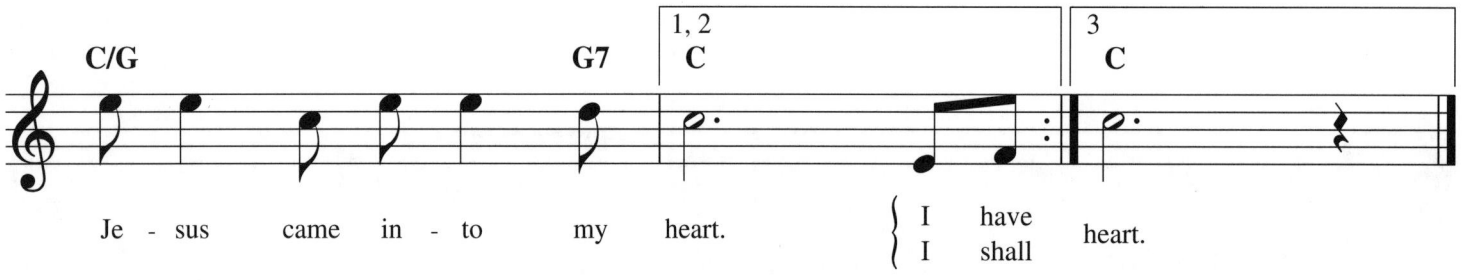

SOMETHING BEAUTIFUL

Words by GLORIA GAITHER
Music by WILLIAM J. GAITHER

Copyright © 1971 (Renewed) William J. Gaither, Inc. (ASCAP)
All Rights Controlled by Gaither Copyright Management
All Rights Reserved   Used by Permission

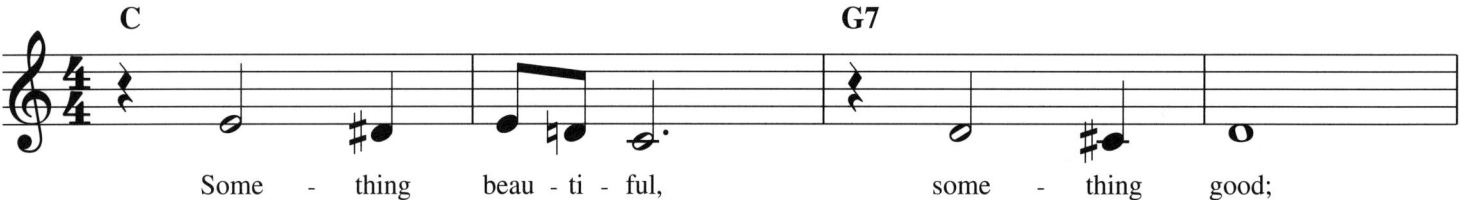

Some - thing beau - ti - ful, some - thing good;

All my con - fu - sion ___ He un - der -

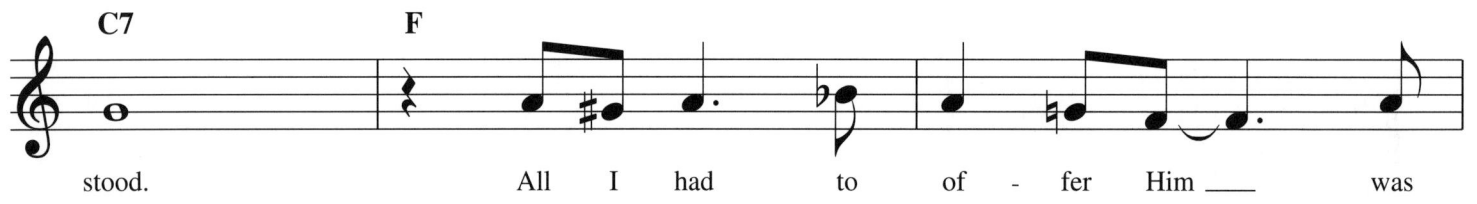

stood. All I had to of - fer Him ___ was

bro - ken - ness and strife, but He made some - thing

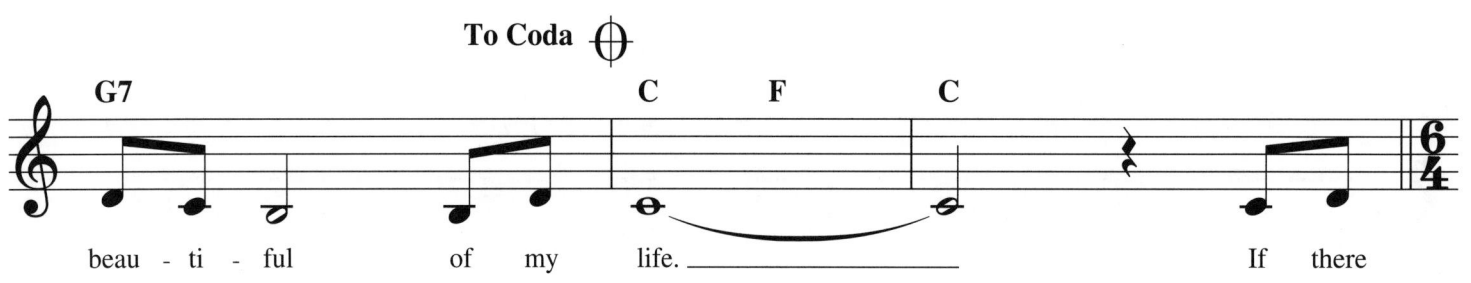

beau - ti - ful of my life. ___ If there

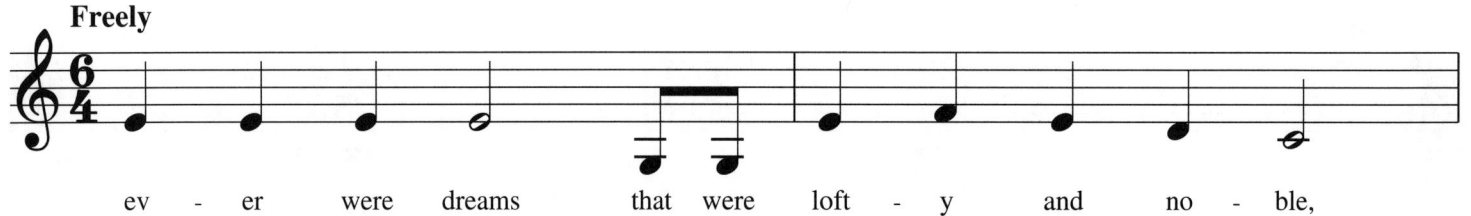

ev - er were dreams that were loft - y and no - ble,

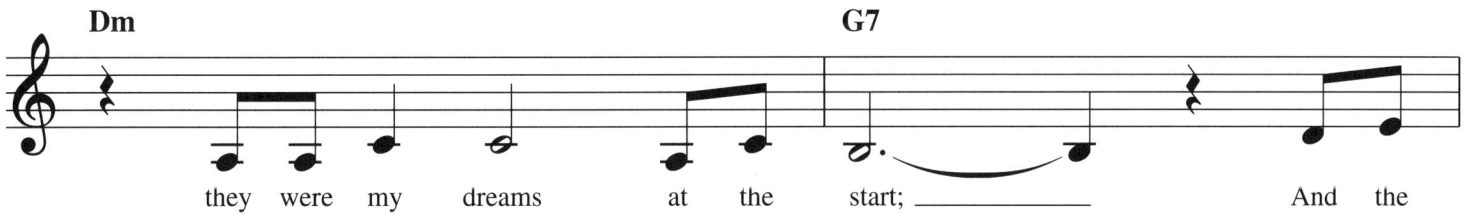

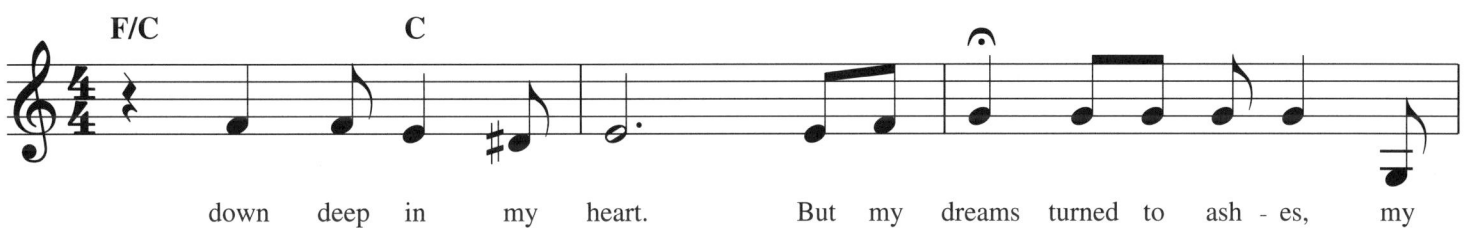
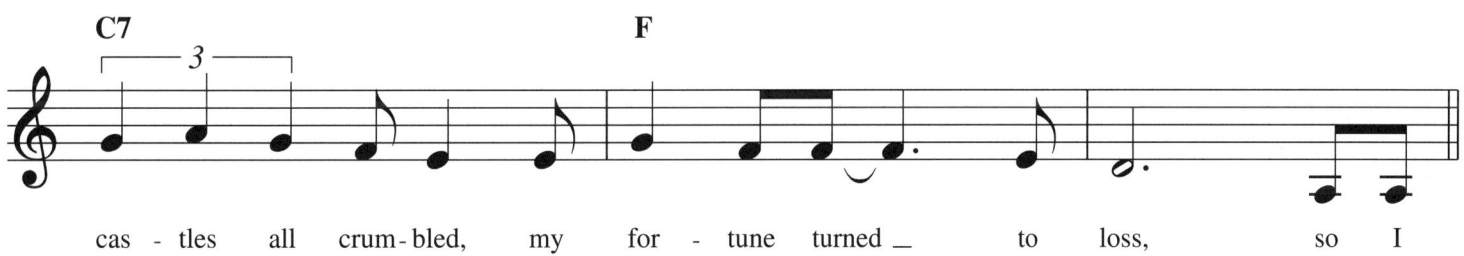
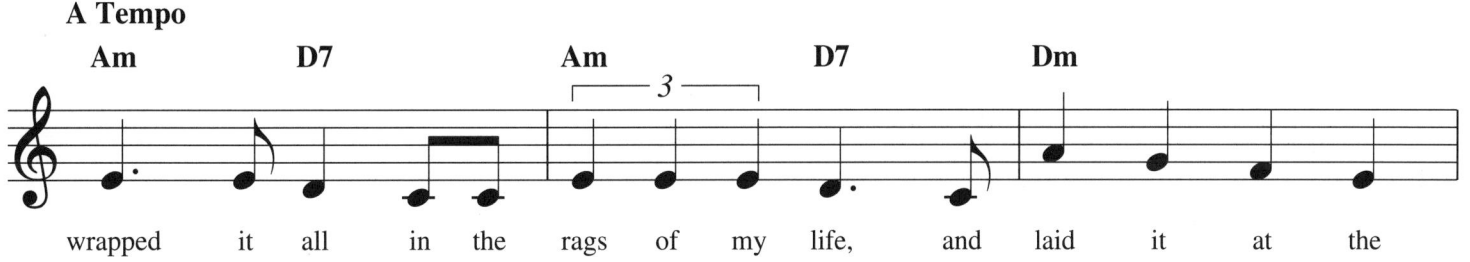
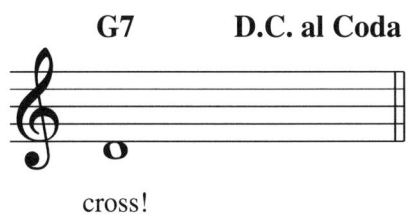
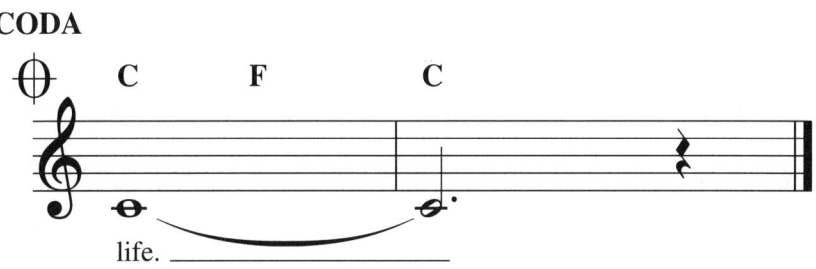

Stepping on the Clouds

120

© 1974 Word Music, Inc.
All Rights Reserved   Used by Permission

Words and Music by
LINDA STALLS

Moderately, in 2

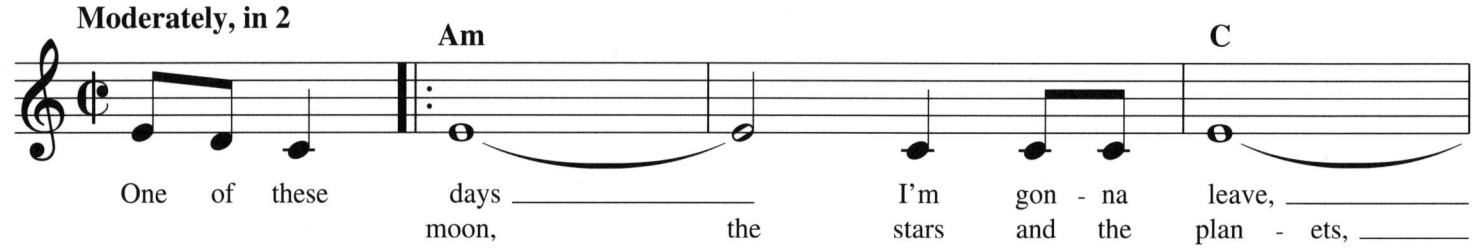
One of these days _____ I'm gon-na leave, _____
moon, the stars and the plan-ets, _____

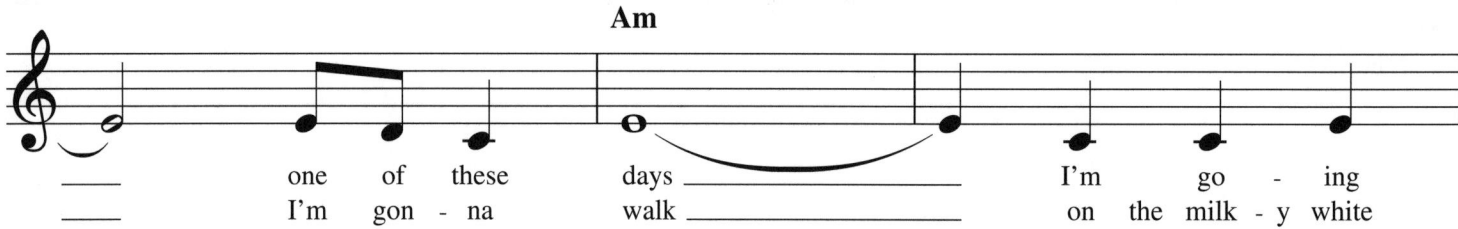
_____ one of these days _____ I'm go-ing
_____ I'm gon-na walk _____ on the milk-y white

home; _____ I'm gon-na take _____
way; _____ When old _____ Ga-briel _____

_____ my fi-nal jour-ney, _____ I'm gon-na
_____ gives the sig-nal, _____ I'm gon-na

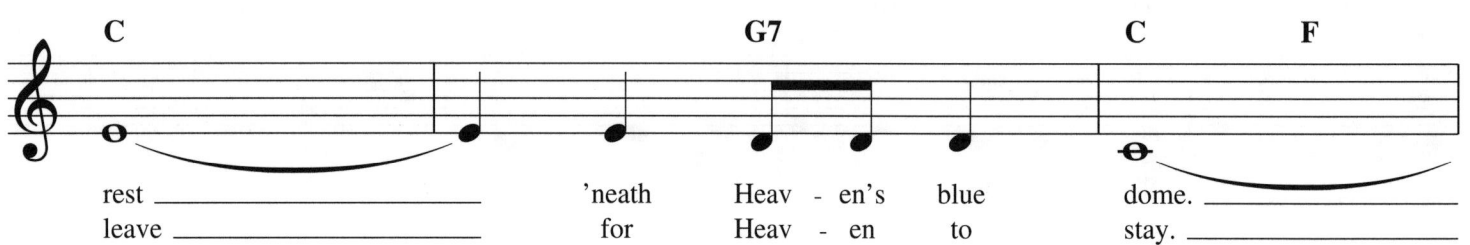
rest _____ 'neath Heav-en's blue dome. _____
leave _____ for Heav-en to stay. _____

_____ Step-ping on the clouds, we'll see Je-sus,

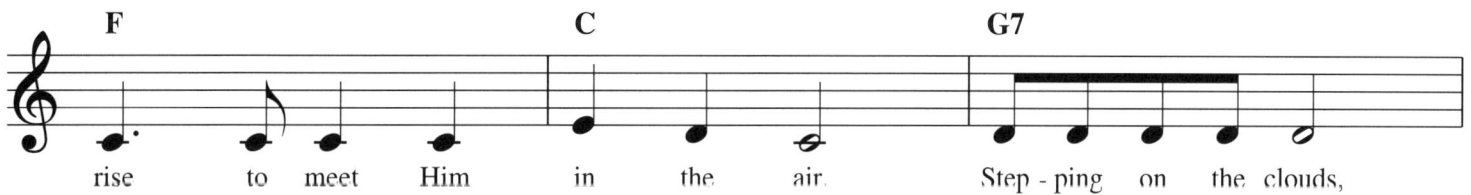
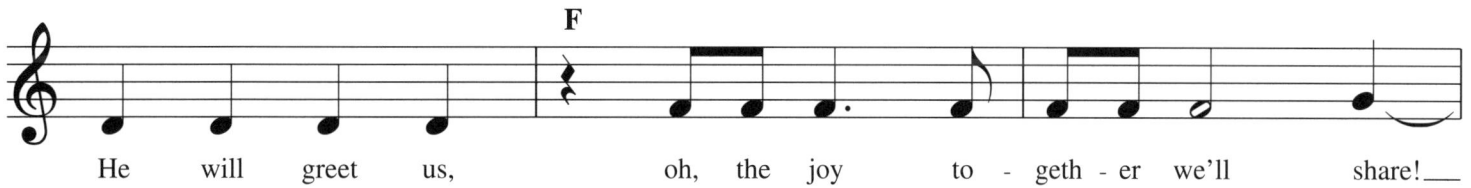
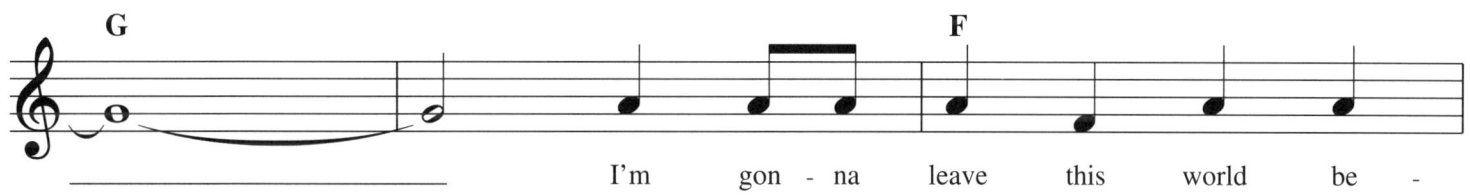
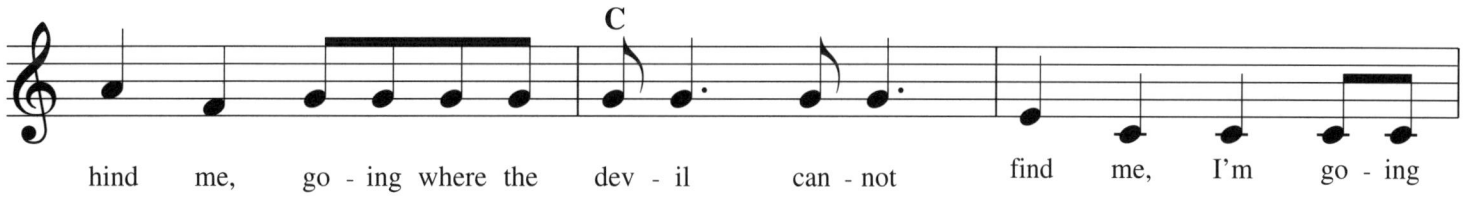
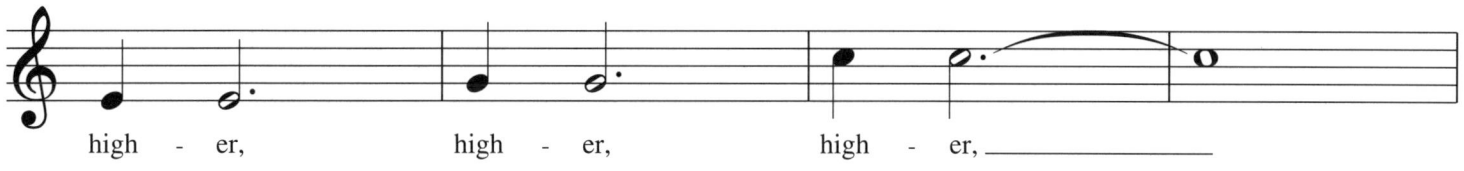

SURELY THE PRESENCE OF THE LORD IS IN THIS PLACE

© Copyright 1977 Lanny Wolfe Music (ASCAP)/admin. by ICG
All Rights Reserved   Used by Permission

Words and Music by
LANNY WOLFE

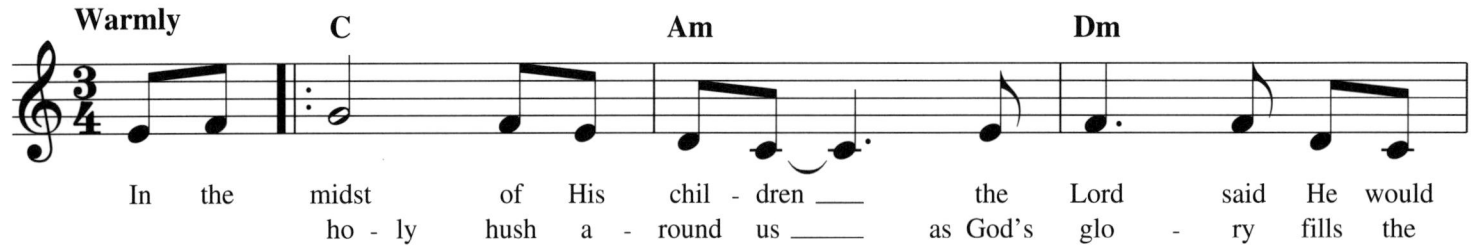

In the midst of His chil - dren ___ the Lord said He would
ho - ly hush a - round us ___ as God's glo - ry fills the

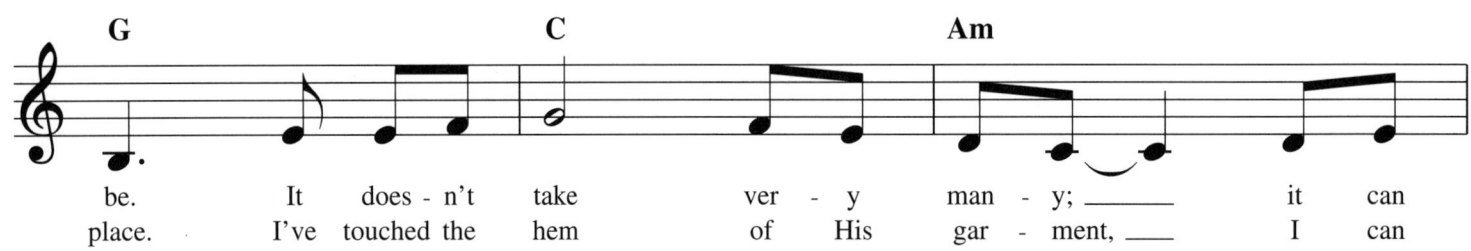

be. It does - n't take ver - y man - y; ___ it can
place. I've touched the hem of His gar - ment, ___ I can

be just two or three, and I feel that same sweet
al - most see His face, and my heart is o - ver -

Spir - it ___ that I've felt oft times be - fore.
flow - ing ___ with the full - ness of His joy;

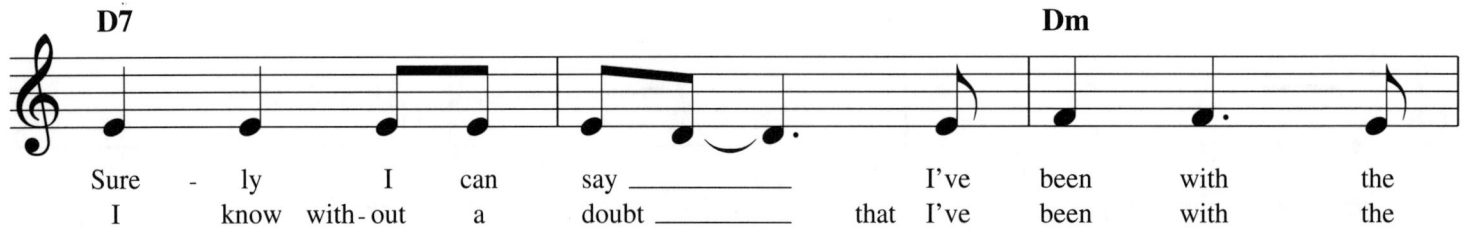

Sure - ly I can say ___ I've been with the
I know with - out a doubt ___ that I've been with the

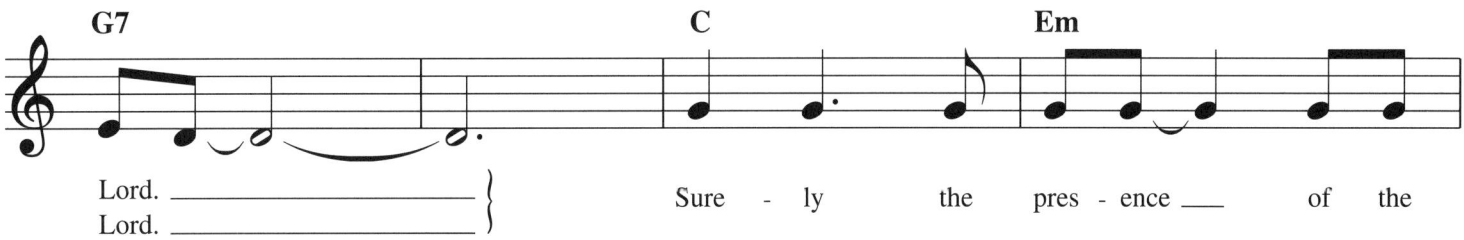
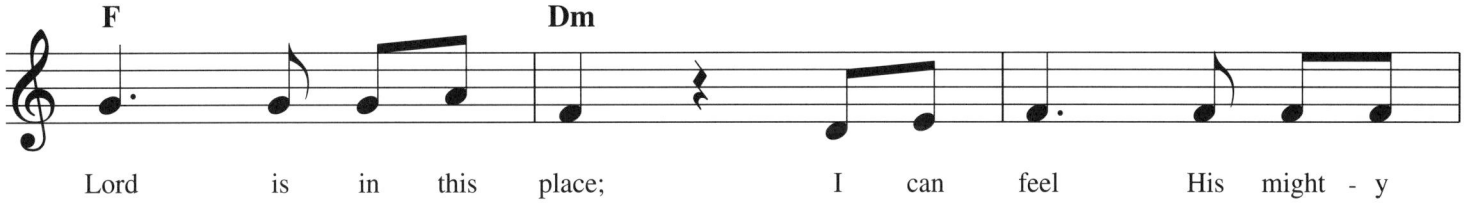
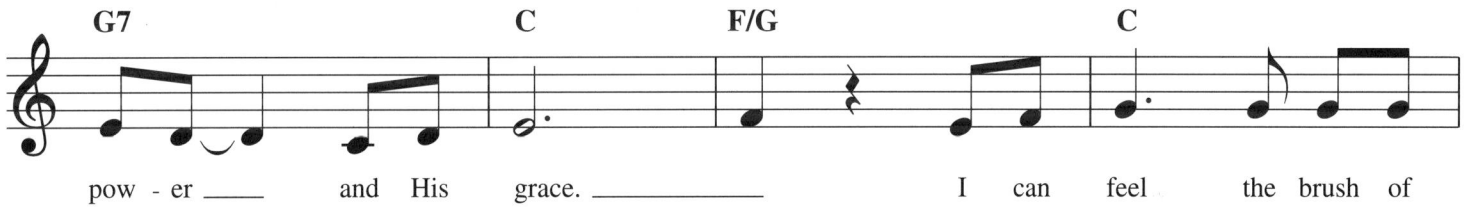

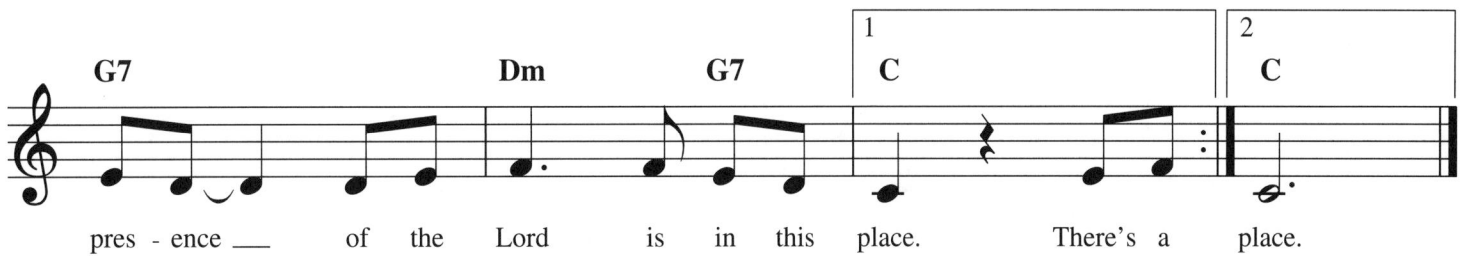

SWEET BY AND BY

Words by SANFORD FILLMORE BENNETT
Music by JOSEPH P. WEBSTER

THERE IS POWER IN THE BLOOD

Words and Music by
LEWIS E. JONES

Triumphantly

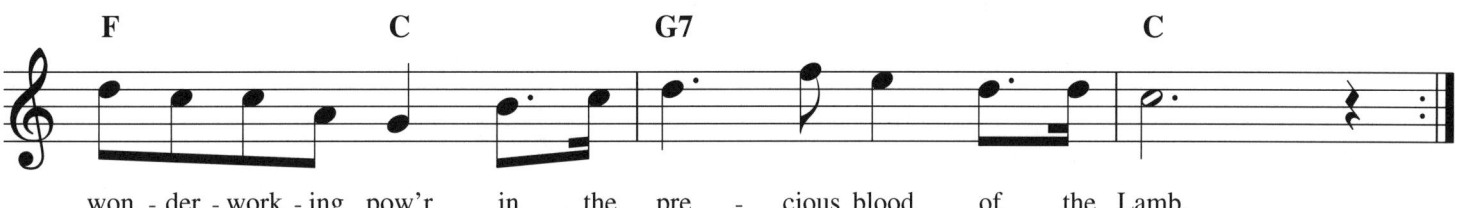

THERE'S SOMETHING ABOUT THAT NAME

Copyright © 1970 (Renewed) William J. Gaither, Inc. (ASCAP)
All Rights Controlled by Gaither Copyright Management
All Rights Reserved   Used by Permission

Words by WILLIAM J. and GLORIA GAITHER
Music by WILLIAM J. GAITHER

Moderately

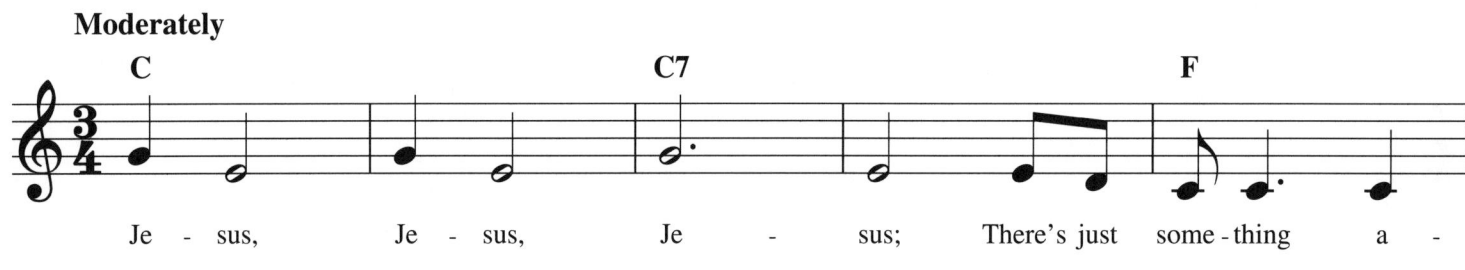

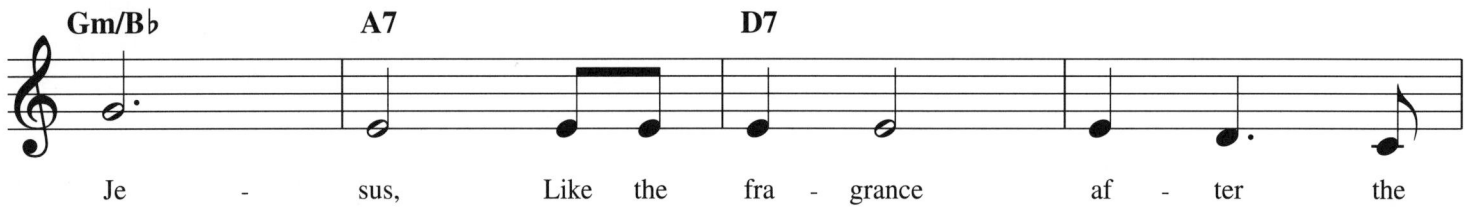

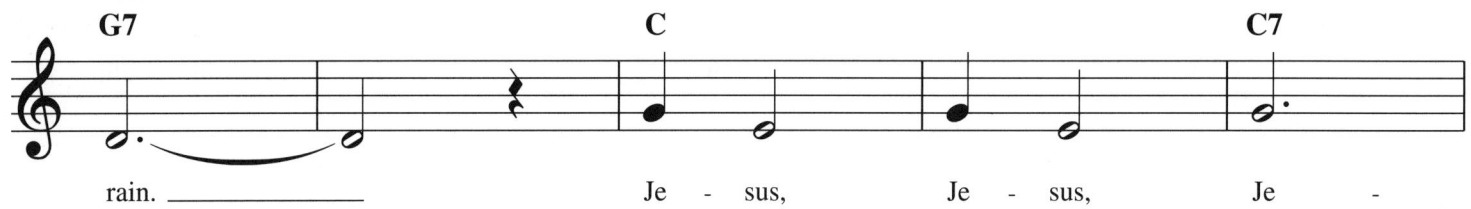

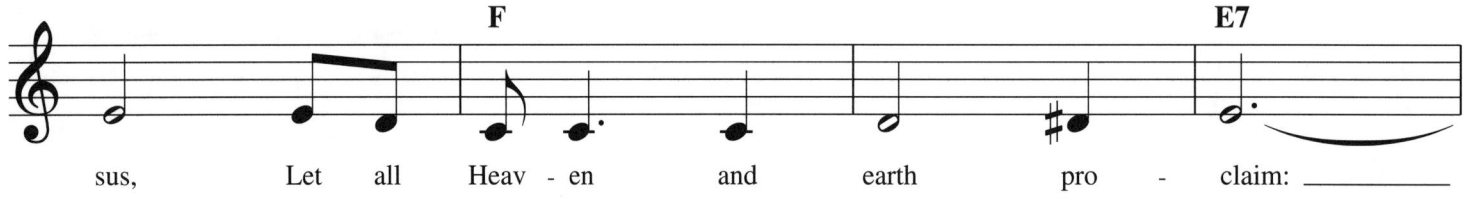

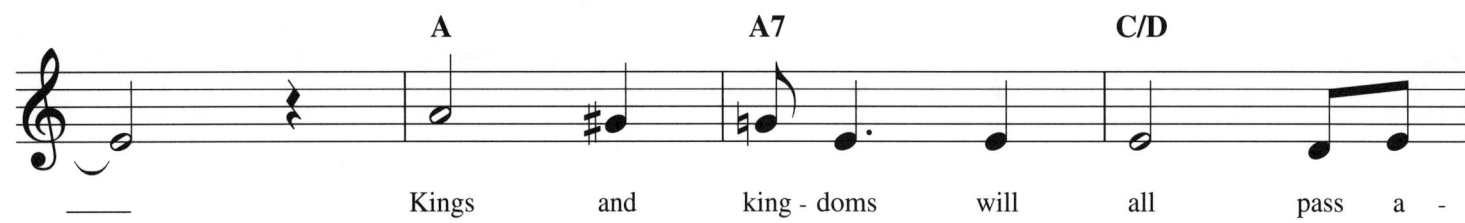

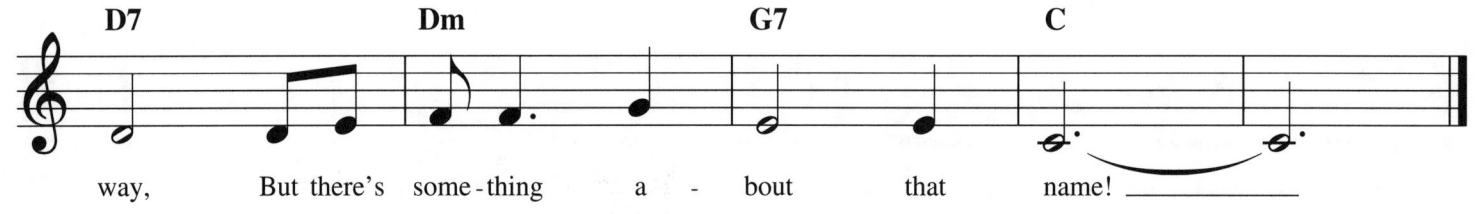

'TIL THE STORM PASSES BY

© 1958 (Renewed 1986) MOSIE LISTER SONGS
(Administered by THE COPYRIGHT COMPANY, Nashville, TN)
All Rights Reserved International Copyright Secured Used by Permission

Words and Music by
MOSIE LISTER

Reflectively

In the dark of the mid-night have I oft hid my face, While the storms howl a-bove me, and there's no hid-ing place; 'Mid the crash of the thun-der, pre-cious Lord, hear my cry, "Keep me safe 'til the storm pass-es by."

Man-y times Sa-tan tells me, "There is no need to try, For there's no end of sor-row; there's no hope by and by." But I know Thou art with me, and to-mor-row I'll rise Where the storms nev-er dark-en the skies.

When the long night has end-ed, and the storms come no more, Let me stand in Thy pres-ence on that bright, peace-ful shore; In that land where the tem-pest nev-er comes, Lord, may I Dwell with Thee when the storm pass-es by?

'Til the storm pass-es o-ver, 'til the thun-der sounds no more, 'Til the clouds roll for-ev-er from the sky, Hold me fast, let me stand in the hol-low of Thy hand; keep me safe 'til the storm pass-es by.

TURN YOUR RADIO ON

© 1938 Stamps-Baxter Music (BMI) (admin. by Brentwood-Benson Music Publishing, Inc.)
Copyright Renewed
All Rights Reserved Used by Permission

Words and Music by
ALBERT E. BRUMLEY

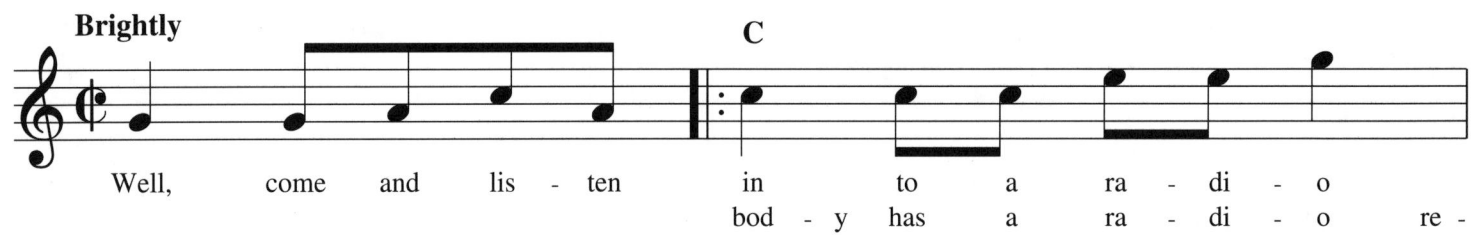

Well, come and listen in to a radio
body has a radio re-

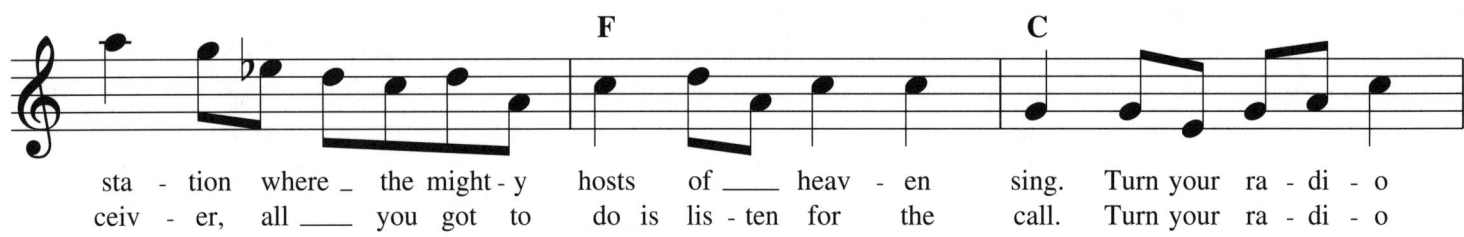

station where the mighty hosts of heaven sing. Turn your ra-di-o
ceiv-er, all you got to do is listen for the call. Turn your ra-di-o

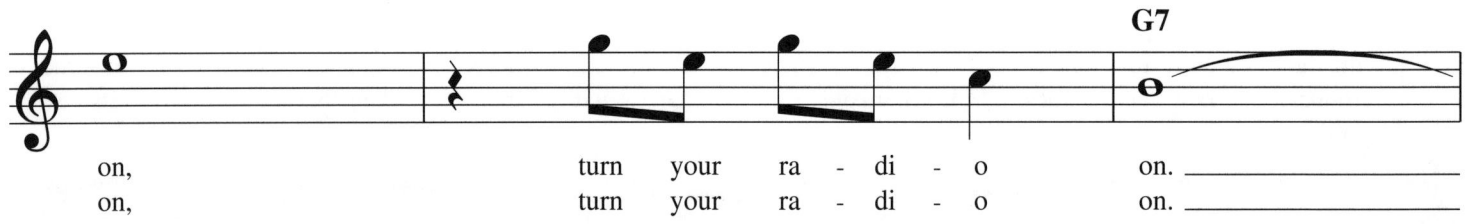

on, turn your ra-di-o on.
on, turn your ra-di-o on.

If you want to feel those good vi-bra-tions com-ing from the
If you lis-ten in, you will be a be-liev-er lean-in' on the

joy that His love can bring, turn your ra-di-o on,
truths that were nev-er false. Get in touch with God,

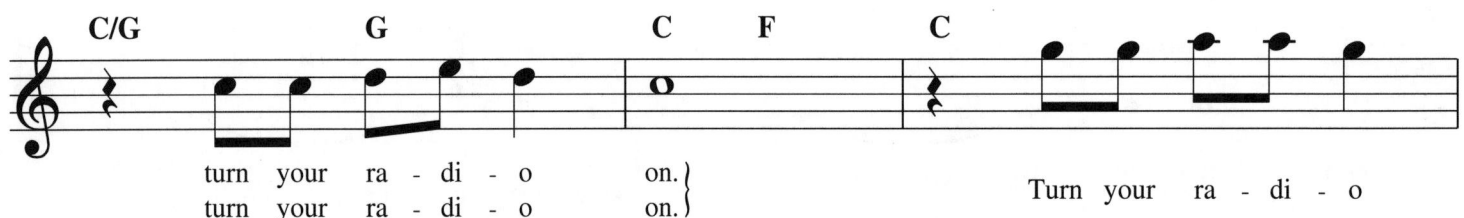

turn your ra-di-o on.
turn your ra-di-o on.

Turn your ra-di-o

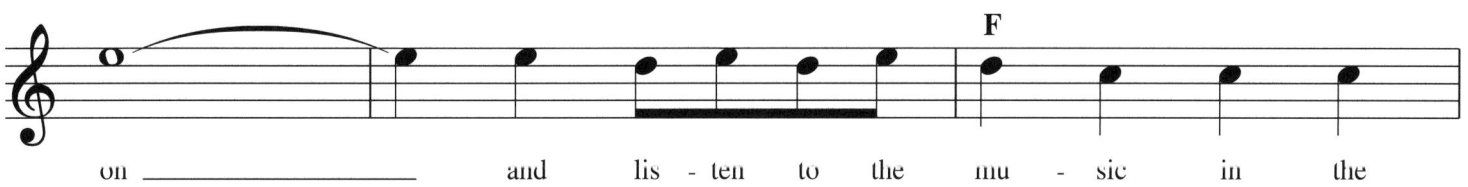
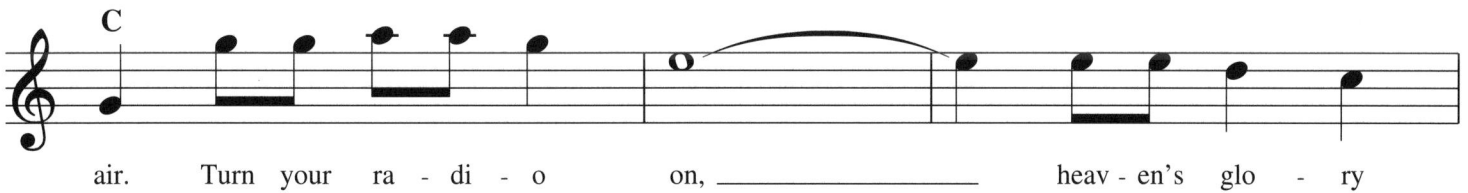

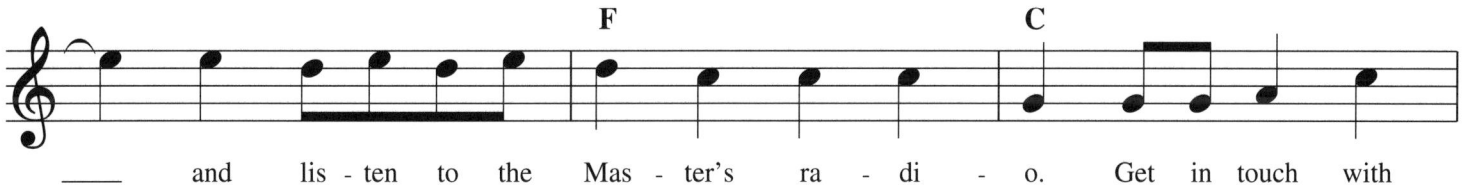
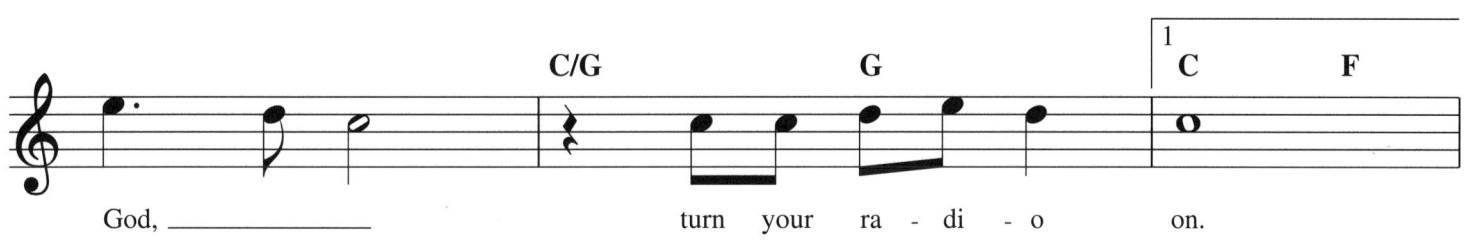
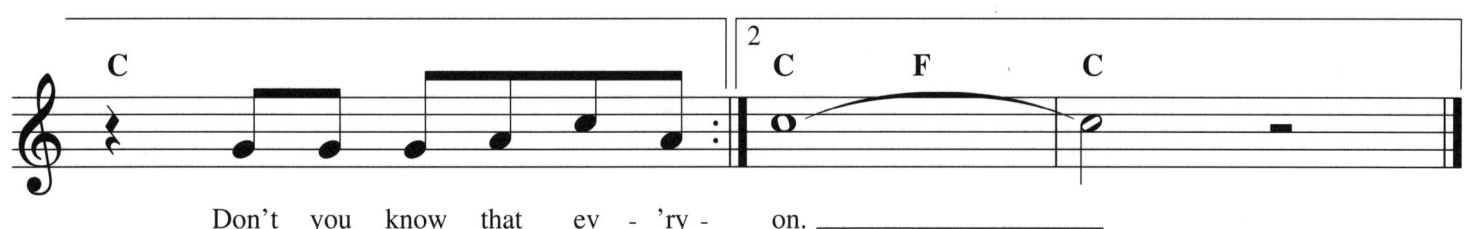

THE UNCLOUDED DAY

UPON THIS ROCK

Words by GLORIA GAITHER
Music by DONY McGUIRE

© 1982, 1983 BUD JOHN SONGS, INC., IT'S-N-ME MUSIC and GAITHER MUSIC COMPANY
BUD JOHN SONGS, INC. and IT'S-N-ME MUSIC Admin. by EMI CHRISTIAN MUSIC PUBLISHING
All Rights Reserved Used by Permission

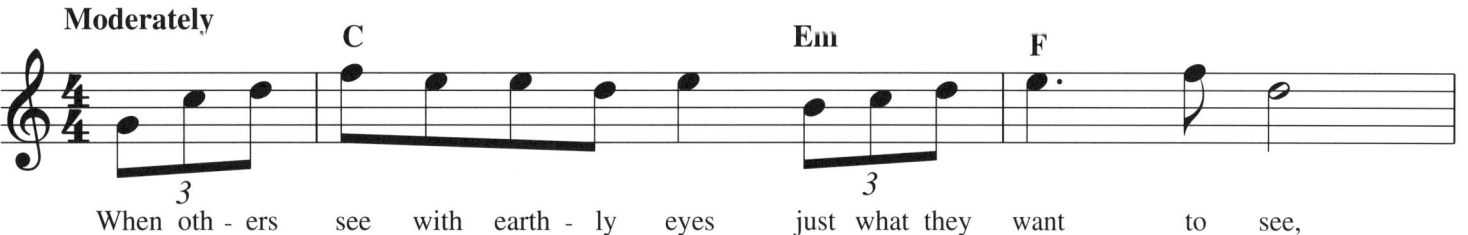

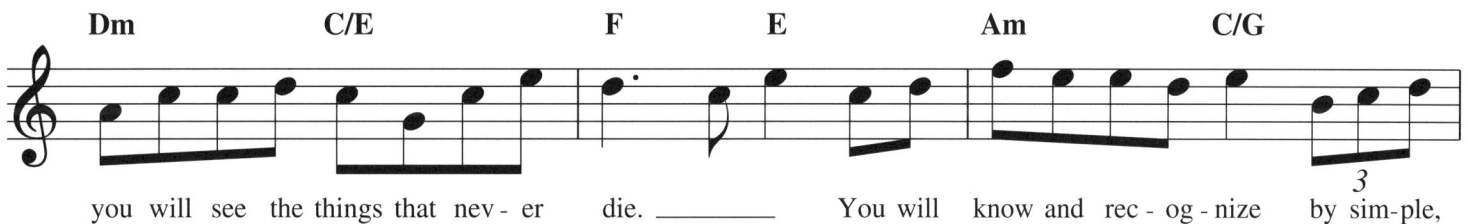

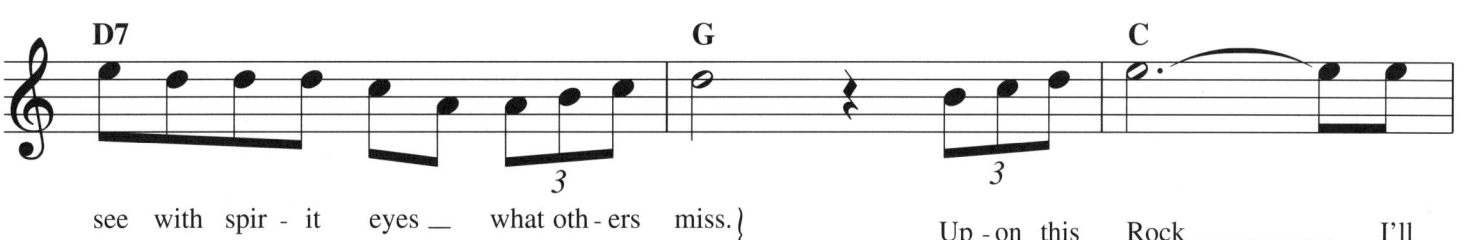

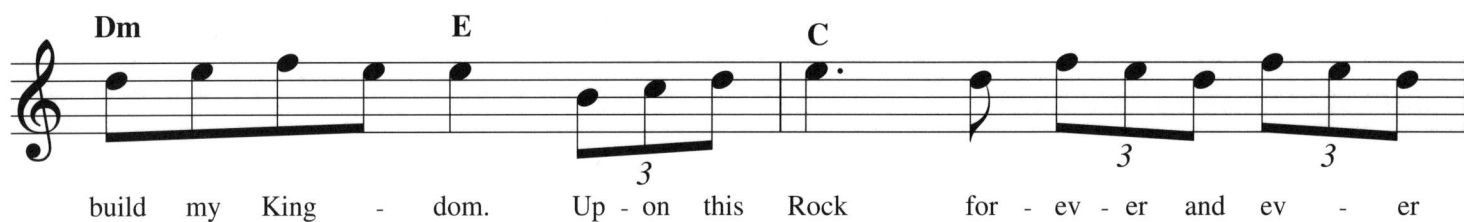

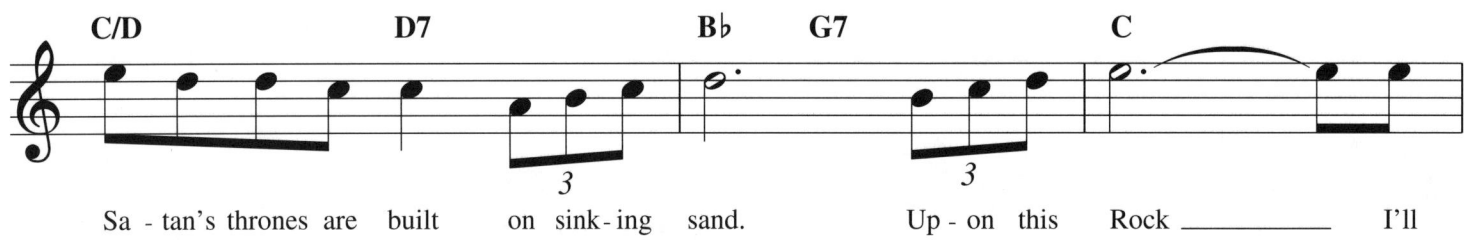
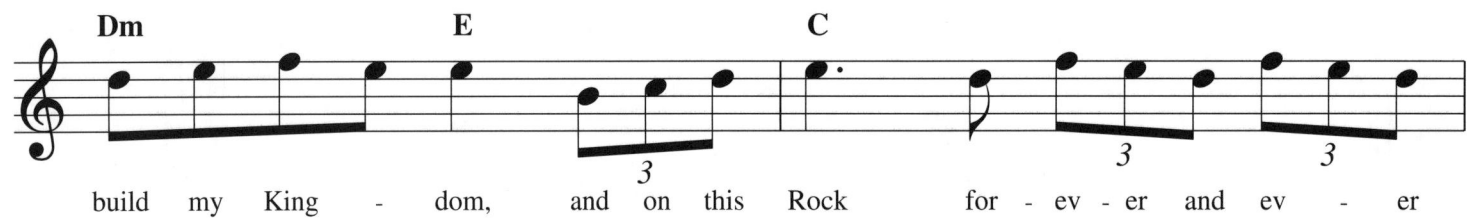
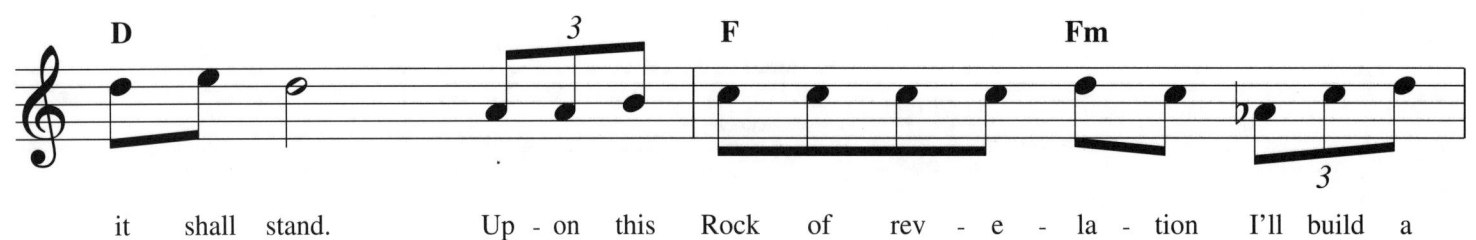

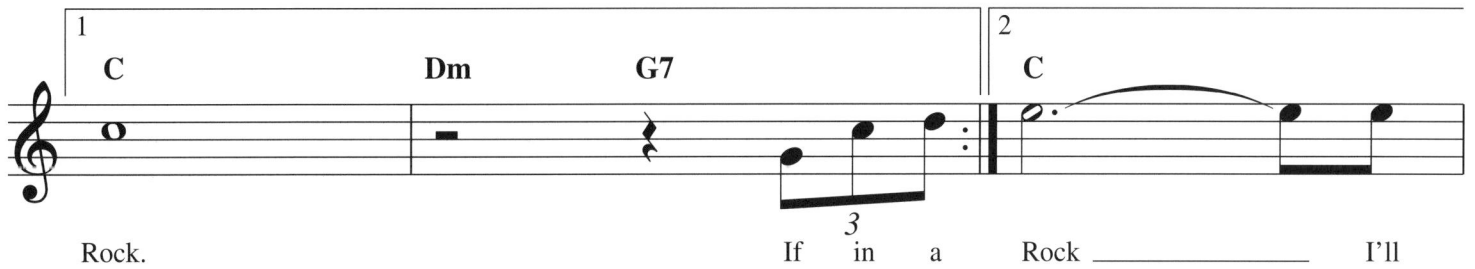
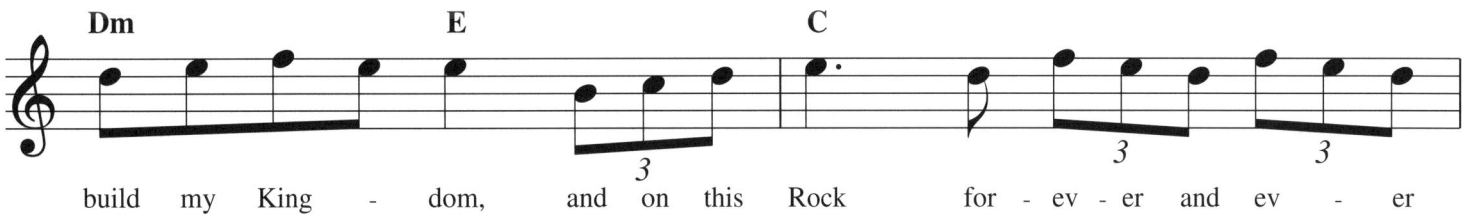
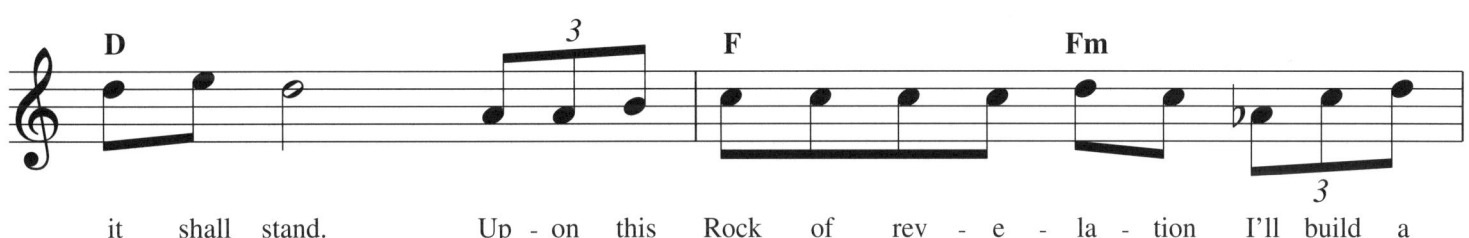
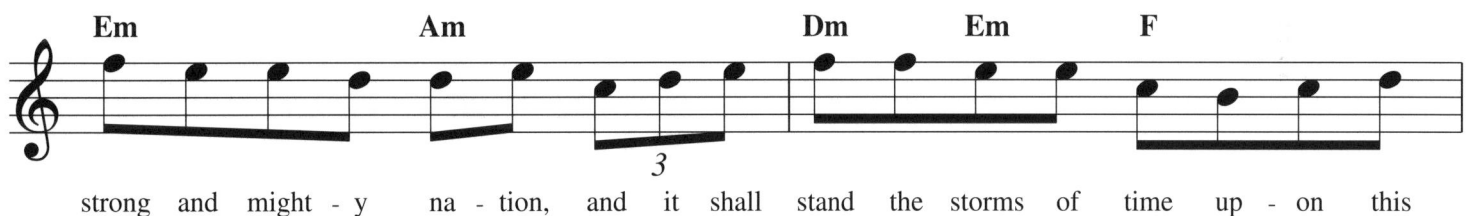
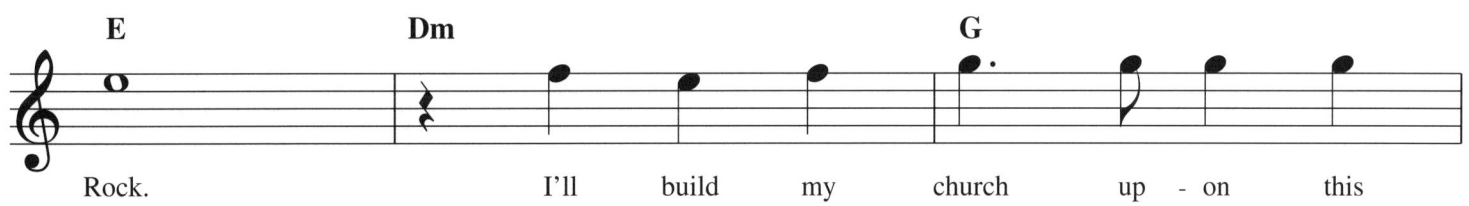
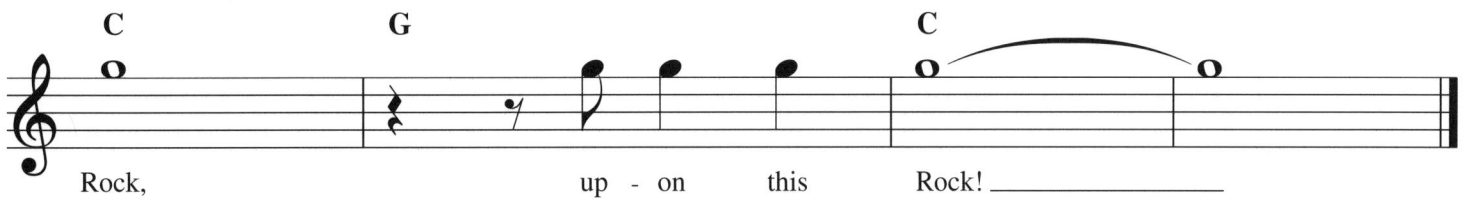

VICTORY IN JESUS

© Copyright 1939 by E.M. Bartlett
© Copyright 1967 by Mrs. E.M. Bartlett, Renewal
Assigned to Albert E. Brumley & Sons (SESAC)/admin. by ICG
All Rights Reserved   Used by Permission

Words and Music by
E.M. BARTLETT

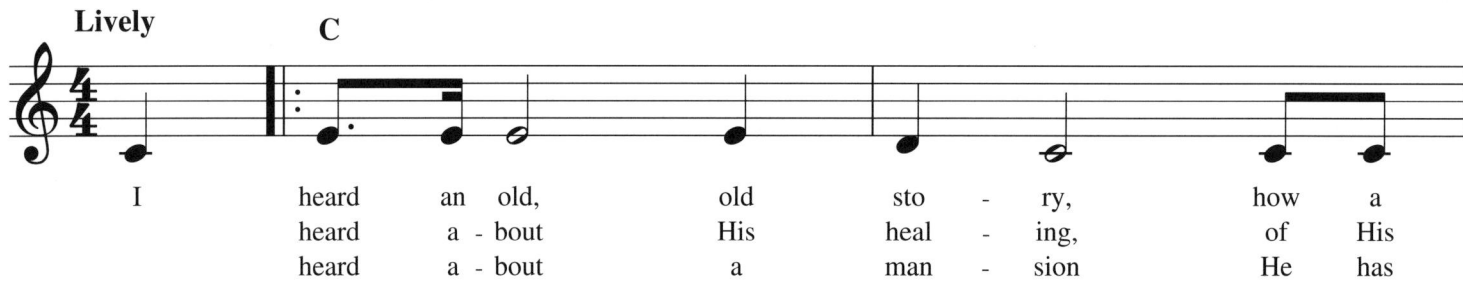

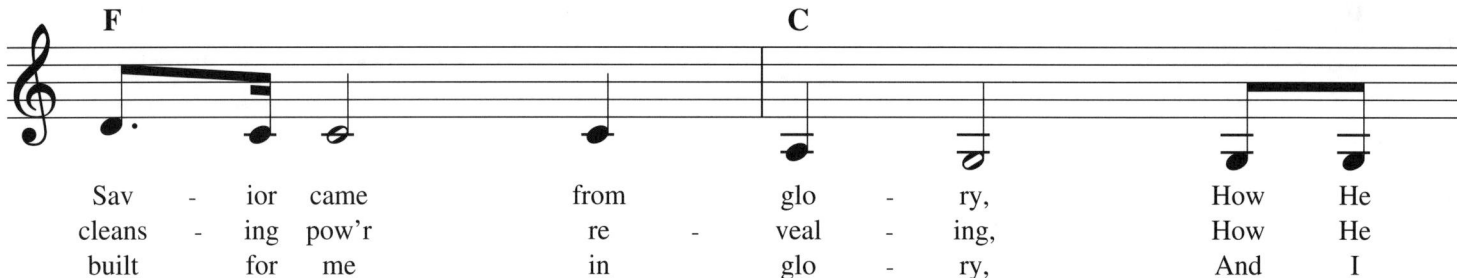

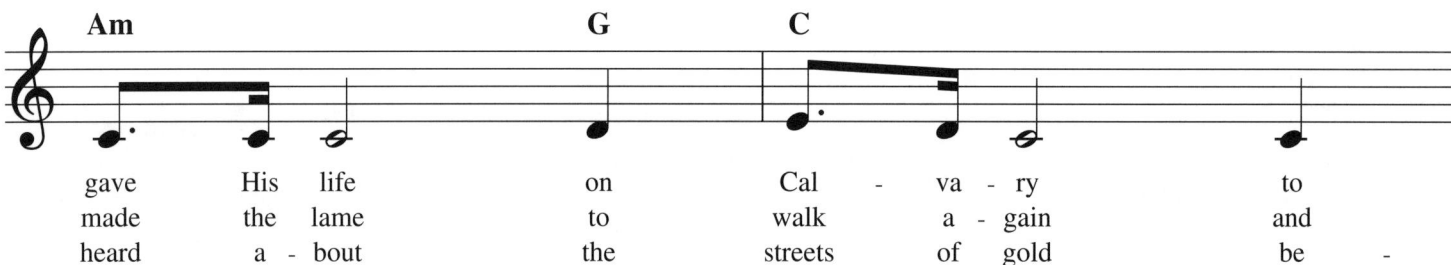

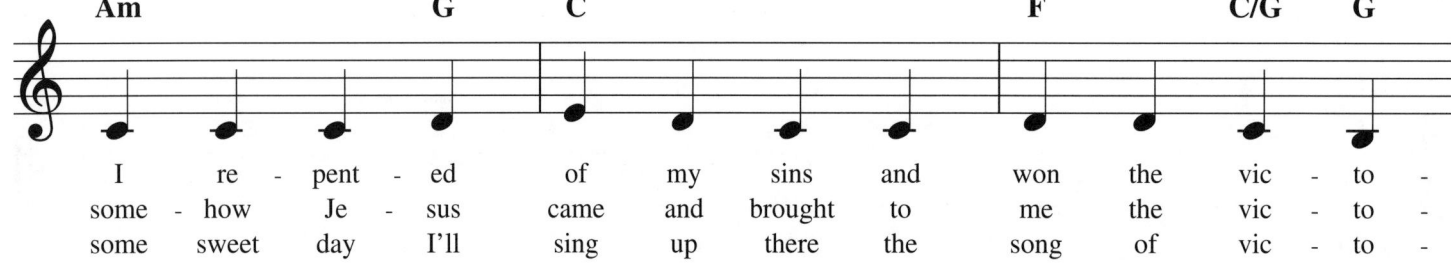

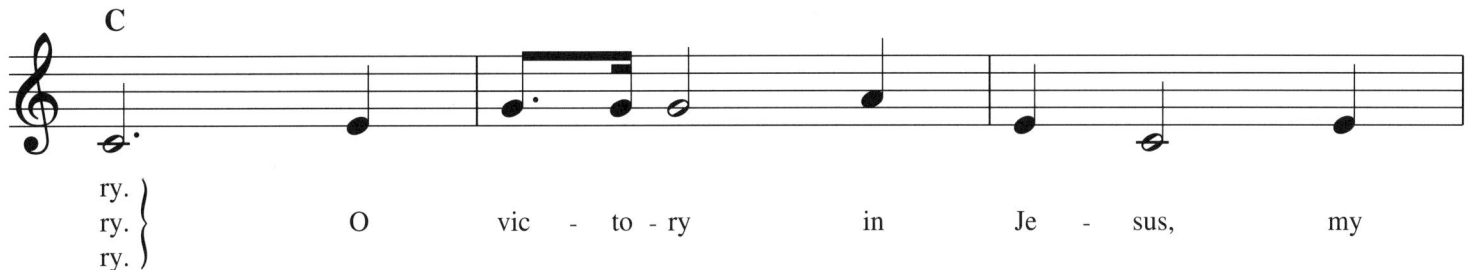
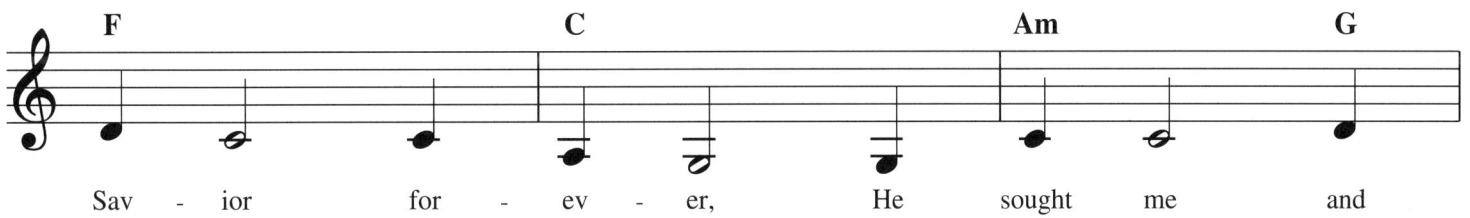
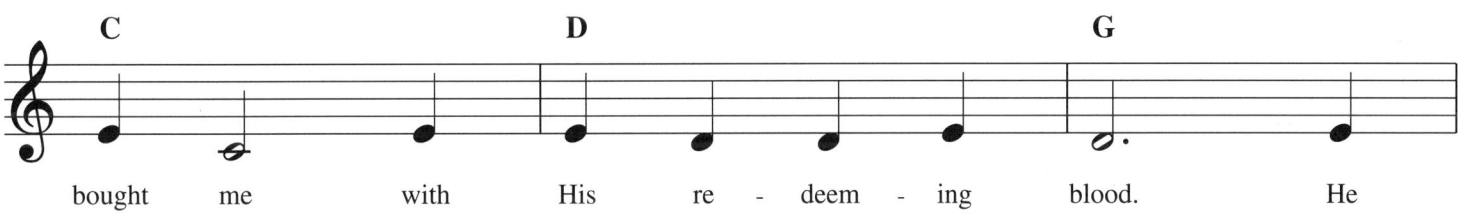

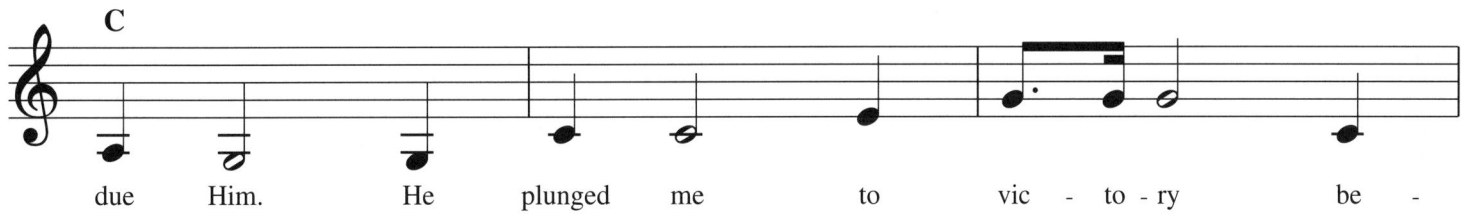
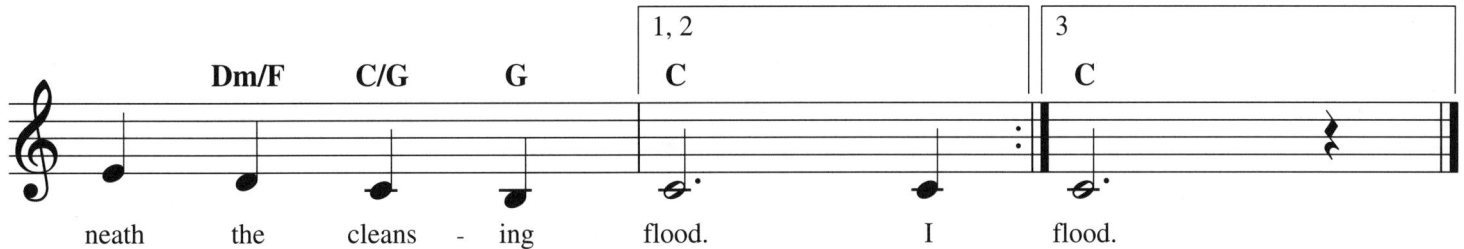

WE SHALL BEHOLD HIM

Words and Music by
DOTTIE RAMBO

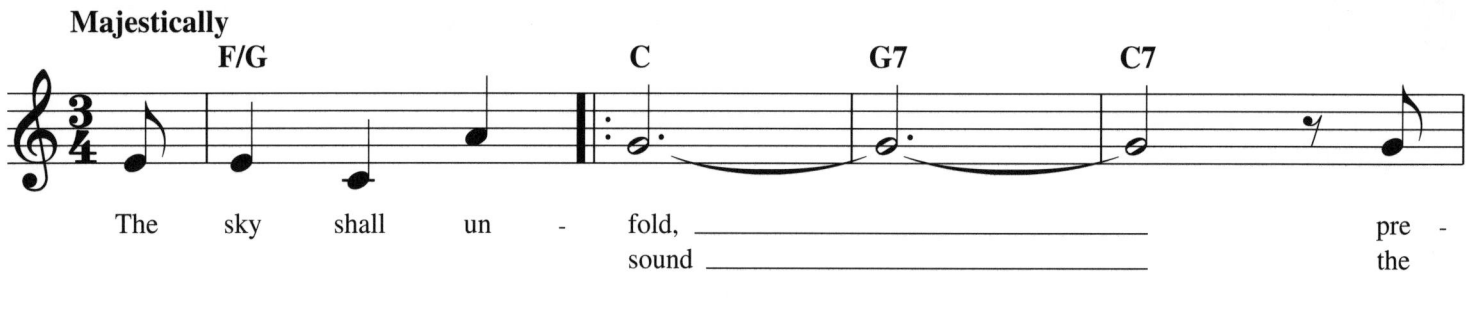

The sky shall un-fold, pre-
sound the

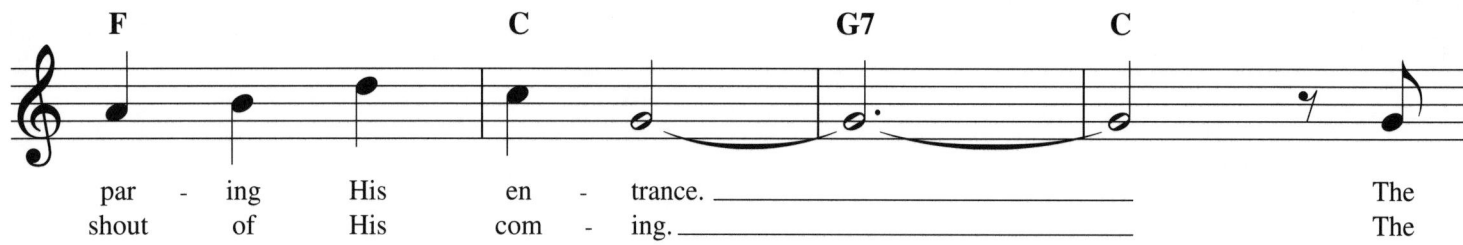

par - ing His en - trance. The
shout of His com - ing. The

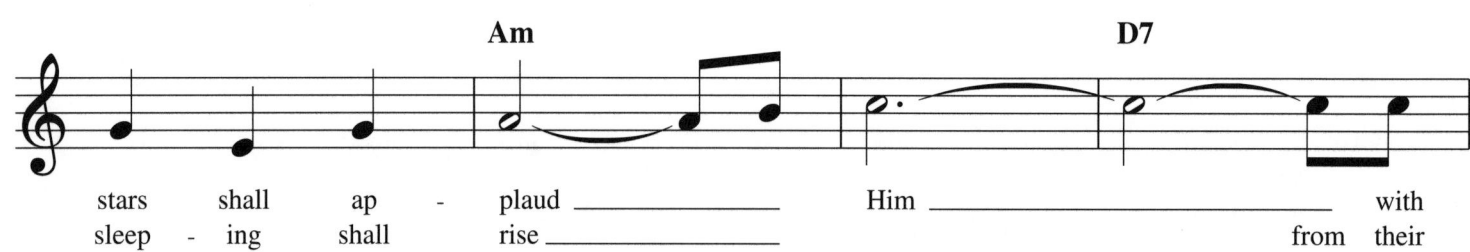

stars shall ap - plaud Him with
sleep - ing shall rise from their

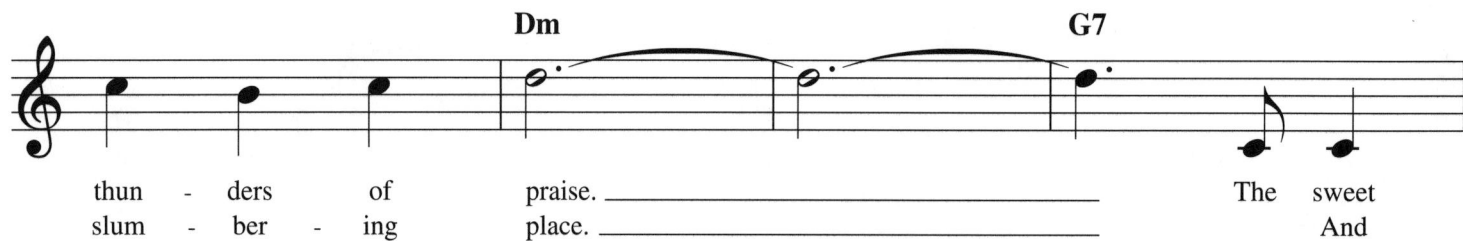

thun - ders of praise. The sweet
slum - ber - ing place. And

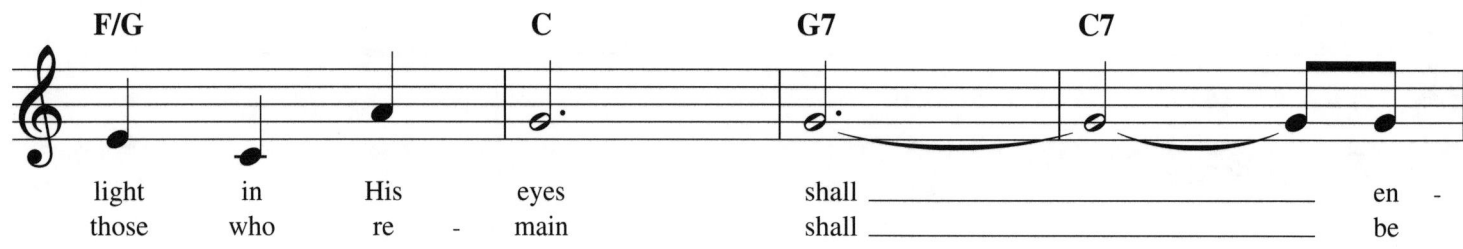

light in His eyes shall en-
those who re - main shall be

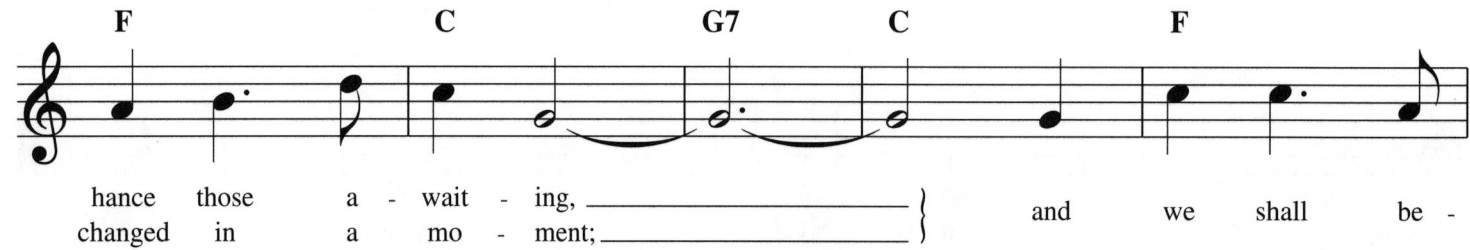

hance those a - wait - ing, and we shall be-
changed in a mo - ment;

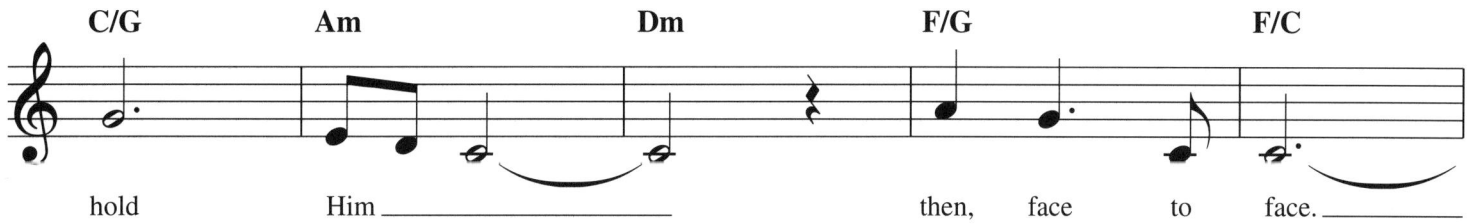
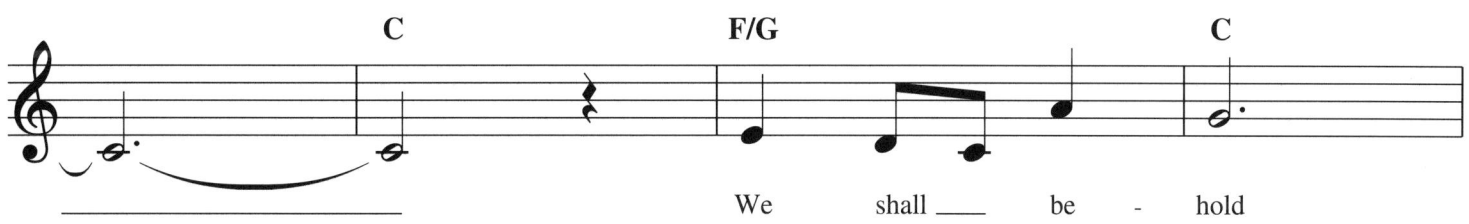
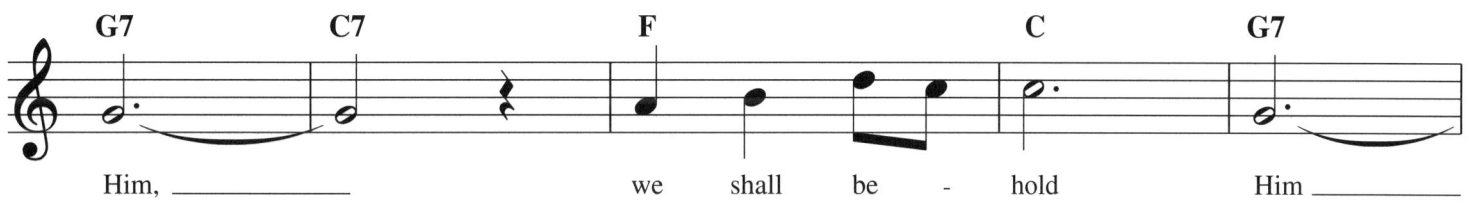
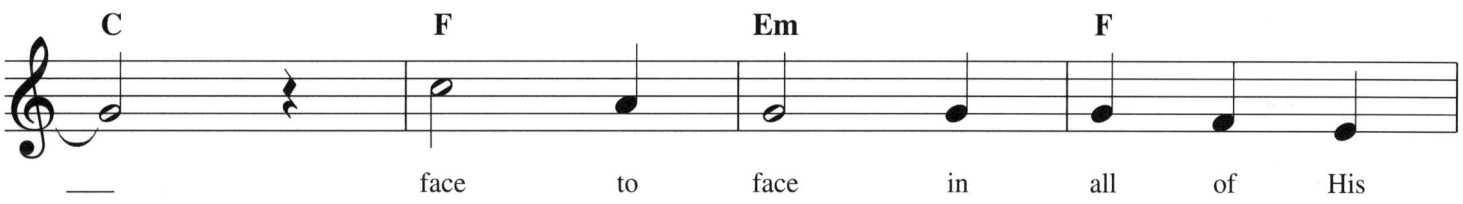
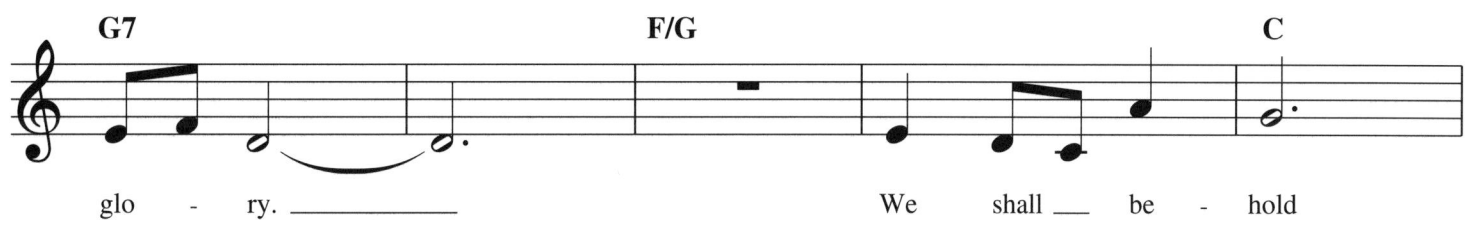
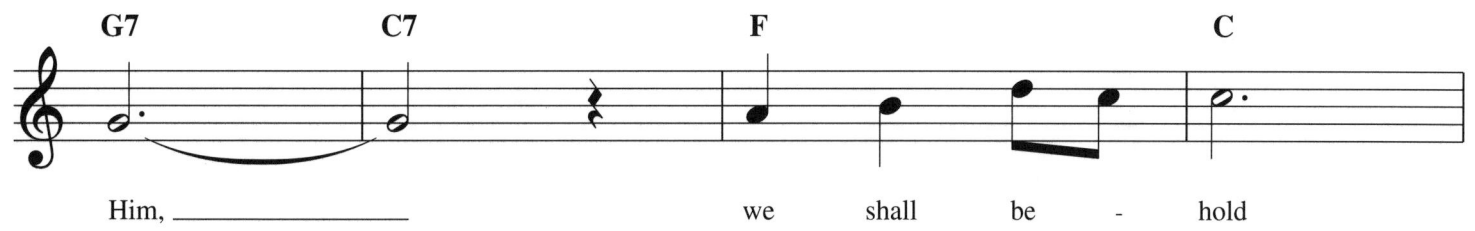

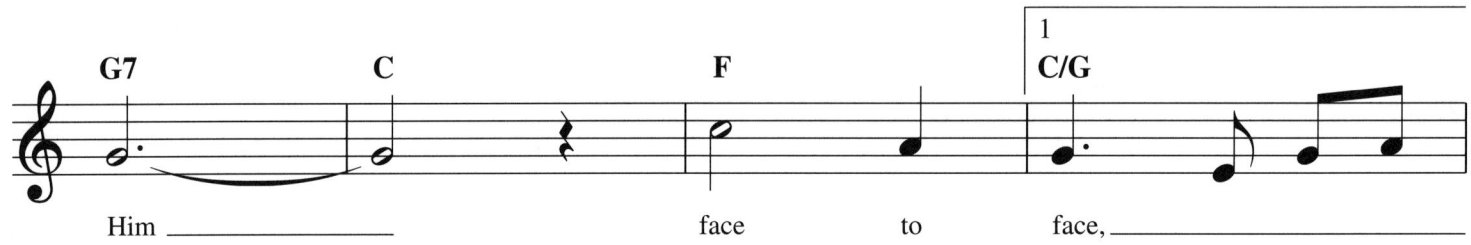
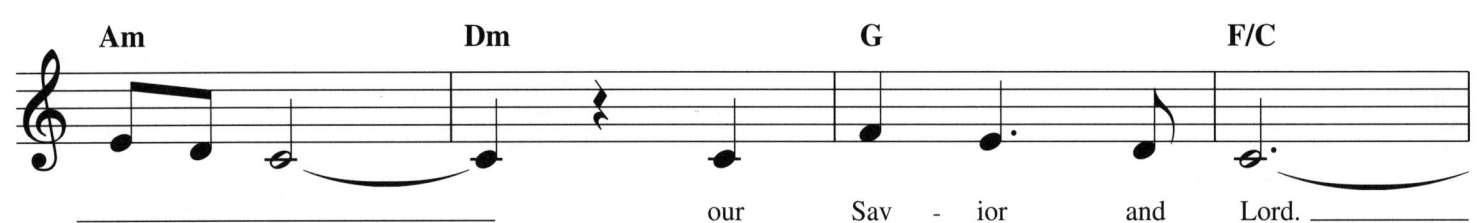
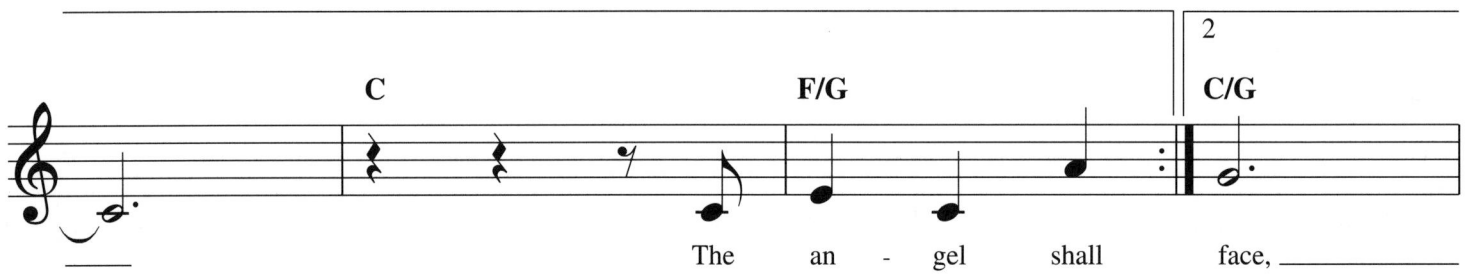
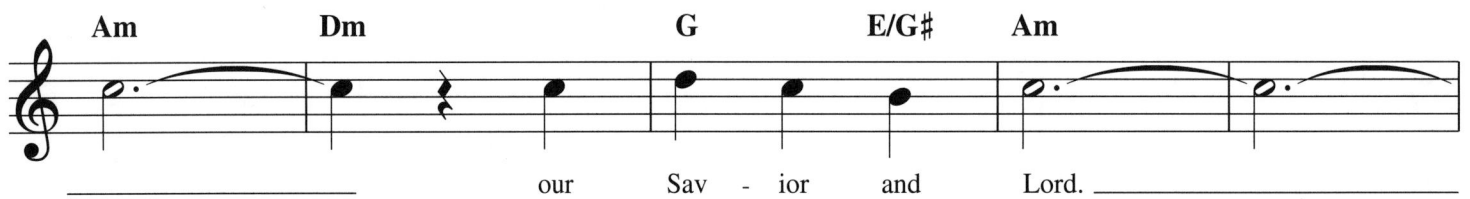
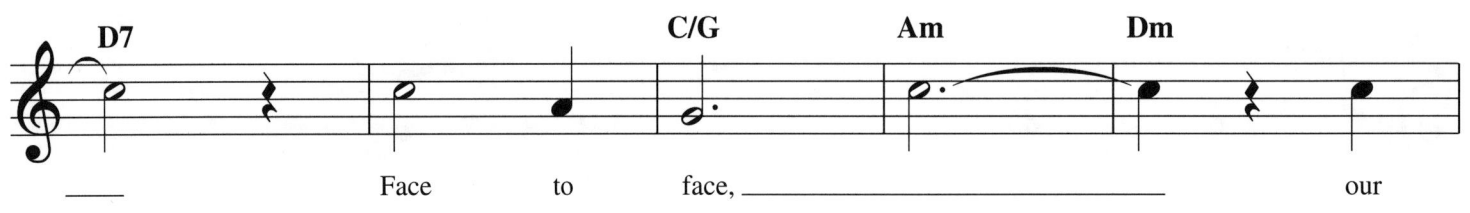
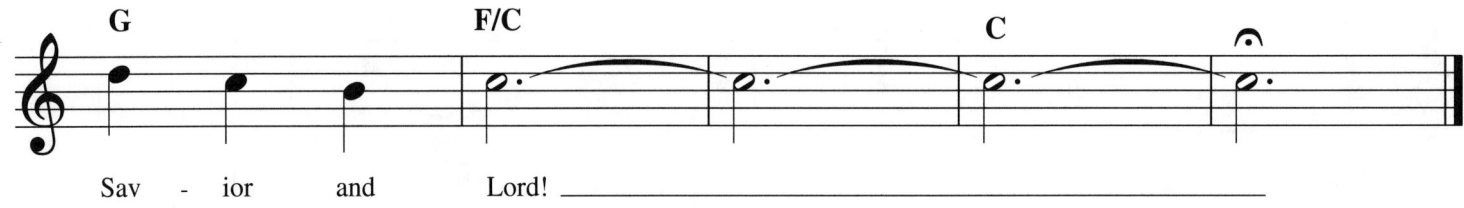

WE'LL UNDERSTAND IT BETTER BY AND BY

Words and Music by
CHARLES A. TINDLEY

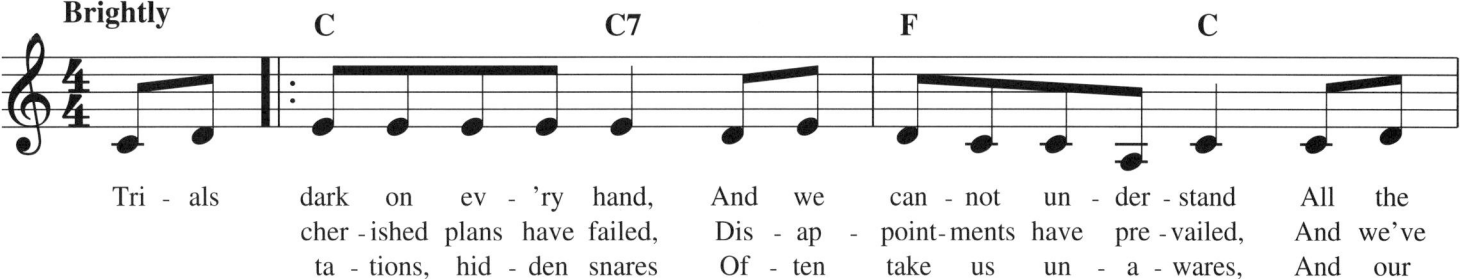

Tri - als dark on ev - 'ry hand, And we can - not un - der - stand All the
cher - ished plans have failed, Dis - ap - point - ments have pre - vailed, And we've
ta - tions, hid - den snares Of - ten take us un - a - wares, And our

ways that God would lead us to that bless - ed Prom - ised Land. But He'll guide us with His eye, And we'll
wan - dered in the dark - ness, heav - y - heart - ed and a - lone. But we're trust - ing in the Lord, And ac -
hearts are made to bleed for some thought - less word or deed; And we won - der why the test When we

fol - low till we die; We will un - der - stand it bet - ter by and by.
cord - ing to His Word, We will un - der - stand it bet - ter by and by.
try to do our best, But we'll un - der - stand it bet - ter by and by.

By and by, when the morn - ing comes, When the saints of

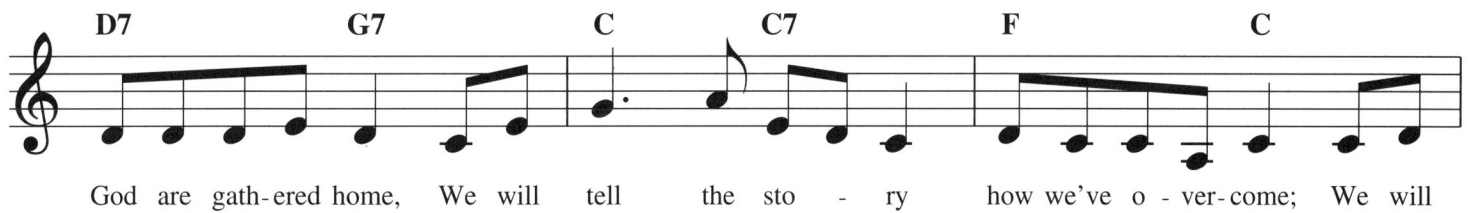

God are gath - ered home, We will tell the sto - ry how we've o - ver - come; We will

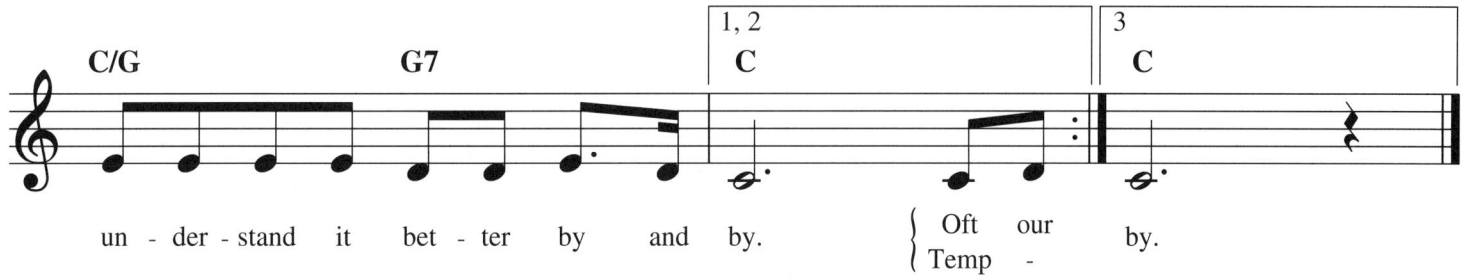

un - der - stand it bet - ter by and by.   Oft our   by.
                                            Temp -

WHEN THE ROLL IS CALLED UP YONDER

Words and Music by
JAMES M. BLACK

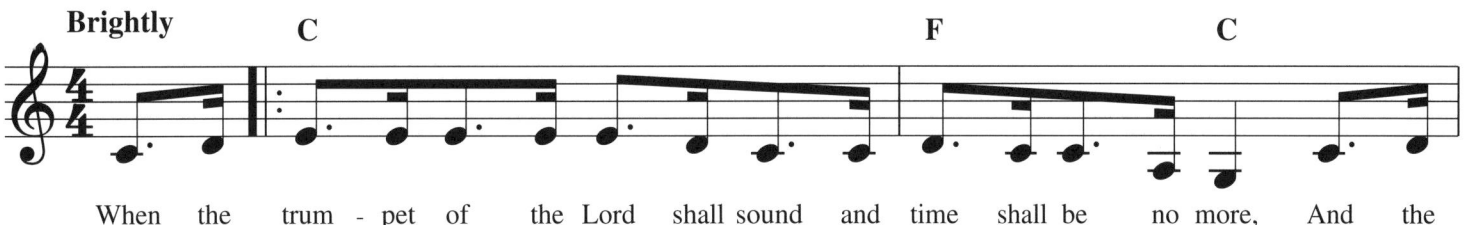

When the trum-pet of the Lord shall sound and time shall be no more, And the
bright and cloud-less morn-ing when the dead in Christ shall rise, And the
la-bor for the Mas-ter from the dawn till set-ting sun; Let us

morn-ing breaks, e-ter-nal, bright and fair; When the saved of earth shall gath-er o-ver
glo-ry of His res-ur-rec-tion share; When His cho-sen ones shall gath-er to their
talk of all His won-drous love and care. Then when all of life is o-ver and our

on the oth-er shore, And the roll is called up yon-der, I'll be there.
home be-yond the skies, And the roll is called up yon-der, I'll be there. When the
work on earth is done, And the roll is called up yon-der, I'll be there.

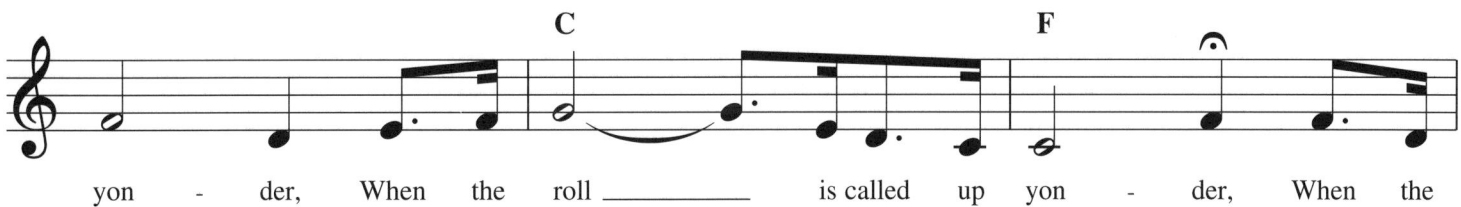

roll _____ is called up yon-der, When the roll _____ is called up
yon-der, When the roll _____ is called up yon-der, When the

roll is called up yon-der, I'll be there.
On that
Let us there.

WHEN WE ALL GET TO HEAVEN

Words by ELIZA E. HEWITT
Music by EMILY D. WILSON

Joyfully

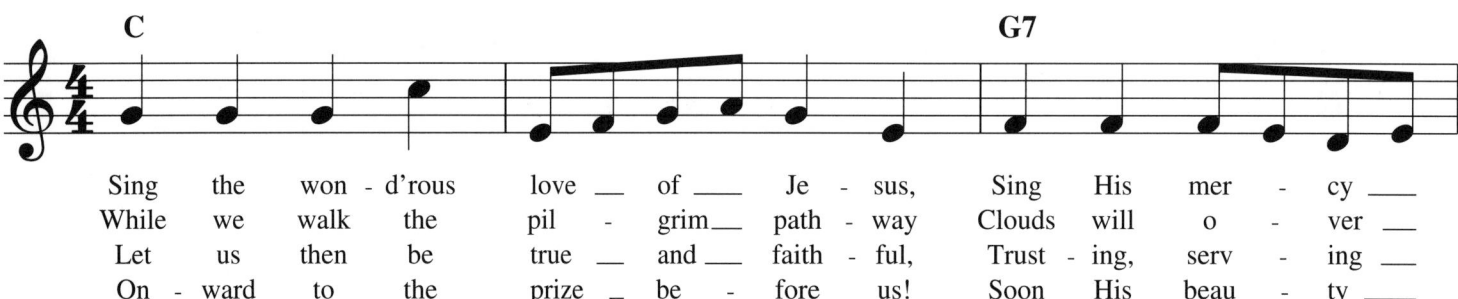

Sing the won-d'rous love ___ of ___ Je-sus, Sing His mer-cy ___
While we walk the pil-grim ___ path-way Clouds will o-ver ___
Let us then be true ___ and ___ faith-ful, Trust-ing, serv-ing ___
On-ward to the prize ___ be-fore us! Soon His beau-ty ___

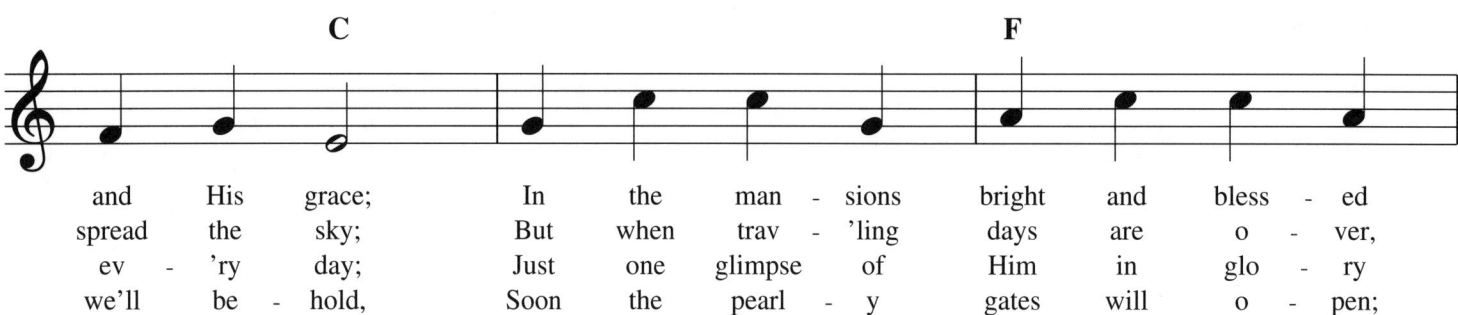

and His grace; In the man-sions bright and bless-ed
spread the sky; But when trav-'ling days are o-ver,
ev-'ry day; Just one glimpse of Him in glo-ry
we'll be-hold, Soon the pearl-y gates will o-pen;

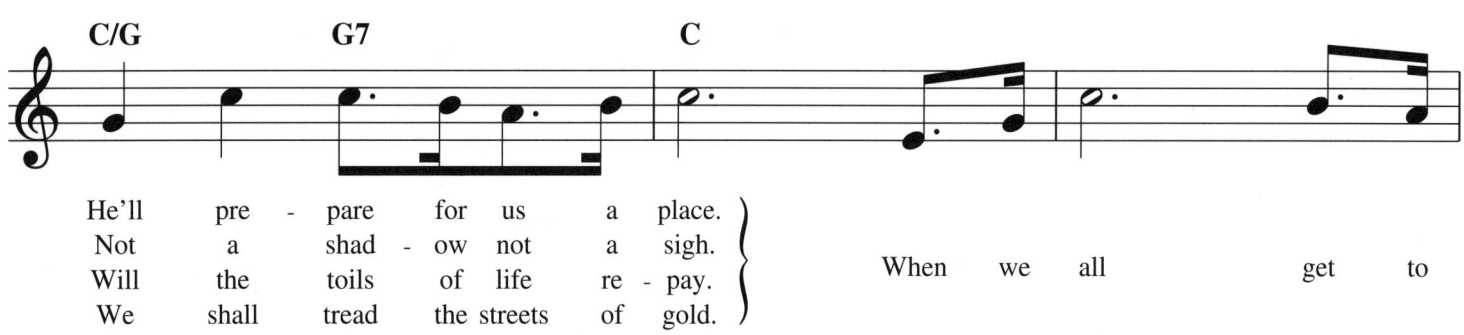

He'll pre-pare for us a place.
Not a shad-ow not a sigh.
Will the toils of life re-pay.   When we all get to
We shall tread the streets of gold.

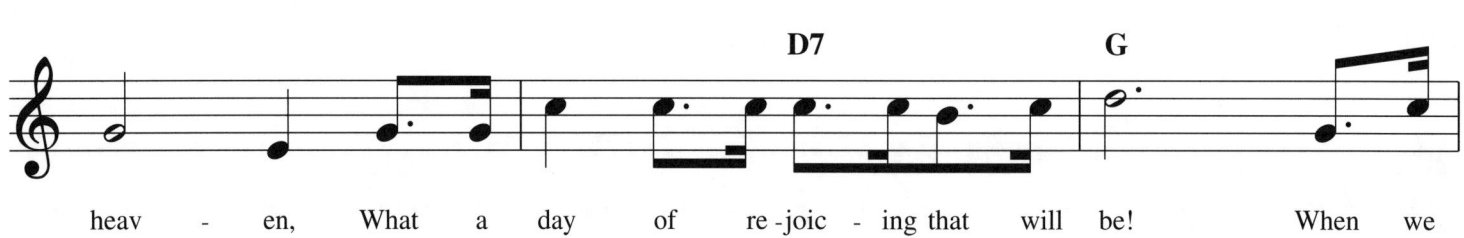

heav-en, What a day of re-joic-ing that will be! When we

all see Je-sus, We'll sing and shout the vic-to-ry.

WHISPERING HOPE

Words and Music by
ALICE HAWTHORNE

Gently

| C | F | C |

Soft as the voice of an an - gel
If, in the dusk of the twi - light,
Hope, as an an - chor so stead - fast,

| G7 | | C |

Breath - ing a les - son un - heard, _____
Dim be the re - gion a - far, _____
Rends the dark veil for the soul, _____

| | F | |

Hope with a gen - tle per - sua - sion
Will not the deep - en - ing dark - ness
Whith - er the Mas - ter has en - tered,

| C/G | G7 | C |

Whis - pers her com - fort - ing word: _____
Bright - en the glim - mer - ing star? _____
Rob - bing the grave of its goal. _____

| | G | C |

Wait till the dark - ness is o - ver,
Then when the night is up - on us,
Come then, O come, glad fru - i - tion,

| G/D | D7 | G |

Wait till the tem - pest is done, _____
Why should the heart sink a - way? _____
Come to my sad wea - ry heart. _____

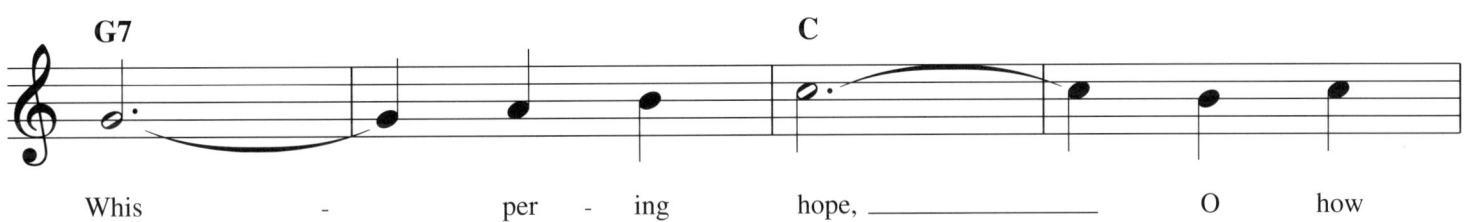
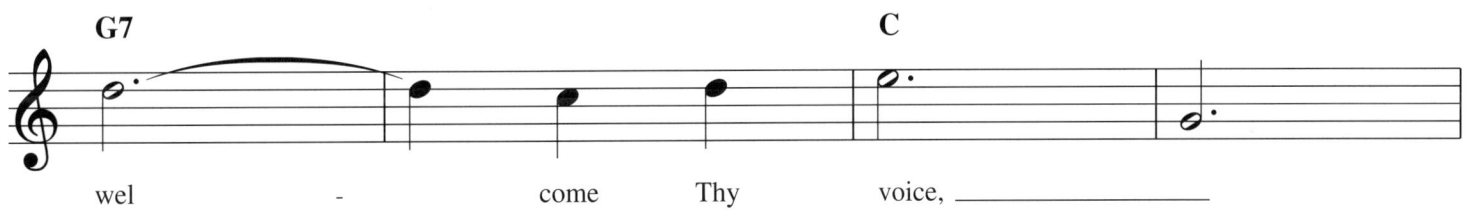
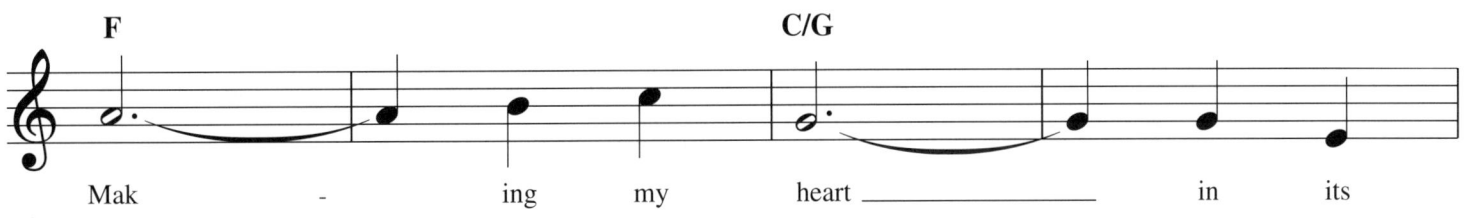
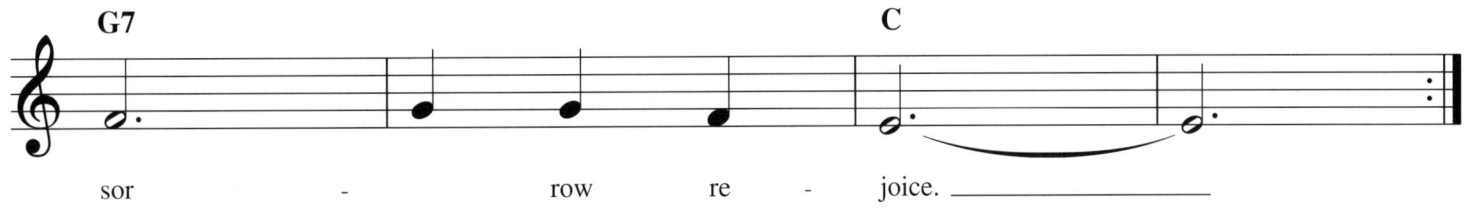

WILL THE CIRCLE BE UNBROKEN

Words by ADA R. HABERSHON
Music by CHARLES H. GABRIEL

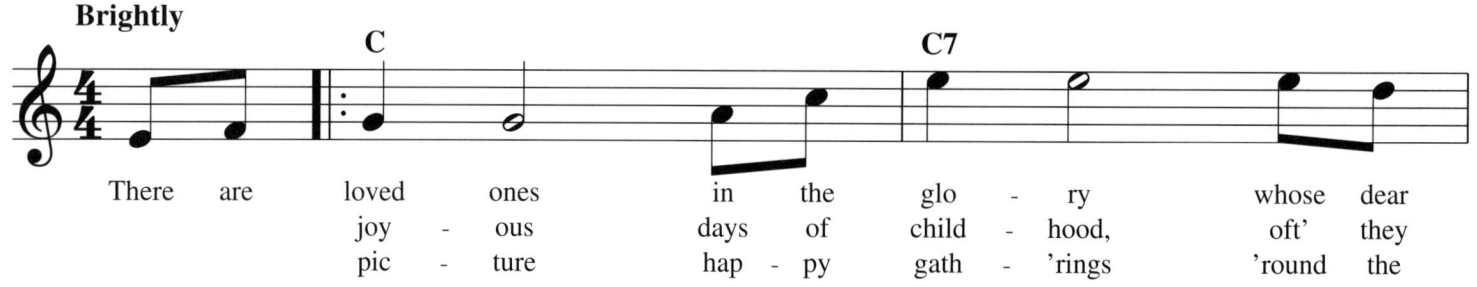
There are loved ones in the glory whose dear
joy-ous days of child-hood, oft' they
pic-ture hap-py gath-'rings 'round the

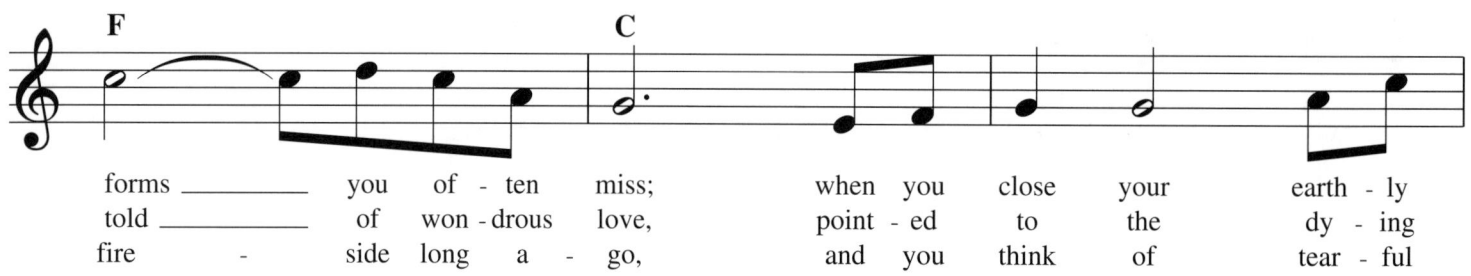
forms you of-ten miss; when you close your earth-ly
told of won-drous love, point-ed to the dy-ing
fire-side long a-go, and you think of tear-ful

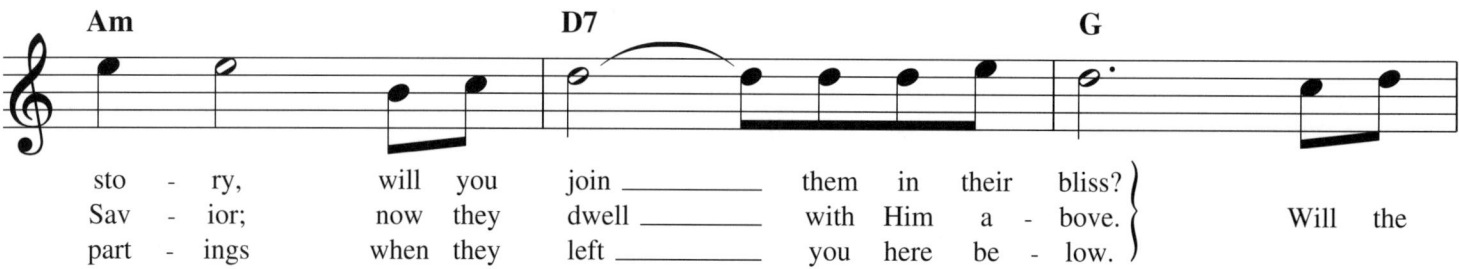
sto-ry, will you join them in their bliss?
Sav-ior; now they dwell with Him a-bove.
part-ings when they left you here be-low.
Will the

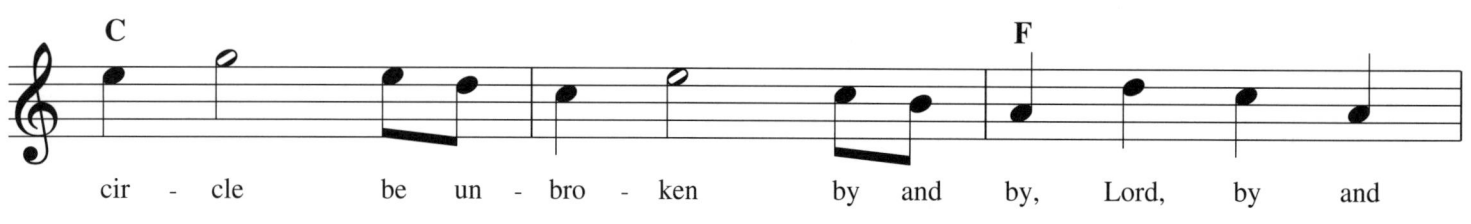
cir-cle be un-bro-ken by and by, Lord, by and

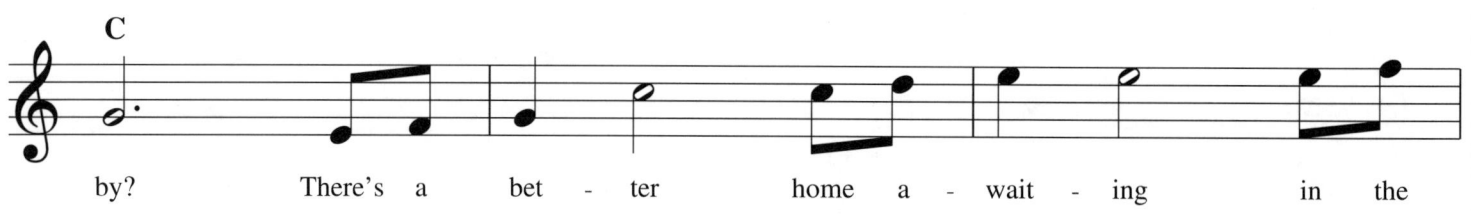
by? There's a bet-ter home a-wait-ing in the

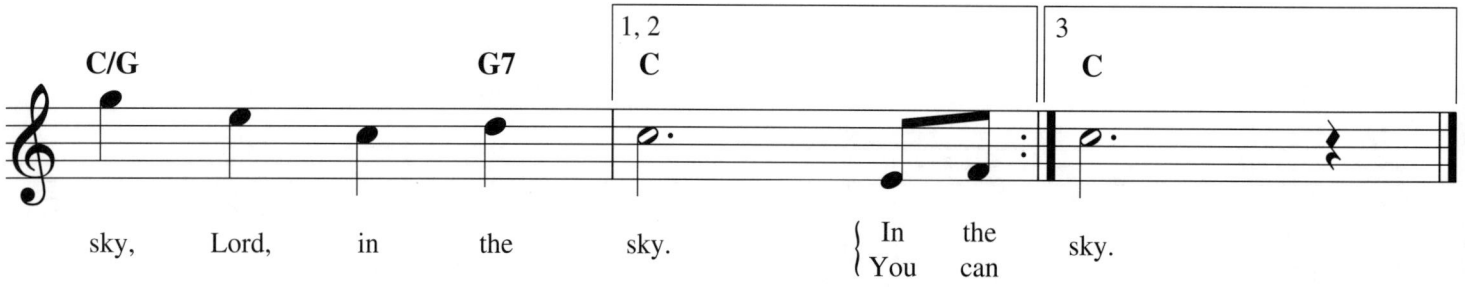
sky, Lord, in the sky. In the sky.
You can

WRITTEN IN RED

© 1984 Word Music, Inc.
All Rights Reserved   Used by Permission

Words and Music by
GORDON JENSEN

In let - ters of crim - son God wrote His love on a hill - side so
Down through the ag - es God wrote His love with the same hands that

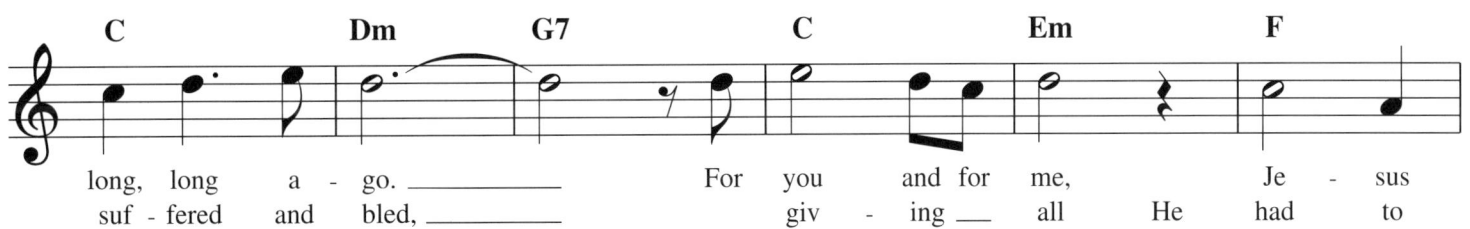

long, long a - go. _____ For you and for me, Je - sus
suf - fered and bled, _____ giv - ing __ all He had to

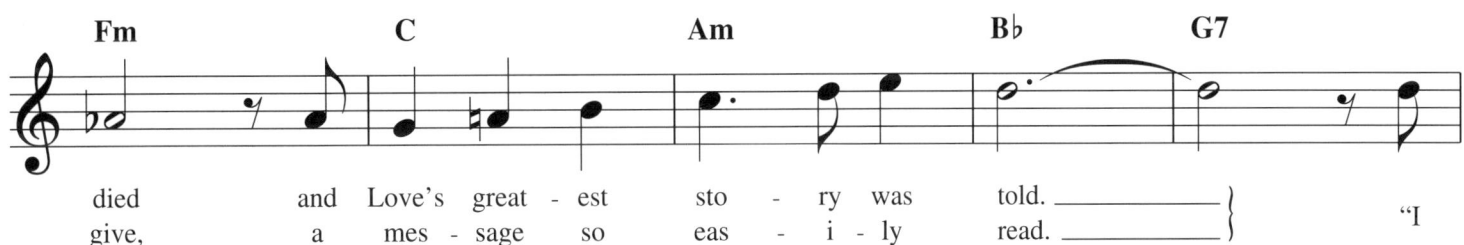

died, and Love's great - est sto - ry was told. _____
give, a mes - sage so eas - i - ly read. _____ } "I

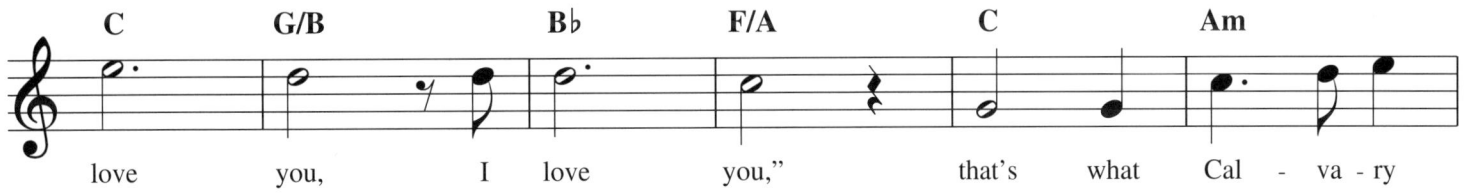

love you, I love you," that's what Cal - va - ry

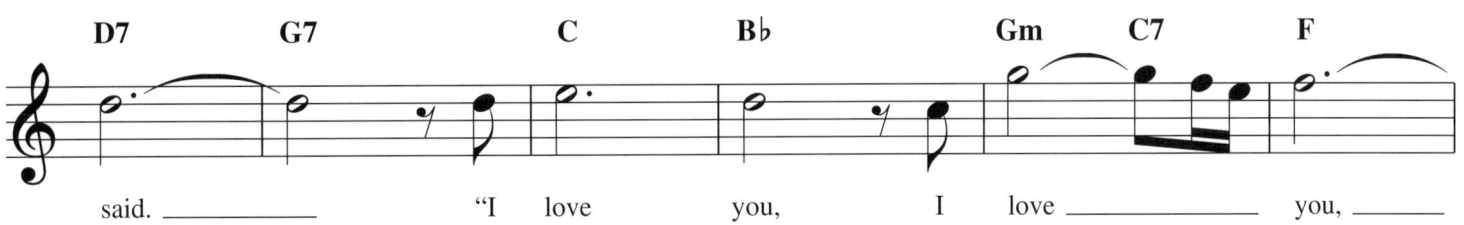

said. _____ "I love you, I love _____ you, _____

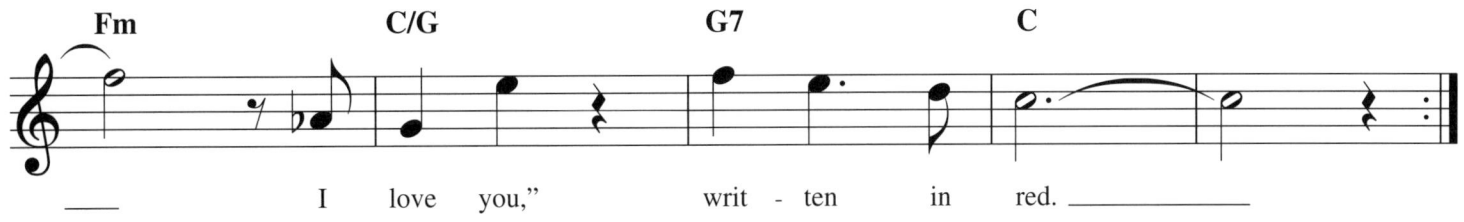

___ I love you," writ - ten in red. _____

Wings Of A Dove

Copyright © 1959 by Husky Music, Inc. and Larrick Music
Copyright Renewed
All Rights for the U.S. and Canada Administered by Unichappell Music Inc.
International Copyright Secured   All Rights Reserved

Words and Music by
BOB FERGUSON

Moderately, in one

When trou - bles sur - round us, _____ When
 drift - ed _____ On the
 down _____ To the

e - vils come, _____ The
flood man - y days, _____
wa - ters that day, _____

bod - y grows weak; _____ The
He searched for land _____ In
He was bap - tized _____ In the

spir - it grows numb. _____ When
var - i - ous ways. _____
u - su - al way. _____

these things be - set us, _____ He
Trou - bles he had some _____ But
When it was done, _____

does - n't for - get us. _____ He
was - n't for - got - ten. _____ He
God blessed His Son. _____ He

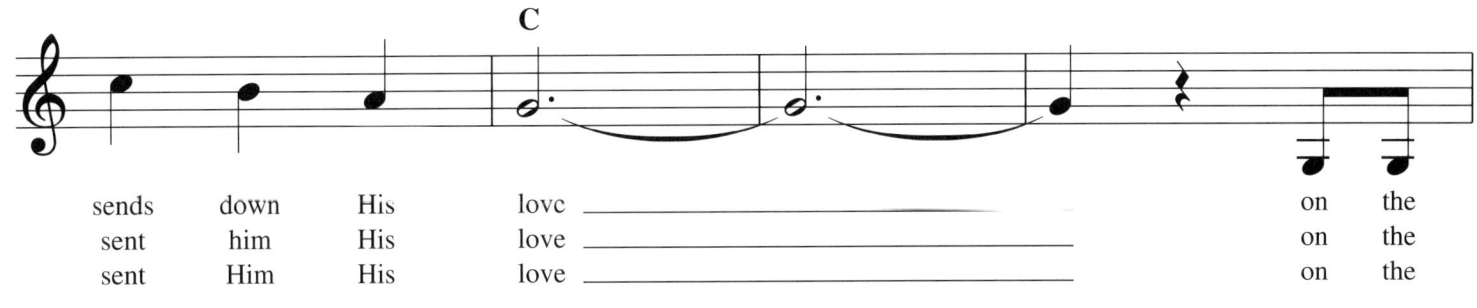
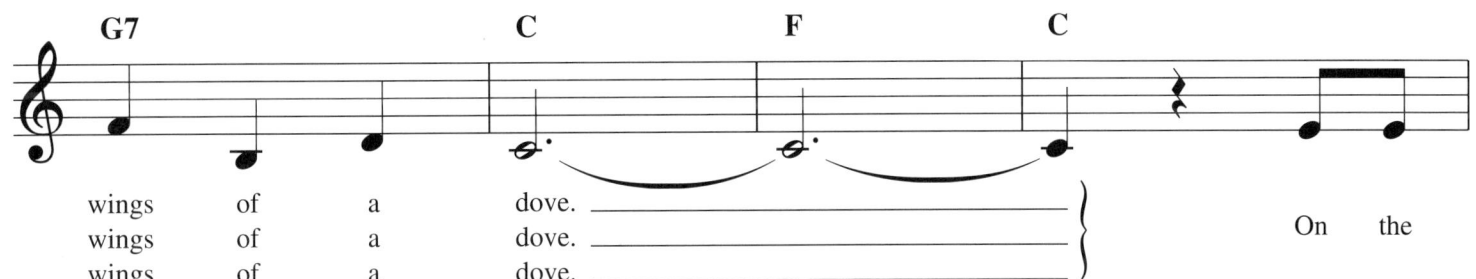
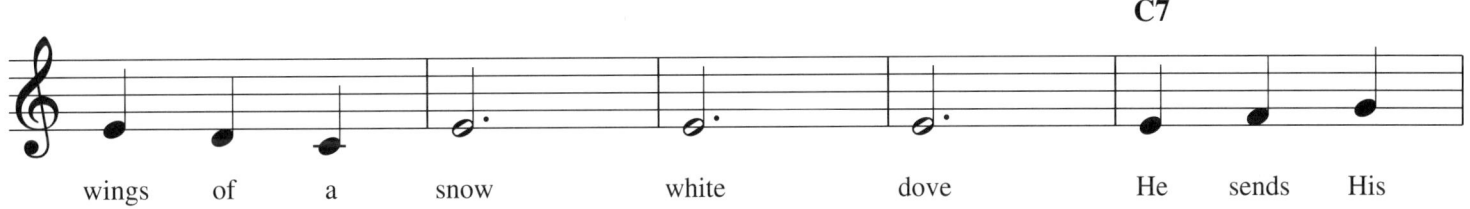
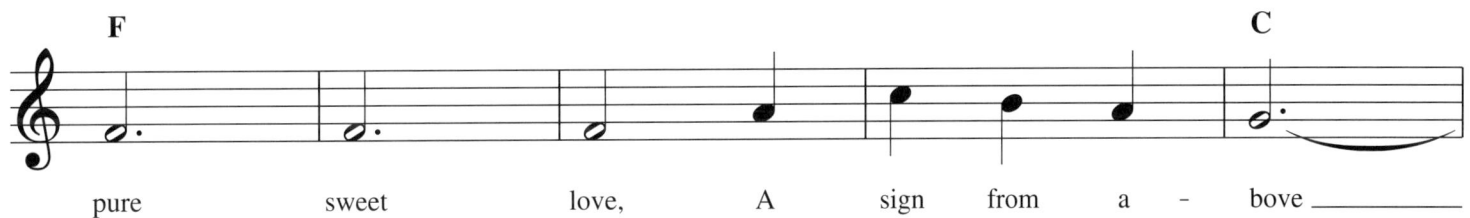
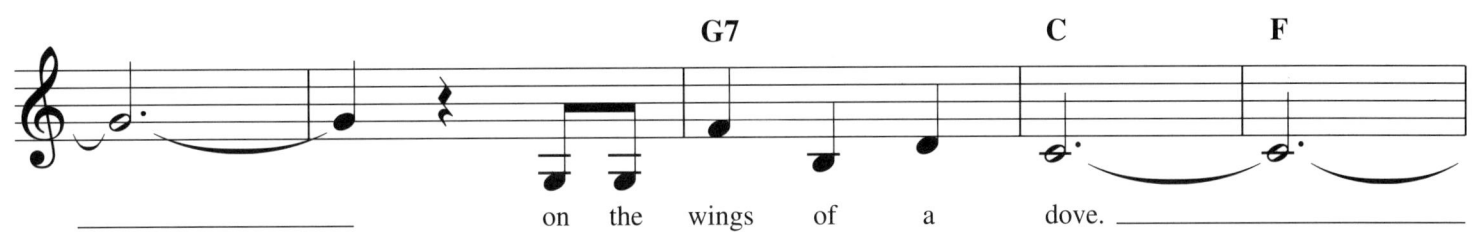

WONDERFUL GRACE OF JESUS

Copyright © 2001 by HAL LEONARD CORPORATION
International Copyright Secured   All Rights Reserved

Words and Music by
HALDOR LILLENAS

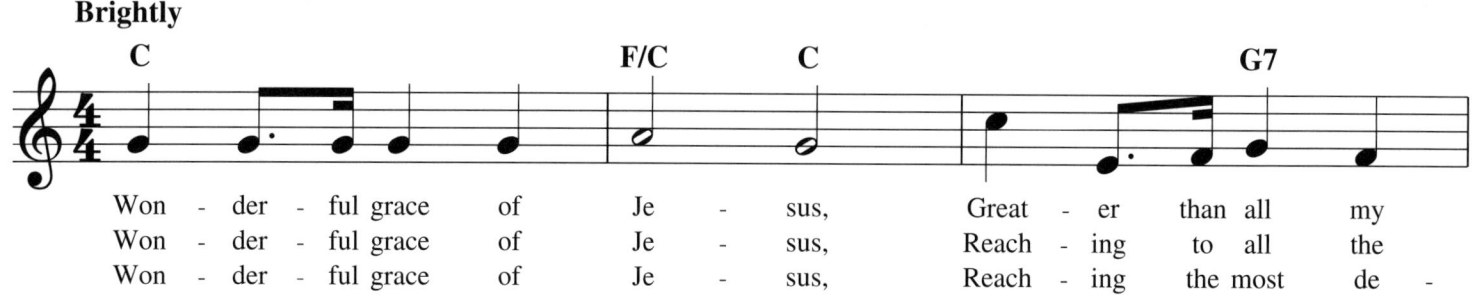

Won - der - ful grace of Je - sus, Great - er than all my
Won - der - ful grace of Je - sus, Reach - ing to all the
Won - der - ful grace of Je - sus, Reach - ing the most de -

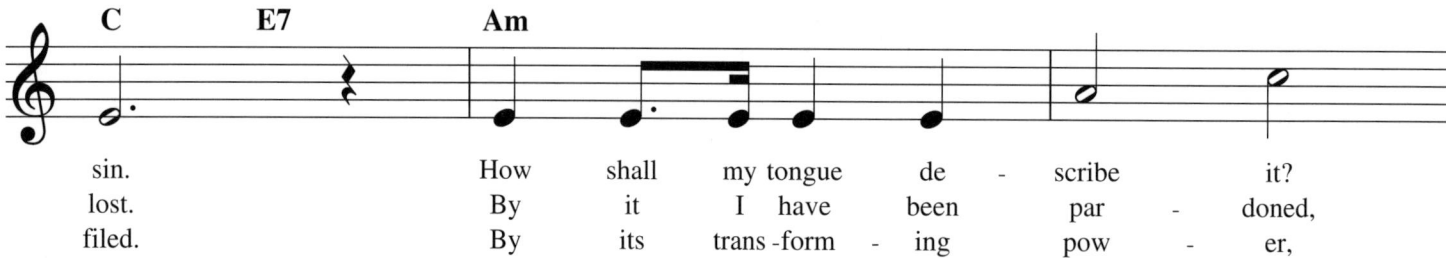

sin. How shall my tongue de - scribe it?
lost. By it I have been par - doned,
filed. By its trans - form - ing pow - er,

Where shall its praise be - gin? Tak - ing a - way my
Saved to the ut - ter - most. Chains have been torn a -
Mak - ing him God's dear child. Pur - chas - ing peace and

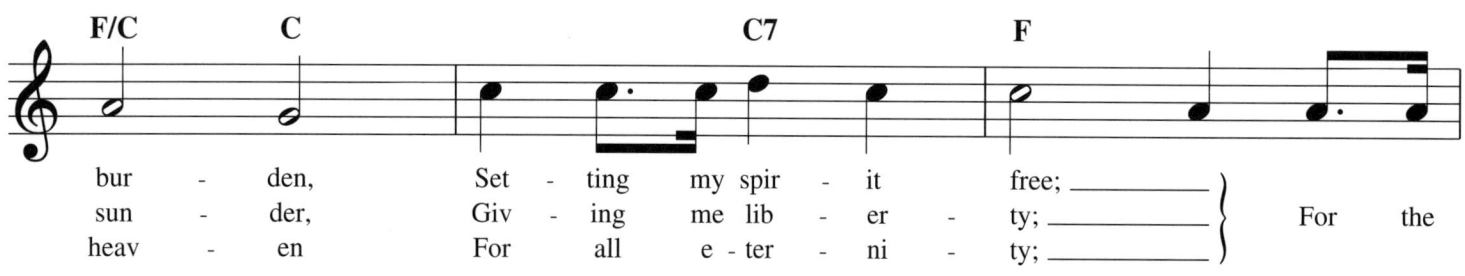

bur - den, Set - ting my spir - it free;⎫
sun - der, Giv - ing me lib - er - ty;⎬ For the
heav - en For all e - ter - ni - ty;⎭

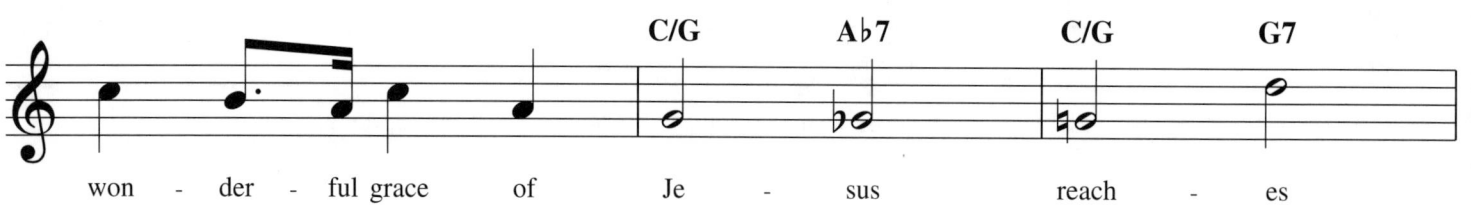

won - der - ful grace of Je - sus reach - es

me. Won - der - ful the match - less grace of

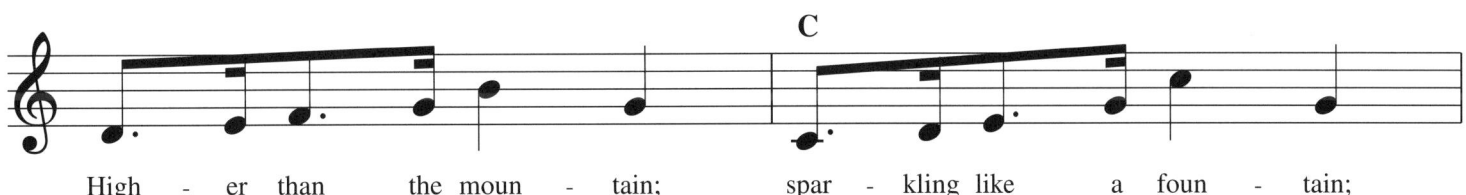

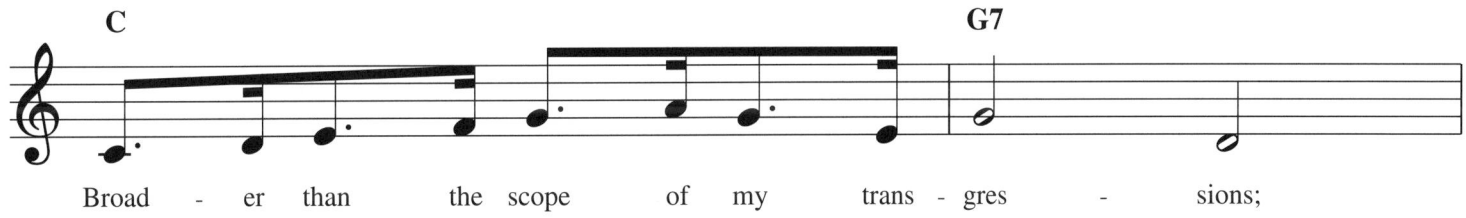

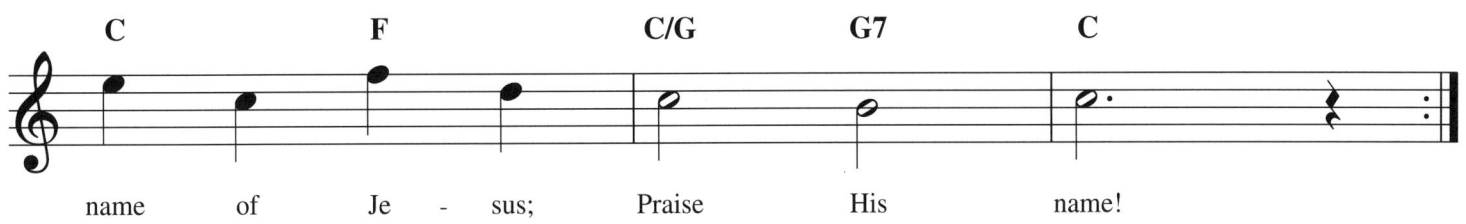

CHORD SPELLER

C chords

C	C–E–G
Cm	C–E♭–G
C7	C–E–G–B♭
Cdim	C–E♭–G♭
C+	C–E–G#

C# or D♭ chords

C#	C#–F–G#
C#m	C#–E–G#
C#7	C#–F–G#–B
C#dim	C#–E–G
C#+	C#–F–A

D chords

D	D–F#–A
Dm	D–F–A
D7	D–F#–A–C
Ddim	D–F–A♭
D+	D–F#–A#

E♭ chords

E♭	E♭–G–B♭
E♭m	E♭–G♭–B♭
E♭7	E♭–G–B♭–D♭
E♭dim	E♭–G♭–A
E♭+	E♭–G–B

E chords

E	E–G#–B
Em	E–G–B
E7	E–G#–B–D
Edim	E–G–B♭
E+	E–G#–C

F chords

F	F–A–C
Fm	F–A♭–C
F7	F–A–C–E♭
Fdim	F–A♭–B
F+	F–A–C#

F# or G♭ chords

F#	F#–A#–C#
F#m	F#–A–C#
F#7	F#–A#–C#–E
F#dim	F#–A–C
F#+	F#–A#–D

G chords

G	G–B–D
Gm	G–B♭–D
G7	G–B–D–F
Gdim	G–B♭–D♭
G+	G–B–D#

G# or A♭ chords

A♭	A♭–C–E♭
A♭m	A♭–B–E♭
A♭7	A♭–C–E♭–G♭
A♭dim	A♭–B–D
A♭+	A♭–C–E

A chords

A	A–C#–E
Am	A–C–E
A7	A–C#–E–G
Adim	A–C–E♭
A+	A–C#–F

B♭ chords

B♭	B♭–D–F
B♭m	B♭–D♭–F
B♭7	B♭–D–F–A♭
B♭dim	B♭–D♭–E
B♭+	B♭–D–F#

B chords

B	B–D#–F#
Bm	B–D–F#
B7	B–D#–F#–A
Bdim	B–D–F
B+	B–D#–G

Important Note: A slash chord (C/E, G/B) tells you that a certain bass note is to be played under a particular harmony. In the case of C/E, the chord is C and the bass note is E.